"The proverb, 'if the blind lead the blind, both shall fall into the ditch,' is far too often the case in the field of leadership studies. In a domain, cluttered with explorations of the obvious, Nigel Nicholson has done it again. His book, The 'I' of Leadership: Strategies for seeing, being and doing, takes a refreshing, extremely original look at this complex subject. The different lens he uses to help leaders acquire deeper insights into the causes of success and failure, is second to none. This book is a must for any serious student of leadership."
Professor Manfred Kets de Vries, INSEAD

"Nigel Nicholson achieves the rare feat of being both original and practical, and entertaining and insightful. This book is genuinely different and thought provoking: it sets leadership in the context of history, evolutionary science and the latest thinking on psychology, but remains grounded in a reality that all leaders will recognise day to day. Richly illustrated with cases from arts, history, business and politics the book is a compelling read."
Jo Owen, author of the best-selling How to Lead

"Most books on leadership leave me cold – not this one. This book is full of wisdom and insight, as well as displaying empathy for business leaders today. It is relevant, intelligent and inspiring yet makes you think. The book also helps you reflect on your own style of leadership in an insightful manner."
Chris Cracknell, CEO, OCS Group Ltd

"Nicholson's The 'I' of Leadership offers a fresh perspective to seemingly non-fresh world of leadership books. By focusing on character, he insightfully charts out differences between leaders (e.g., Bush versus Blair), and highlights what the rest of us can do to become great leaders. Nicholson's examples make the book a page turner, while enticing the reader to gain tremendous self-insight into their own leadership roles."
Max H. Bazerman, Straus Professor, Harvard Business School

"Leaders do face different challenges as time progresses. But the essence of what makes one decide in what we can in hindsight call 'the right way' does not change. Nigel Nicholson has captured the answers to those always intriguing questions why some people succeed in becoming great leaders and which ingredients make a good leader. Nicholson has a researched view, based on his own academic observations of how individual people develop, but Nigel is at the same time refreshingly pragmatic in his approach. A must read for every leader (to be)!"
Marten Pieters LLM, MD and CEO, Vodafone India Ltd

"A brilliant book brimming with insights. It's a fascinating blend of knowledge synthesized from history, psychology, organizational experience, and principles of evolution. Readers are treated to deep insights into leadership, followership, and even the nature of human nature. It's by far the best book I've read this year."
David M. Buss, author of *Evolutionary Psychology: The New Science of the Mind*

"What a wonderfully fresh and direct way of writing about human behaviour. For sheer observational skill, range of scientific knowledge and story-telling ability, it is reminiscent of the insights of Erving Goffman, but applied to the intriguing topic of what sets leaders apart. The Seeing-Being-Doing Model is a landmark contribution to psychology."
Jules Goddard, author of *Uncommon Sense, Common Nonsense*

"Leadership is both a broad and specific field, there are many types of leader in many different areas but they nevertheless share some key traits, this book does a great job of delving into this contradiction and sets itself apart from the crowd of leadership manuals by providing insight and enough expertise to interest even a casual reader. It could certainly be of use to a great number of my colleagues who might have some grasp of political leadership but often know very little about business leadership and it is certainly one of the most comprehensive looks at leadership that I've come across."
Rt. Hon. Peter Hain, MP, former Labour Cabinet Minister

"In these times of transformation there is a lot of talk about leadership but not enough clear analysis. That is what this book brings – not just on the skills but on the nature of leadership itself. This book is profound, practical and compelling reading. Its many stories and ideas provide the strategic and tactical guidance that any of us might need when called upon to lead."
Jesús Díaz de la Hoz, Executive Partner, PwC

"Alpha males are driven by self-interest. They can either serve others' interest at the same time or operate at the expense of others. In chimpanzees, as in humans, the first kind of leader is very popular, but the second kind better watches his back. Nigel Nicholson engagingly explains all possible variations on this theme for our own species."
Frans de Waal, author of *The Bonobo and the Atheist*

"Oh no, not another book on leadership. Nope, this is not just another book. It is THE book. It is a lifetime's work. It could not be further from the glib easy-to-follow biz books out there, celebrating the latest fad. The scope of it is huge – covering philosophy, science, anthropology, history, politics, psychology and especially narrative. We can be authors of our lives. And this book reads like a great story. From Nicholson's rigour emerge some simple, highly useful models. Keep it close by. I intend to."
Neil Mullarkey, founder-member of London's Comedy Store Players and communication consultant

"A magnificent sweep on the different ways to approach and improve leadership, with many original insights and observations on what distinguishes the great leaders from those who have failed to have the lasting impact which is demanded of a person in a leadership position."
Stuart Roden, Senior Partner, Lansdowne Partners

THE "I" OF LEADERSHIP

Strategies for Seeing, Being and Doing

Nigel Nicholson

JB JOSSEY-BASS™

A Wiley Brand

© 2013 John Wiley & Sons, Ltd.

Registered office
John Wiley & Sons, Ltd., The Atrium, Southern Gate, Chichester, West Sussex, PO19 8SQ, United Kingdom

For details of our global editorial offices, for customer services and for information about how to apply for permission to reuse the copyright material in this book please see our website at www .wiley.com.

Reprinted August 2013

Wiley publishes in a variety of print and electronic formats and by print-on-demand. Some material included with standard print versions of this book may not be included in e-books or in print-on-demand. If this book refers to media such as a CD or DVD that is not included in the version you purchased, you may download this material at http://booksupport.wiley.com. For more information about Wiley products, visit www.wiley.com.

Library of Congress Cataloging-In-Publication Data
Nicholson, Nigel.
  The "I" of leadership : strategies for seeing, being and doing / Nigel Nicholson.
    pages cm
  Includes bibliographical references and index.
  ISBN 978-1-118-56743-2 (hbk.) – ISBN 978-1-118-56744-9 (ebk.) –
ISBN 978-1-118-56745-6 (ebk.) – ISBN 978-1-118-56746-3 (ebk.)   1. Leadership.
2. Strategic planning.   I. Title.
  HM1261.N53 2013
  303.3'4–dc23   2012049029

A catalogue record for this book is available from the British Library.

ISBN 978-1-118-56743-2 (hardback)   ISBN 978-1-118-56744-9 (ebk)
ISBN 978-1-118-56745-6 (ebk)   ISBN 978-1-118-56746-3 (ebk)

Cover design: Jason Anscomb, Rawshock design

Set in 11.5/15pt Minion Pro by Toppan Best-set Premedia Limited, Hong Kong
Printed in Great Britain by TJ International Ltd, Padstow, Cornwall, UK

For Oliver
My leader

CONTENTS

ACKNOWLEDGEMENTS

I owe London Business School and its enlightened leaders – Sir George Bain, John Quelch, Laura Tyson, Robin Buchanan, and Sir Andrew Likierman – a huge debt of gratitude. Over the 22 years of my tenure they gave unqualified support to all the trials, errors, experiments, innovations and personal transformations that have culminated in this book. I came to the School having enjoyed a rich intellectual development at the wonderful Social and Applied Psychology Unit in Sheffield, including a spell in the USA with Lou Pondy and his legendary group at the U of I at Urbana–Champaign – but I found at London Business School a totally new and challenging environment. There were three strands to this challenge, all strongly represented in this book. First was discovery of how teaching sophisticated and smart leaders can be a hugely rewarding and enlightening reciprocal process. Second, was my personal experience of leadership, of the OB Group (twice) and as a member of the School's top team as a Deputy Dean. These showed me the pain, burden, joy, privilege and above all, the experienced truth of leading. Third, was the support I was given to be bold, innovative, and courageous in building new ways of learning: via the diagnostic field trip I designed for the Executive MBAs, my transformation of the open enrolment program from "Interpersonal Skills for Senior Managers" into "High Performance People Skills for Leaders", and most of all, the chance to really push the envelope by developing the amazing Proteus Programme, which came to embody my total belief in the idea that seeing is the key to new ways of being and doing.

At the School I have had a fabulous set of colleagues – never more than right now – who were marvellously helpful and responsive in my pleas for research insights on particular points in this book. It is such a staggering privilege to be able to exchange thoughts with such a brilliantly talented bunch of young minds. Thanks guys! Many of the best times in life are conversations. Throughout my life the chance to explore through dialogue with some of the smartest people on the planet has been a most profound joy, and again this book owes much to you all: sadly passed away: my dear friends the great Dan Gowler and Avery Sharon, and thankfully still with us: John Downer, Michael Frese, Toni Gillham, Jules Goddard, Siegfried Greif, Bob Hogan, Dominic Houlder, Laurance and Jos Kuper, Rob Kurzban, Geoff Miller, Adele Nicholson, Madan Pillutla, Janet Radcliffe-Richards, Norbert Semmer , Zak Van Straaten, Michael West, Sadie Williams, Bob Wood, and too many more to mention.

All are eclipsed by one person with whom I have had the most profound meditations on the nature of self, reality and leadership – my amazing son, Oliver (aged 10), to whom I have dedicated this book because he has infused me with the spirit to realize the deepest ambitions of this project, as a later life companion and conversationalist par-excellence. My other sons and daughters have been no less inspiring – Alice, Nell, Sam and Leo are all deeply ingrained in everything I try to do as affirmations of integrity, intelligence, humor, growth, joy and love. All of these qualities, plus the commitment of partnership comes too from the love of my life, Adele, who for the last 15 years gave me purpose, faith, loving kindness and the most meaningful meeting of minds.

This is all very well, but a book is a work of production, and how lucky I was to find a team at Jossey-Bass at the top of their game, and happily in love with this project. First and foremost is Rosemary Nixon whom I have known, liked and respected for several decades, but we really found a new connection through this work, in which she has consistently shown a deep appreciation of what it is all about. Her support has meant more than I can say through times of doubt and difficulty. At her elbow is a great line-up of professionals at Wiley. Thank you. I have also had great help from Karis Benford, who was a fabulous aid in my biographical peregrinations, and Patti Luong, my right arm, left arm, head and legs in helping me to avoid dropping the ridiculous number of juggling balls in my overstuffed life. Brilliant!

Lucky me! Thank you. All of you.

– 1 –

IT GOES WITH THE TERRITORY – LEADERSHIP MOMENTS

There is a tide in the affairs of men
Which, taken at the flood, leads on to fortune.

William Shakespeare

TWO MOMENTS

Moment 1

An African-American female teacher faces around 30 young children in a Florida elementary school classroom. Behind their heads you can hear the click and whirr of motorized camera lenses. Next to her, also facing the class, sits a man, legs folded, observing the scene with the appearance of relaxed geniality. After a couple of minutes, as the teacher is drilling the class on its reading, a second man comes hurriedly up behind the seated man, bends at the waist and whispers something in his ear. The seated man looks momentarily startled, then distracted, but quickly resumes the appearance of following the class.

Yet now his face betrays that he is distracted. He picks up a school book, flipping the pages. He looks like he is going through the motions of paying attention to the class. He holds a composed demeanor to the end of the class – some six minutes later. At this point he asks the class a question, smiles at their response and warmly, yet unhurriedly, congratulates the children and their teacher on their impressive reading skills. He stands and calmly takes his leave.

It is September 11th 2001 and the man is George W. Bush. We are witnessing him at a turning point in his presidency; a recorded moment that became an instant source of controversy in the US media. Shortly before the class, Bush had heard that a plane had crashed into the twin towers of the World Trade Center in New York, but, up to this point, had assumed it was an accident with a light aircraft. Now, a voice has just spoken in his ear the fateful words: "America is under attack." Soon he will learn that a second passenger liner has been flown into the twin towers, resulting in nearly 3000 deaths.

Bush's moment of truth, captured on video, has been pored over on YouTube by countless commentators. For some observers his muted and delayed reaction was a sign of weakness, folly and indecision. Others praised his composure as a mark of real leadership.

At one level what he did or might have done in that six minutes hardly matters. It is difficult to see what he could have done to change what was happening. Yet, people watch leaders and especially their reactions at critical moments. The question they ask – seldom from a neutral point of view – is what is going on in the leader's head? They are quick to judge one way or the other, and whichever way that is, it is a story. We cannot see into other people's heads. In fact, psychology shows us we struggle to see into our own. So what we have is a story – our story of why others act as they do. The leader also has a story. This is George W. Bush's.[1]

My first reaction was outrage. Someone had dared to attack America. They were going to pay. Then I looked at the faces of the children in front of me. I thought about the contrast between the brutality of the attackers and the innocence of those children. Millions like them

2

would soon be counting on me to protect them. I was determined not to let them down.

I saw the reporters at the back of the room, learning the news on their cell phones and pagers. Instinct kicked in. I knew my reaction would be recorded and beamed throughout the world. The nation would be in shock; the president could not be. If I stormed out hastily, it would scare the children and send ripples of panic throughout the country. The reading lesson continued, but my mind raced far from the classroom. Who could have done this? How bad was the damage? What did the government need to do?

Press Secretary Ari Fleischer positioned himself between the reporters and me. He held up a sign that read "Don't say anything yet." I didn't plan to. I had settled on a plan of action: when the lesson ended, I would leave the classroom calmly, gather the facts, and speak to the nation.

Is what he is saying a "true" account? This is not an easy question to answer. Let us assume he has tried faithfully to recollect his exact sensations. We know that, even with the most strenuous attempt to recall and report accurately, all memory is "reconstructive". Each time we bring something up from the vaults of memory it changes its shape, even as we lay our hands on it. With the best will in the world, our stories change with the telling, and perhaps especially when we write them down for posterity. But, even so, from this account, Bush is trying to tell us about the "I" of his leadership – the mental process he is engaged in. This is clearly important, since it has consequences.

Let's go a few thousand miles east across the Atlantic, four years later, to witness a similar big-time "I" moment for another leader, who also happens to be a good friend of Bush.

Moment 2

I thought inconsequentially of all the times I'd been there, and pictured it now in my mind: the bus, with the roof blown off; limbs, bones and blood strewn everywhere. And for what? In the name of God? Anger, pity and determination jostled like queue-jumpers barging into each other. I took a deep breath. Cut out the emotion, just think. Get a sense of the magnitude, work out the emotions of the country but do so in a way that leaves you free to describe them, but not to share them, except for the purpose of description, so as to leave your mind clear. Do I leave the G8? Do we cancel it? How can I chair it waiting for news? Do we hand the enemy a victory by altering our arrangements? Do we show insensitivity to the victims by carrying on? I know it sounds callous but calculations have to be made. There will be a time for me to weep later. Now, you are the leader, so lead.[2]

The time is July 7th 2005 and the speaker is British Prime Minister Tony Blair. In the midst of chairing the G8 summit at Gleneagles in Scotland, he has just received the news of terrorist tube train and bus bombings in central London that have left 56 people dead and around 700 injured.

This time we have no video record but you can imagine the man, standing by a window, thoughts whirring as he stares into space. As he does so, three big things are happening to him, just as they were for Bush.

One big thing here is the Self and its machinations; talking to itself as it stumbles through the thickets of thought and feeling. This is self-regulation,[3] and it can be done in bad ways and good ways. It is critical to a leader's effectiveness – how does one process the moments and assemble a coherent performance?

The second big thing is Strategy. How does one, as a leader, choose between courses of action? Strategy means going beyond perception and impulse and constructing a plan that delivers the outcomes one wants. It means making decisions, such as when to stand back; when to engage; when to take the lead; when to follow the voice of others. Leadership is implicit in action that goes beyond reaction.

The third big thing is History. Blair and Bush are political leaders, well aware of where they stand in the landscape of events. What they do connects with elements that were there before them and will be there after them. History evolves, and leaders with it.[4] Evolution here means something way beyond this or that man or woman and their times. It is about leadership in all times. We have had leaders since the dawn of history. What have they been doing and why? Leaders' responses to the events of their times are part of, and sometimes important drivers of, cultural evolution.[5]

So let's return to Bush and Blair at their moments. Actions by people remote from these leaders have sent their shock waves into the space they occupy. As the waves break on the shore of the leader's consciousness, the mind first turns in on itself, absorbing feelings, memories, impressions and impulses, before moving out to take in a broader landscape – the model of the world that the leader possesses, and the question of the leader's identity. Leaders' answers to the "who am I?" question are critical to their actions and effectiveness. Most of the time the answer hangs implicit and latent behind the curtain of consciousness, but it may be awakened and activated by the leader or evoked by those followers and friends who see themselves as part of the leader's story.

For both Bush and Blair, in our frozen moments, leadership resides in the special responsibility they have in such circumstances – to deflect, direct, focus the wave of energy that is suffusing them. They are intensely aware of the momentous responsibility that sits on their shoulders and of their power, though this has limits. They know that they are actors in a drama that is materializing around them but which was not of their making. They know that their responses will affect the process and the aftermath, but also that much of what follows will happen regardless of what they think and do. They do know that they are on the cusp of history and that they can change the future. At another level, they are just men surfing a mental tsunami.

Such is the nature of leadership and its moments. Some of these we can all identify with. There are always times – yes, rare for many of us – where being the person on point duty means we have no choice but to respond on behalf of others – there is no one else to turn to. *Carpe diem* – seize the day. Any one of us can find ourselves thrust into a leadership moment. How we see that moment, how we view ourselves as actors in the moment and what we do, or plan to do, in that moment is the "I" of leadership. It is seeing, being and doing.

ANOTHER BOOK ABOUT LEADERSHIP?

There are so many. Some have recipes. Some tell stories. Some construct theories. Some dig in the entrails of a particular period of history. Some contain ancient wisdom.[6]

There has to be a good reason for one more – this book. Forgive the pun but it is an "I" opener. The underlying thought running through this book is that leaders are the prisoners of many overwhelming forces and constraints, and yet there is a kernel of indeterminacy, of awareness, will and choice – seeing, being and doing – that can take the leader and the led in many different directions. For Bush it was six minutes of dissembling. For Blair it was a strident call to arms. Both could have been different.

I have written this book not just for leaders, designated or self-proclaimed. It is for anyone who has suffered or been thankful for a leader, and would like to know why. What leaders do matters. At any time, any of us may be momentarily called upon to lead. This book is for anyone who wants to understand what is happening in the world around them because of leaders, and for anyone who wants to understand the role of leaders in history, how this has changed and why. The story is told in three stages.

History: This book is rooted in evolutionary science, through which we shall seek to provide an integrated scientific account of the role leadership plays in history.[7] This matters because we face a crisis on our planet that requires leaders to be more part of the solution than part of the problem. It is important that we have ways of looking at leadership in our society that enlighten our efforts to choose, direct and accept our leaders.

Strategy: Leadership is strategic. It works through what is immediate and challenging to what is difficult and distant – the goals of leadership. Much of what we shall highlight here is intensely practical, yet strategic. When should the leader lead her people, and when should she follow them? How can the leader fuse elements of her identity with those of her people –

their culture and institution? How does a leader balance her role in shaping events with responding to them fluently and flexibly? To answer these questions we shall be using a powerful but simple framework – SPQ[8] – which I have developed over 20 years to guide leadership development. SPQ stands for Situations, Processes and Qualities – seeing, doing and being. The strategy of leadership consists of the different ways in which these three fundamental elements can be linked and controlled.[9]

Self-management: The hardest part of leadership is to achieve the right kind of self-control. The wrong kind is too much control being applied to the wrong impulses. Leaders have to endure, sacrifice, be brave, take risks and give to others. Every day we are assaulted by images and stories of failing leaders. We see good people doing bad and stupid things. We see leaders who build great success and then fall down just at the point where they should be standing tall. In this book we will be examining tools for self-management, and how leaders can think themselves into effectiveness; looking at situations in new ways and by talking to themselves in some new ways. At the heart of self-management is the story – the interior narrative that the Self constructs to make sense, integrate and direct action, thought and feeling. We humans are instinctively story-telling animals.[10]

For Bush, the story – the title of his memoir – is *Decision Points*: a man who sees himself throughout his life as making tough calls to discipline himself and make things happen in the world. A point of departure early in the book recounts his decision to foreswear alcohol after concluding he has a drink problem.

Blair's book, equally tellingly, is called *A Journey* and starts with his awakening to the meaning of political leadership in the British system after his landslide election victory in 1997. This title reflects a quite different narrative to Bush's. Blair's is the story of a man deeply immersed in the leadership landscape – constantly analyzing, learning and growing in confidence.

Figure 1.1:   The "I" of leadership

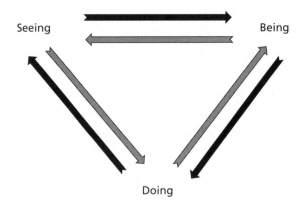

The two stories are strongly contrasting and very consequential for them and the world around them.

Both Bush and Blair have implicit strategies for seeing, being and doing.

A strategy for seeing is having a philosophy and a methodology for interrogating reality and extracting from it meaning and purpose, which sometimes means challenging and shaping the world around you. A strategy for being means having a story of who you are and why you act as you do. A strategy for doing is knowledge and confidence in your repertoire of tactics, ideas, habits and skills – it is self-control, the art of constructing sequences of actions that are plausible and serve your ends. The three are linked – see Figure 1.1.

Graffito:
Rousseau: To do is to be
Sartre: To be is to do
Sinatra: Dooby dooby do

Let's add better, if less funny, fourth and fifth lines "To see is to be; To see is to do."[11]

In business it is said that structure follows strategy, but actually the reverse also happens – strategy emerges from structure. Rationally, the business should be shaped around its purposes (Rousseau), but actually often the shape of the business constrains its purpose (Sartre). This duality is also a pivotal insight into leadership. Some leaders are shapers and some are adaptors, and the best are judicially both. The shaper's strength of character defines the enterprise. The adaptors help organizations, states or cultures to become what they need to be to do what they have to. Think of Steve Jobs vs. Eric Schmidt – Apple vs. Google – the former led by a vision, the latter by an awakening. Both vision and awakening require eyes to be opened. What Jobs and Schmidt saw shaped what they did. What they saw came from who they were: Jobs burning with impulses and images; Schmidt entranced by the worlds of possibility he glimpsed emerging in the digital era.

Can leaders choose who they are, what they see and what they do? If they can, then they can claim the power to achieve their goals. If not, they are constrained; the prisoners of their identity, knowledge and capability. Changing who you are is a slow and, some would say, impossible road. Changing what you do is challenging. Changing how you see is the only trick that can be pulled off in an instant, and if seeing is being – look at Saul's legendary transition to becoming St Paul, the founder of the Christian church, through a vision at a cross-roads in Damascus – then almost anything is possible.

LEADERSHIP MOMENTS

Every instant of our lives is a confluence of experience – world and mind come together in the moving moment, the stream of awareness we call consciousness. Mostly we breeze along this stream, since most of the riverbank landscape is predictable, ordered and unchallenging. Yet, at any point, we may be confronted by big, unpredictable events that spark the kind of mental dialog Bush and Blair are recollecting. The difference is that they are leaders with a special designation to be ready to respond to and take responsibility every day for a range of unbidden events. It goes with the territory. Leadership can be so defined – as a territory within which we have responsibility for action and reaction. It is taking charge – something we all have to do, even if only from time to time.

So what is your territory? If you are a supermarket shelf-stacker it is pretty small. Events may happen around you. A trolley crash in aisle 13 may hand you a leadership moment, fleeting though it may be. Most of us have a variety of interpersonal responsibilities and material duties to which the leadership call may come more frequently – situations where, like Blair, we have to pull ourselves up mid-stream and say to ourselves, "Now, be a leader."

Ah, but is this what it's like? Mike Useem has written about the inspirational stories of real-life leaders who seized the day.[12] In a rich variety of instances, leaders defined their style, values and potentialities to the world through some act of courage, thoughtfulness and/or high moral style. Yet what about all the other moments? What worries many leaders is that their leadership might be defined by things that they let happen, by oversight, ignorance or default. What happens if you miss your leadership moment?

My argument here is that for people in leadership roles – and many who are not or do not think of themselves as leaders (a surprisingly common self-denial among mid-level managers, by the way) – every moment is a leadership moment. This is a statement about the consciousness of leadership – even at our idlest moments it is surely better that we have actively chosen to be passive than to be so by default, following the drift of things. A Buddhist monk might disagree. But in business, passively floating with the tide does not always lead to good places. Leaders get washed up this way.

This book is about self-control, versatility and mastery. It is about the leader in all of us, and especially those who have to bear the responsibility in the eyes of others for leading. It is about the most intimate instances of leaders' thought, feeling and decision-making. It is about the deepest origins of leadership in our animal natures and our ways of living for millennia. It is about people and their stories – the what, the why and the might-have-been. Here's an example.

What Happened to George S. Patton

George S. Patton was an extraordinary man – a US general of vision, great force of personality, tactical brilliance, immense personal courage and an esoteric erudition in the classics of ancient Greece and Rome.[13] He first revealed his military brilliance in skirmishes in WWI, languished uncomfortably through the inter-war years and then came into his own in WWII as a peerless attack machine – disciplining and inspiring his armies to victories across Africa and in the Battle of the Bulge that effectively terminated the war in Europe. So many leadership moments, but, tragically, one of the most defining – memorably captured by George C. Scott in the eponymous movie – took place in a field hospital where he slapped the head of a shell-shocked soldier hospitalized from battle fatigue, calling him a coward. The disgrace of the incident removed Patton from the front line of war for the best part of a year and cost him the chance of becoming the Commander-in-Chief of the entire Allied armies in the European theater of war. This also possibly prolonged the conflict by as long, for Patton was an attack dog – a force of nature greatly feared by the Axis powers.

It has been said that all of the most important of life's battles are fought within the Self. This was Patton's problem. He was larger than life; his Self was a neurotic and tortured organ, bound into his story of himself – his "destiny" as a hero. His personal vision was a source of magnetic power but was rendered useless when found shorn of the rudimentary forms of self-control that enable etiquette, protocol and correct behavior to be carried off without error. Poor Patton – his affronted beliefs triggered him straight into a monumental anti-leadership moment.

LEADERSHIP AS CHARACTER

Let's lift some names out of the air: Henry Ford; Barack Obama; Bill Gates; Duke Ellington; Ernest Shackleton; Steve Jobs; Carly Fiorina; Ratan Tata; Lee Kuan Yew; Margaret Thatcher . . . pick your own.

Now let's pick some other names: Susan Mason; Roy Makeba; Pablo Gonzales; Kim Sun Joy; Oscar Levinson . . .

You won't know the second list. If you do spot a familiar name, it's a fluke. I made them all up. Imagine them to be ordinary men and women who occupy positions where their job is *to make decisions or take responsibility for the coordination and direction of other people*. The part in italics will do as a working definition of formal leadership.

My point is that in the first list we can see larger-than-life figures. They all have "made history," one may say, and some are still making it. This raises a question that will occupy us throughout this book – did they make history or did history make them? How different would their organizations, nations and the people around be if someone else had occupied their role?[14]

Two Arguments

Argument 1: The world (or their part of it) would be very different. These people shaped institutions, relationships and the tide of events around them. As Emerson said, "There is no history, only biography." The world has been made by the shaping force of human willpower; by agents and actors, especially those in positions of leadership. Indeed, that is one reason why we choose or allow them to lead us, because they promise to be the agents of renewal, revolution and restoration.

Argument 2: Although people make a difference, the world turns on the logic of larger forces. It, in effect, selects the people it needs at the time. It lures those who have the motives and the profiles to accept and be acceptable. It uses them and spits them out. Put another leader in their place and there will be short-term deviation, but in the long run the river of history will be drawn by the gravitational forces of the moment to find its way to the same estuary.

Both arguments contain truth. Leaders are both the servants and the architects of history. This is also true of my fictitious and largely anonymous list of leaders. They, in their smaller worlds – a man running a downtown garage, a woman office manager, a sports coach, a film producer – all do things that change the world, and for some of their close associates, do so radically. A person only has to fall in love to change the world, by altering the life of another person. Yet, how much difference do we really make? We cause ripples on the surface of time that dissipate as it moves on its relentless course; if we look down on our ant-like perambulations from a height, they seem to signify little. Little? Maybe, but sometimes individuals and groups of these moving specks really do change the course of history.

But, as much for our fictitious Susan Mason as for the very real Barack Obama, character is destiny. This also is a two-way street of cause and effect. Who we are determines what we do; and what we do determines who we are. Make no mistake, all of these people have impacts on the world, which depend as much on the forces within them as on those outside them. Patton's place in history was defined by the jumble of passions that seemed to rage within him, at every stage. Tony Blair, a more coolly calculative person, was, par excellence, a reader of his context, yet it was his reading of that context that defined his actions. To see is to do. His memoir on his time as British Prime Minister is striking for its relentless analytical flavor, but his analysis was always deeply personal and linked to his moral identity. Who you are matters. What you *do* with who you are matters even more.

Warren Buffett – Driven by His Compass

Warren Buffett never seemed to enjoy being a leader much.[15] For the brief time in 1991 he was the savior of scandal-mired Salomon Brothers investment bank when called in to restore its tarnished reputation, he set rules for probity, destroyed the bonus culture (a good thing in today's climate!) and handed off day-to-day leadership as fast as he could, preferring to "lead" from a distance, whilst continuing to nurse his favored projects and live according to his habits. Economists talk about "revealed preference" – what you do is what you are – to do is to be. That is Buffett to a tee – a man whose actions always reflected choice, as is true of many eccentrics. From the earliest age he played obsessively with numbers, and very early on conceived a burning desire to make money through enterprise. These instincts, nurtured by his father's haunted memories of the Great Depression, combined to create the architecture of his ambitions in financial markets. Subsequently, this became embodied in his spectacularly successful enterprise, Berkshire Hathaway, and built his distinctive philosophy and methodology of investment, founded on his faith in his ability to discern "true value" in assets and stocks.

Buffett was a man who always knew in what direction his compass was pointing and where he wanted to go.

WHO ARE YOU? THE COMPASS QUESTION

For all of us, life is a succession of choices. Many happen by default. Stuff happens that we just don't have the power or the inclination to stop. Yet there are occasions in life when we find ourselves at a choice point that we know is critical. Shall I take this job, marry that person, move to this country? Faced with dilemmas of this magnitude some people seek the power of reason to be the arbiter. They sit down and draw up lists of pros and cons, but are shocked when they discover that this method doesn't deliver the answer, or they continue to feel uneasy about its solution.

Most people don't go through this rigmarole, or if they do start using a calculus, they give up after a while and fall back on "gut feeling." Of course this then leaves one with the puzzling aftermath of wondering, why did I lean one way rather than the other way? Only self-knowledge will answer such questions. This is not as easy as it seems, and many people prefer not to enter this zone. It's too problematic. Hidden desires and fears often drive choice.[16] We don't always want to be confronted with our dark side, or even just the sloppy mess of our mixed motives. Many leaders prefer the bliss of ignorance when it comes to their compass. They know it tells them unerringly what to do and where to go, but they fear they could lose their sense of confident purpose if they interrogate their own motives too closely. One can sympathize, yet be acutely aware of the dangers such willful ignorance invites. We will plumb the depths of this question later, considering how leaders can achieve secure self-knowledge without loss of confidence or control.

The interior conversation – question and answer – is something leaders need. It can be "self-talk,"[17] a conversation that goes on in the leader's head. It is a story, or, if you do it properly and work through the options, a bunch of stories that a leader can construct, each of which will take the leader plus followers in a different direction. Some of these stories work better than others. Leadership success and failure is a question of whether a leader has settled on a story that works best for herself, her goals and the surrounding world. Yet stories enchain stories, so, before you know it, the leader's story becomes their life journey and the followers' story.

This is another pillar of our analysis of leadership – to look at the lives of leaders, something we shall do throughout this book. We will use an analytic schema to understand how the life of the leader, or indeed any of us, unfolds: Destiny + Drama × Deliberation. Destiny comprises the forces impelling the leader along her path; Drama consists of the unpredicted events and pressures blowing her this way and that; Deliberation is the process that takes place when a leader is able to take a step back, think and make choices. The Bush/Blair testimonies exemplify all three.

Lives make history. From the fragments of the leadership moment, through the chain of such moments that make a life story are constructed the longer narratives of power, politics, succession and revolution.[18] These are adaptive processes because, ultimately, leadership is an essential attribute of our species and many other mammalian social systems, to enable the coordination and mobilization of effort to do what is needed.

THE "I" OF LEADERSHIP – THE STORY OF THIS BOOK

We started with two fragmentary moments of leadership. From such fragments are woven the fabric of a life story. Bush called his book *Decision Points* to reflect his stance as an embattled man facing down his inner and outer demons, starting with his decision to quit drinking. Blair called his book *A Journey* because he felt that he ended up, at the end of his ten years as Britain's Prime Minister, in a very different place than he started from. Both are highly reflective books, but even these brief quotes illustrate subtle but important differences in their thought processes, and thus what leadership means to them.

All leaders have narratives.[19] Some are clearly more about making sense of the past after it happened – Bush's is of this type. It takes him in certain directions. Others are much more about shaping the future – to be the author of their story. Blair seems to be going more in this direction. That's the way with stories, without them we are just reactors – responding to things that befall us, or to the impulses that arise within us. The narrative is a control device. It makes sense of the present by connecting with the past, and projects us onward into the future with a sense of purpose.

Should we worry about the truth of the story? It is clear that some leaders are fantasists about their mission – Patton came close – others seem highly objective. Yet a story is a story, and could be told in other ways. This is not a philosophical question but a practical one. The story you tell opens some doors and closes others.

The "I" of leadership raises other questions, such as how does leadership change leaders? What happens to the "I" on its journey? Blair is at pains to tell us what he learned about the political landscape of leadership and his own responses. He ends up much more definite about his confidence as a leader and more certain in his view of the world just at the point where he has to step aside. It is a paradox he recognizes ruefully.

All of us face parallel struggles – to apply ourselves to a changing world and learn how to be more effective. How leaders meet this challenge has consequences for the rest of us, so we'd better understand how they can be helped and guided.

The journey of this book starts with our animal nature, moves on to take in the sweep of human history since the dawn of time to explain the varieties of leadership and their effects, before closing in on the territory leaders inhabit and what it means to be strategic. We shall continue beyond this point to penetrate the leader's mind and the drama that takes place within the Self – the "I" of leadership. Throughout, we will meet leaders – some famous, some not – whose stories we can learn from. This is only a "self-help book" in two respects. It is my aim that the analysis I offer will be compelling and helpful to leaders in every walk of life, and to their followers. Near the end of this book I will also suggest disciplines that can be practiced – in seeing, being and doing – which will help you, dear reader, to be what you can be.

We start our journey in the next chapter by coming back to basics – to our animal identity and what leadership means in the world of social animals.

IMPLICATIONS AND OBSERVATIONS FOR LEADERS AND ORGANIZATIONS

This book is about the telescopic link between the most intimate parts of leadership – from the "I" that sees, feels and acts through to the global impact leaders have on the world. They do so by the path of strategy – how the leader's story is assembled from moments. Some key thoughts:

- Leadership is about taking charge – seizing the moment. Many leaders fail by taking the world for granted or not recognizing that this could be a moment for them to step up and be the leader the situation needs.

- What you see and how you see are at least partially under the leader's control – this means data analysis and (fast) reflection rather than chasing one's impulses.

- The leader needs to know her story, but remember that it is a work in progress. She should not become its prisoner.

- The people around the leader have a duty to help her – especially in what the leader sees.

– 2 –

LEADERSHIP IN THE WILD – THE EVOLUTION OF POWER

Man is the only animal that laughs and weeps, for he is the only animal that is struck with the difference between what things are and what they ought to be.

Hazlitt

LEADING BY FEAR

Steve Jobs, the genius who created Apple, perfected the art of fixing people with a relentless, silent and unblinking stare in order to unnerve them.[1] He was notoriously volatile, given to bursts of extreme emotion. He would scream at people and abuse their work, yet turn on sweetness and charm when in a buoyant mood or if he felt it was required. He would burst into tears at moments when he needed the indulgence of others.

Larry Ellison ruthlessly cut a swathe through Oracle – eliminating rivals and weaklings as he went in order to secure absolute control.[2]

Michael Eisner, Andy Grove, Rupert Murdoch, Al "Chainsaw" Dunlap and Carly Fiorina are among the many business leaders who have, or had, the capacity to intimidate by force of will and raw power.

A dark example was publishing magnate Robert Maxwell.[3] Born into poverty, he was a Czech war hero who came to England and clawed his way to the top, achieving celebrity status for his high-profile political and charitable work, all the time robbing his company's pension fund. He inexplicably vanished off his yacht in 1991, presumed drowned, just as the scandal of his criminality was unfolding around him. I once worked with one of his top team, who told me what it was like when the boss walked into the office:

> Immediately the atmosphere changes. Maxwell is a big man and physically dominates the space. Tension hangs like a fog in the air. The more nervous people present feel a knot in the pit of their gut, hoping that the leader's gaze won't light on them. Everyone searches for signs in his demeanor as to his mood. Is today going to be one where silky smiles and broad good humor will diffuse the tension, or is it going to be one of those dreaded occasions when the gaze is a dagger, silence a threat and a question a blow? Everyone fears that the arbitrary axe of the leader's malignant attention will fall on them, for everyone present knows that Maxwell is famous for picking out people and publicly humiliating them.

It is said that unpredictable creatures are the most dangerous.[4] The predictably aggressive can be avoided, attacked or contained. Randomness is a winning strategy in games such as scissors–paper–stone – every other strategy can be outsmarted by an opponent.[5] Randomness is especially powerful where the alternatives to fire are milk and honey. The capacity of great intimidators to charm and allure is also part of their power.

When leaders evoke such visceral feelings in followers, we are in the territory of pure animal instinct. The leaders know what they are doing – they get a deep animal satisfaction from their dominance. So many in history have sucked on this drug: Hitler, Pol Pot, Gaddafi, Idi Amin, Saddam Hussein, Stalin and many more. Joseph Stalin – with whom even eye contact was a deadly risk – delighted in forcing his most senior henchman to dance along to an absurdist novelty record in which howling dogs replaced human voices.[6]

It is a model of leadership that has its roots in the deepest areas of animal response – where the most basic emotions of fear and need reside.

The Uncle Joe Strategy

Joseph Stalin's surname was a personal invention, partly mimicking his first mentor Lenin, and means "man of steel," which indeed he was.[7] Stalin grew up in his native Georgia as a supremely gifted young man, stunningly bright, artful as a singer and a poet, but tough as hell, hardened by the regular beatings of a drunken father; abuse also administered by his doting mother as an act of duty. This was followed by the brutalizing environment of the seminary school – many more beatings and fights – from which he escaped, along with most of his peers, to become a street revolutionary. In the chaotic times of the late Tsarist empire this meant conducting derring-do acts of armed robbery, which became a principal means of financing his ideological hero, the morose and bookish exile Vladimir Lenin.

Stalin's rise through the Bolshevik ranks was marked by repeated close shaves as he kept a pace or two ahead of the Tsarist police; pursuing him through the stream of intelligence reaching them from a self-renewing network of double agents. No one could be trusted. Everyone, in times where outcomes could swing either way, had to back more than one horse to win, except for the hardened ideologues, such as Stalin, Lenin and their cronies. As betrayal mounted upon betrayal, even Jo Stalin, the legendary escapologist, was eventually turned in to the authorities by one of his most trusted associates, the rising Bolshevik star Roman Malinovsky, who turned out to be a highly paid double agent. Stalin was exiled as a political prisoner, surviving for two years under the hardest conditions imaginable in Kureika, a village in the frozen wastes of northern Russia above the Arctic Circle.

Curiously, these probably turned out to be the most contented times of his life. Although under nominal guard, he roamed the barren landscape hunting and fishing for his sustenance, ruminating, singing and writing. His return to the centers of power revealed a man of unusual dominance, discipline and self-reliance; suffused in an over-whelming belief that no one was to be trusted. The story of Stalin's Russia exemplifies the power of leaders to make history. He enacted continual purges of any potential power sources, including many in the military that he turned out desperately to need as the second great world war loomed. Stalin's paranoia was justified and self-justifying – the more you persecute the more enemies you accumulate – but it was also personal. Anyone who got close to him was at risk, and his personal history was littered with defensive malevolence and tragedy, as friends, family and lovers went mad, killed themselves or were assassinated.

ANIMAL DOMINANCE

In *The Call of the Wild*[8] the great American writer Jack London describes the ordeals of dog packs in the Klondike, and in particular a large dog, Buck by name, stolen from a household and shipped to haul sleds in harness with a team of tough husky dogs across the icy terrain of the Yukon. Buck suffers many indignities from his human masters but learns painfully how to control his rebellious instincts. He also finds himself subject to the authority of the leading dog. He learns to bide his time and then fights the leader to the death, before Buck assumes the position of top dog.

This is marvelous stuff – anthropomorphized, of course, but London has clearly spent a lot of time around dogs and wolves to capture, as well as any human can, the instincts of our closest non-human associates (members of the dog family have been our "best friends" since the dawn of time, long before the first domestication of any other species).

Leadership here means dominance. But with an intelligent species like the dog, this is not just a matter of tooth and claw supremacy but also of intelligence – the brains required to effect control. Over what? Over impulse, relationships and events. In his other marvelous work of animal fiction, *White Fang*,[9] London explores this in the context of the wolf pack. The leader of the pack is not always the biggest and toughest, but the one that can keep peace in the pack.[10] This is one of the main benefits of leadership – to help keep the social order intact. Not every member of the group is going to aspire to be leader. There is both instinct and calculus involved, for humans no less than dogs. The instinct question is: do I have enough natural raw drive for domination to enter a contest? The calculus is: what are the chances of my getting beaten and losing what I have?

Evolutionary science tells us that the point of contests for dominance is to get good genes into the next generation.[11] There are huge variations in how this game is played out by different species. The female praying mantis and some spider females consume the smaller and weaker male victor immediately after he has consummated his union, so they can ingest the nutritional value of his flesh to enrich the life chances of their offspring. I guess this outcome comes as a surprise to him, but he has fulfilled the point of his existence. He is doing no less than many executives who sacrifice their lives to joyless labor-filled days in order to store up resources to secure the life chances of the next generation.[12]

Not all contests for dominance are physical. When attempting to mate, birds don't compete by trying to push each other out of the trees. Rather, they see who can sing the most elaborate song or build the most fantastic nest. These are displays of behaviors within their capabilities in order to signal that they possess good genes – a promise for the next generation. Again, the human parallels are not hard to spot. These signals have to be valid and not fakeable to fulfill their evolutionary goal – which is what evolutionists call "costly signaling" of their "reproductive fitness."[13] This fitness resides in whatever qualities or features will help an organism to survive and reproduce its genes. In most mating species, females have the upper hand. They just have to signal availability and wait for the cabaret of males strutting their stuff to prove their strength, health, stealth, resilience, intelligence, creativity or whatever is valued in their micro-world.[14] Most species stick to criteria that are relevant to their design and environmental niche. For humans, because our niche has become human culture – something that changes over time and place – and because we are remarkably versatile in our range of qualities and behaviors, the currency of fitness indicators is a constantly shifting game.[15] This happens over the breadth of history and over quite short time spans.

It raises some important questions for leadership. One is whether leadership is akin to reaching a peak of achievement in a pecking order. Answer: yes and no. Yes – many people do aspire to leadership as a "fitness peak," but in human society there are many other ways of achieving distinction and becoming a winner in the sexual selection stakes, such as via artistic endeavor, vocation, entertainment or specialist knowledge.[16] Indeed, in some societies being the leader may be a sterile, powerless calling of personal sacrifice, where others pull the strings and reap the rewards. Modern monarchies come to mind. We shall explore the reasons for these variations.

One of the most interesting and pertinent today is the role of women in leadership. Women are as fitted to leadership as men in many contexts, yet they remain a rarity. This, too, we shall resolve through our analysis in Chapter 15, by examining the dependence of corporate leadership on an unfriendly male paradigm of primal pecking orders.

When one looks at dominance, for many herding species it is a relatively simple matter – the victor commands the harem and offspring. One might be tempted to fall into the common error of seeing this as a constant struggle for supremacy amongst the boys. But, as we have noted, this is qualified by a risk–reward calculus.[17] What's the point of chancing your luck in contests that you have no hope of winning, and indeed where you could get seriously hurt or humiliated? None of the others in the group will thank you for disturbing the peace with useless contest. Jack London's fictitious saga of pack dogs does a good job in conveying how naturally this logic unfolds, with scarcely a conscious thought required. The desire to fight and win doesn't even enter the thoughts of many humans who find contentment in less dramatic strategies. There are advantages to being a follower. You don't have to fight, parade or pretend – you can just do your thing under the protection of a leader.

THE POLITICS OF LEADERSHIP

Yeroen and Luit are old comrades. They joined the community near its start. Yeroen, the elder, is a big, dominant guy – devious, willful and confident – when he's in the driving seat. He is impressive but easily gets tired; then he seems to take a time-out. Luit is slighter, more sociable and good natured. Although there is no formal hierarchy in the community, the way everyone greets Yeroen tells you he's the top guy. But things seem to be changing. Yeroen's age is showing and, on a couple of occasions in meetings, Luit has seemed to challenge him. Now fights between them are becoming more open. So far, people are playing it safe and keeping onside with Yeroen, but you can see gossip is spreading. He could soon lose the support of the community – especially some of the key women, for the balance of their opinion and support matters here. The tide does indeed turn, and Yeroen starts giving way to Luit, letting him be the one who resolves conflicts in the group. But one of Yeroen's buddies, a relatively young fellow, Nicky, comes into the fray, increasingly challenging Luit in public. Other alliances start shifting and before long it is Nicky who has outflanked them both to become the acknowledged leader in the community.

These are the politics of leadership – if one defines politics as the alignment of interests. As you might have guessed, the characters in the story are not humans but chimpanzees (I have deliberately humanized my summary of the story). These, our nearest cousins genetically, were closely observed by Frans de Waal in their Arnhem Zoo colony, and the story is adapted from his fascinating book *Chimpanzee Politics*,[18] which, from painstakingly recorded observations, offers a brilliantly vivid depiction of the games of contest, alliance, revenge, spite and submission that are played out within this primate community. The daily theater of our human social existence is disconcertingly mirrored in their themes. Jane Goodall and her team's pioneering observation studies in the wild of gorillas and chimpanzees echo the point,[19] underscoring what shapes these politics: individual differences and context. The behavior of every chimp and gorilla is a function of its DNA-encoded character, the resources and status it possesses and the pressures that surround it. Not much different to us really.

25

Though you might reflect that our relationships are a lot more regulated than chimpanzees', cast your mind back to your childhood and you may recall strong echoes of the shifting alliances of the playground, for mentally chimps are pretty much at the level of infant school.[20] This still elevates their model of leadership to something way above a simple "might is right" dominance. Indeed, even wolves and dogs, as Jack London shows, play games not just of dominance but also of trust. The game depends on the context. We can only make sense of leadership within a context.

One of the most interesting parallels between human and primate leadership comes from experiments with colonies of macaque monkeys.[21] Researchers experimented with different ways of organizing their food supply – contrasting centralized distribution with decentralized provisioning. The results were startling. The two approaches gave rise to radically different patterns of social power and interaction. The centralized model reinforced the tough, competitive dominance model; the decentralized model yielded a much more harmonious, cooperative and democratic order. A simulated game with students produced a very similar contrast of social patterns.[22]

In both cases there is leadership. The difference is that in the one it is highly visible in the open contests of alpha males; in the other, they have to secure trust as much as inspire fear.

HUMAN LEADERSHIP

When a flock of birds simultaneously takes to the air, or when a herd of buffalo wheel and turn as one, it is a miracle of coordination. Who is leading? This is a very human question and presumption. Sit in a packed stadium with other members of your species and watch the crowd rather than the sports and you will see waves of emotion and expression, uncoordinated except by the spontaneous urges of people infecting each other with thought and feeling. Not a leader in sight.

Join a small team of strangers and engage in a complicated group task against the clock, and look at how people behave. It depends greatly on who is in the room. You may be "blessed" with a "natural" leader – typically a dominant male – who will see it as his role and right practically to tell everyone what to do and how to do it.[23] The result may not be great, for the best results will come when the group members interact spontaneously, share information and influence each other freely as the task unfolds. This is akin to the hunting party organization of our tribal forebears. Leadership at its best is often organic – a shared function of the group.[24] One member takes the lead to get things moving; others join in at junctures where they are most needed to contribute, focus, coordinate and solve problems. Sure, the group needs focus and direction, but it also needs reflective observation, generosity of spirit, warmth, humor and invention. This is what industrial psychologists call "self-managed teams," showing it to be an efficient and effective way of organizing industrial production.[25] Many business leaders have discovered intuitively the refreshing results of empowering and liberating their workers. Ricardo Semler, taking over his dad's Brazilian manufacturing business, experimentally but triumphantly created a "natural" order of fluid self-management.[26] W. L. Gore, another family firm, did much the same, rather more systematically.[27]

Indeed, although it is clear you don't always need a "leader" to coordinate, it is curious how infatuated we are with the idea of leadership. Quite often, before I have set a bunch of executives to do some group task, I ask them what the prerequisites are for successful group work and they will often assert that there has to be a leader. For sure, at the end of such a task they will generally agree about who talked most, had most influence over outcomes, kept the group together and so on, but often there is no clear leader and everything goes fine. Why? It seems to be stuck in people's minds that we need leaders, even though, actually, it is within their experience that they don't.[28] On the golf course, at a dinner party or over lunch at the office we do pretty well without leaders. Yet, with the least provocation, we jump at the option of attributing consequences to leaders. It is part of human nature that we hold the belief that good (and bad) things only happen because some individual is responsible. You can see it in every Hollywood movie, folk saga and historical text – a manifest yearning for heroes, god-like parents and saviors; plus a handy array of villains to blame the bad stuff on. More on this later, but the fact is that *leaders really matter much more under some circumstances than others*, whatever stories people tell about leadership. We also seem to prefer the idea of bad leaders to no leaders. We are spoilt for choice in exemplars! Leaders can be a downright nuisance.

Here's a vivid instance. A major client of mine was a French bank, and the new Chief Executive came to speak after dinner at an executive program I was running. I had asked him to talk about, amongst other things, his personal experience of leadership. This man – very French, but also very cosmopolitan and sophisticated; a fast-talking, highly personable and confident man, with a reputation for dazzling brilliance in the highly technical world of high finance, with the kind of intellectual pedigree only the French know how to nurture – astounded the assembled executives, whom, up to this point, had been gazing at him with eyes shining in adulation, when he pronounced: "Leadership is a lousy way to run a company."

Now, actually, the company needed this man's leadership and especially at the time he made this comment, but he was making a point. He was reminding them that reliance on leaders is a sign of organizational weakness. If the company falls over when the CEO does, it is an ill-resourced business. He was saying good leaders create great companies that transcend leadership. This is done by institution-building, creating organizations that will stand the test of time. In their classic *Built to Last*,[29] Collins and Porras do a great job in showing the benefits of leaders who put themselves behind, rather than in front of, their organizations.

In the case I am describing, the company was Société Générale and the speaker was Jean-Pierre Mustier, wunderkind and CEO of the investment banking division, and, whether consciously or not, he was reflecting on the dramatic manner of his succession to the leadership role. This was brutally sudden, untimely and occasioned by tragedy. His predecessor, the visionary Xavier Debonneuil, was killed in a car crash, along with his daughter, in a head-on collision on a rainy highway outside Paris on the day after Christmas in 2002.

When you have been pitched into the top job by such a traumatic event, humility seems appropriate and, indeed, he was right. Mustier had to learn about the reality of top-level leadership from that sudden tragic instant. And what he learned, as he eloquently elaborated before his assembled lieutenants, was that you can forget all you might have assumed about the job. Think again. He confessed that when he took over he was a case-hardened ops guy, who had been skeptical when the then Chairman, Daniel Bouton, expressed the view that 30% of the top job was human resources. Mustier told his audience how he had come to realize the truth of his mentor's assertion. Leadership of one of the most complex organizations of our age is not principally to do with keeping the system running but about people – whom to hire, and how to manage, motivate, tool them up and coordinate them to get the best out of them.

Much the same insight came to Jack Welch, when he moved the HQ of GE to the training center at Crotonville, with an avowed intent to devote the majority of board time to the all-important process of getting, keeping and motivating talent.[30]

"WE DON'T NEED ANOTHER HERO"

The words are pop diva Tina Turner's and one is often moved to agree when we see what feet of clay are revealed under the robes of the high and mighty. And as we look around, we are entitled to ask the question: do we really need a leader? As we have seen, the answer turns out to be less often than one might imagine. Management writers have coined the phrase "substitutes for leadership" to capture the various arrangements through which this can be achieved.[31] Operating systems, rules, norms and collective agreements can render personal leadership redundant. Indeed, often when there appears to be a boss in charge, lots of decisions are actually diffused and semi-automated. On trading floors, algorithms are regularly preferred to error-prone human decision-makers.

But only in theory can we abandon leadership. It is in our DNA to want leaders and also that we differ substantially in our desires to lead and to be led – that is, there will always be individuals driven to take charge, and others content to let them.[32] Our bias in favor of leadership colors our perceptions. We not only hold within us primitive yearnings for the perfection of god-like, parent-like figures to take the burden of responsibility from our shoulders, but we see the hand of individual willpower in all human events.

The great accidents of modern times – Bhopal, Chernobyl, Deepwater Horizon, Fukushima – like most calamities are a mix of complexity, pressure and negligence.[33] Is there leadership culpability in such cases? Of course there is! But to err is human. Complexity stretches comprehension. Pressure encourages sloppy practice, shortcuts and poor data handling. Negligence is rarely willed, but we demand accountability. So we should, if this means learning lessons and fixing problems. But accountability has cultural overtones, and all too often it means, let's blame someone.[34] More deeply, we hate the idea that shit just happens, and reject even more the thought that we're out of our depth with our own ridiculously complex and challenging self-created systems – such as markets or information networks. We harbor deep yearnings for the simple morality play of our ancestors – where good and evil spirits inhabit men and drive them forward to their destinies.

THE POINT OF LEADERSHIP

We need leaders to be more than just figureheads and fall-guys. The primate studies we have discussed demonstrate that leadership is not a thing but a process – as we have defined it – to coordinate and direct. Studies of tribal peoples tell the same stories. Leadership is a function of social systems – it is one of the most economical and acceptable ways to get things done. What are those things? Three are paramount in tribal societies (see Figure 2.1):[35]

1. **Direction.** If your life consists of following the herds, planning for the seasons and dealing with other groups, a call has to be made about where to camp, where to hunt, when to build shelter, when to run and when to fight. These can be

Figure 2.1: Rediscovering leadership: lessons from anthropology

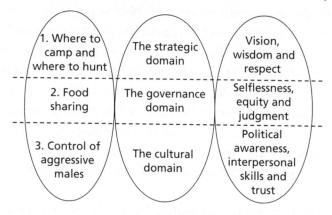

considered strategic decisions in a world of short horizons. The call can be made by the group, but often we prefer to vest it in an individual. Either way, leadership decisions have to be taken. Getting the timescale right is a measure of leadership wisdom – when to plunge into action; when to pause and deliberate. It is a test of the leader's compass that the accumulation of short-term, quick-fix decisions amounts to a coherent strategy and emanates from vision. Buffett's whole life has consisted of him defining his preferred hunting grounds and taking others with him.[36] The corporate graveyard contains the bones of many firms whose leaders made bad strategic calls: Lehman Brothers, Enron, Sun Microsystems, Satyam, Vivendi and many, many more.

2. **Food sharing.** There are always resource allocation issues. It may be to divide a surplus or to cope with a famine. This is a process of alignment – of creating a social order that will satisfy people's wants and focus power where you want it. It can be done in a lot of different ways. Individuals will give to each other in ways that tell us about status and hierarchy – who scratches whose back.[37] Food sharing can be done to bind a community – giving charity to the needy; building networks of cooperation and mutuality. It sets parameters for

reward and exchange. Leaders are prime architects of these models, and sometimes get it horribly wrong. One of the most disturbing outcomes of the financial crisis that overtook the world in 2007 was that it laid bare how one section of the community, bankers, had been gorging on the ever-higher piles of wealth created in one big hothouse of money. The rest of society stood agog at the sight of this plunder. The collapse of Lehman owed much to the extreme self-seeking greed of its leadership cadre: leaders who paid themselves and their cronies disproportionate shares of the food at the table.[38]

3. **Controlling aggressive males.** De Waal's apes display a raw and naked kind of politics in their community. His chimpanzees scream, scratch, bite, debase, self-abase, trick and betray each other. Just down the evolutionary road, their first cousins – the pygmy chimpanzees or bonobos – are making love not war. For them, sex is everywhere, and there is no time, energy or inclination to play bully-my-neighbor.[39] The sex is between pairs of the opposite sex, same sex, solo, in groups, conventional and exotic. We humans have plentiful diversions too, to prevent continual contests among the group who have most to gain and least to lose – the young males. We also have laws – "substitutes for leadership" – but in many communities all the law is informal, and the leader's job is to keep the peace. Legions of young men, pumped by their hormones and itching for some action, need to be put to some purpose. Fighting wars against your enemies is one solution, but is often self-defeating. Leaders who build cultures of cooperation and find acceptable outlets for young male striving (build a sports arena) will thrive, enjoy harmony and tolerate manageable levels of conflict. Enron got rich and famous by giving its young Turks the freedom of the house and look what happened – they tore the place down.[40] But the leader here is a role model – "a culture carrier," as expressed to me by an HR Director – able to set the tenor of relationships and build norms to support them. Daniel Goleman and others

have identified emotional intelligence as a prime leadership quality, and it is in this domain that it chiefly operates.[41]

It is clear that leadership is a burden. If so, why would anyone want to take it on? There are rewards – status, bounty, adulation and, of course, mating opportunities – but also big risks and potential costs. Look at President John F. Kennedy – compulsively consuming sexual opportunities provided by his supreme status but also paying the ultimate price of leadership risk through an assassin's bullet.[42] Being a leader means having to watch your back and continually prove your fitness for the role – keeping yourself in good shape, resourced and supported.

For us humans, the apparatus of leadership includes an armory of power, legitimacy and supporters. This includes "friends" who will do whatever they can to build you up and make you look good.[43] That is until you falter; when you're in danger of falling down and failing them, don't be surprised to see them on the other side of the river waving you goodbye.[44] As we shall see, leaders often get massaged into delusions about their own greatness and infallibility, yet they can also find what looked like solid support melting away like spring snow. The stories of King Lear's loss of power, not far from that of Jimmy Carter (former US President), Dick Fuld of Lehman Brothers and Fred Goodwin of Royal Bank of Scotland, show that the rapid desertion of fallen leaders is only a dressed-up version of the chimp who held the ring for his brief hour and now skulks in the shadows, living on the remnants of reputation and resources.

Leadership can be very hard – and very easy. Just when you're about to throw it in, you hear the people calling for you. Just when you think you've got it made . . .

In the next chapter we shall look at leadership across the sweep of human history, and what we can learn from it.

IMPLICATIONS AND OBSERVATIONS FOR LEADERS AND ORGANIZATIONS

We are animals, after all, so we should connect with our raw nature to understand why we act as we do. From our observations of ourselves and our close cousins in the primate world, some thoughts include:

- Fear works because it is powerful and visceral, but it is not sustainable as an instrument of leadership unless you bend the whole apparatus of the organization behind it, and that invariably takes leaders and followers to an ugly endgame.

- Leaders need to understand what kinds of dominance games are played, and how they are played. Some are visible; some are concealed. In particular, leaders should note the risk calculus of people – those who would like to strive for leadership but are afraid to do so. They can be especially dangerous as hidden enemies.

- Dominance games change with context. Don't assume that what keeps your reputation in place will endure. Pick your battlegrounds with care.

- Consider the motives of people who come to you for protection or guidance. What are the politics of their alliances and what do they really want from you?

- How you organize (centralized vs. decentralized; hierarchical vs. flat) creates a climate that may push you more towards some models of leadership than others.

- Groups need leadership not leaders. Don't fall into the trap of unnecessarily designating individuals as "leaders."

- Leadership is a lousy way to run a company. Make sure you have good "substitutes for leadership" to cover what you may not be able to attend to.

- Watch out for people's over-attribution of the leader as the cause of whatever happens.

- Leadership is a privilege, a service and a burden. If you're going to be a leader, make sure your shoulders are broad and strong – you will be the scapegoat for much that goes on.

- Remember the essentials of what leaders need to do – set direction, food sharing and control of aggressive males.

- Leaders are culture carriers. Remember, everything you do as a leader has cultural significance.

- 3 -

A VERY SHORT
HISTORY OF
LEADERSHIP

The greatest pleasure is to vanquish your enemies, to chase them before you, to rob them of their wealth, to see their near and dear bathed in tears, to ride their horses and sleep on the bellies of their wives and daughters.

Genghis Khan

Twenty-six is a nice age. You are properly into adulthood, full of vitality and ready for life's challenges. Sure you have a lot to learn, but you have plenty of time, don't you . . . ?

Not if your name is Hannibal the Great or Elizabeth Tudor. Both these individuals assumed command of their peoples at this age: one in Carthage in 219 BC, the other of the great maritime nation of England a while later in 1565. Neither had much time to figure out the meaning of leadership.

Hannibal – given a refined education by his father, and also schooled in the ways of war from the age of 9 – acceded to the military leadership of his people after his older brother-in-law was assassinated.[1] Seething at the oppression of the distant Romans and their threats to come into his country to subdue it with force, Hannibal conceived a bold plan to challenge their domination of the Mediterranean. Leading a polyglot mercenary army he descended on the Romans from where they least expected it. Traveling from Spain, he fought his way through France and came down through the Alps, rather than the protected coast road – holding his force together by his confident inspiration, plus the "shock and awe" tactic of elephants to convey them to the battlefield. He was a brilliant general who fought 22 battles undefeated against the Romans over 14 years before withdrawing from the gates of Rome at the last. In the end, he and his people were unable to withstand the power of the Roman Empire, but he had changed the course of its history and prefigured the decline and fall of Rome.

Elizabeth I of England succeeded to the throne as an unlikely heir – her father having disavowed his marriage to her mother Anne Boleyn after having chopped Anne's head off for treason and adultery.[2] Even her paternity was the subject of whisperings. She had been raised in seclusion, though not immune from the sexually predatory advances of her godfather, which she courageously resisted, until, at the age of 15, she found herself hauled before the Privy Council, an intimidating court of the highest noblemen, to face demands that she confess. She faced them down and surprised them with her fierce conviction in her innocence. Her survival of these ordeals and handicaps proved her single-minded commitment, which she channeled into a populist dedication to lead her people – foreswearing marriage to discharge her destiny. Thus, she constructed a foundation for her nation's lasting peace and prosperity through selfless dedication and tough-minded commitment.

Hannibal and Elizabeth had both been thrust into a world of danger and uncertainty. Each, through force of character, forged a path that changed history.

THE BEGINNING OF HISTORY

Our race of hominids – humans – was born under conditions of extreme adversity. Like many other species, it started when a sub-group – a "deme" in the language of paleontology – got cut off from the parent population.[3] Some random mutation appeared in the deme that proved to have distinct adaptive value under the persistent local conditions facing the group. Over several generations the new feature spread. Other variations followed, to the point where the new standard turned out to be incompatible with its long-lost parent model. A new species had been born, which, through its superior adaptive capabilities, in time came to displace its forebears completely and drive them to extinction.

This oft-repeated process of speciation through the millennia is reminiscent of the battle for standards in the technology industry – it is an analogous process.[4] It is evolution at work.

Leadership has special significance for humans and takes many forms, though with two underlying motifs. One is pure dominance – power comes to those who demonstrate, by force of will, their ability to make things happen. But power alone is not enough, or at least it is unstable and hard to sustain. Stalin was one of the most successful. More commonly, the pure dominance model has its day and then dissolves. Look at the so-called Arab Spring of 2011–12. The second motif in human leadership is reputation.[5] We inhabit a world of intelligence, language, consciousness, identity and understanding. You can get away with being the biggest, smartest or baddest guy in the room for only a short while. People will talk about you, weigh you, judge you, and if you fall short, ultimately plot about you and remove you.

If you are to lay any claim to lead people, then you will need a rationale that will command credibility and trust. If you ask people what they want in a leader, a short list recurs time and time again:[6]

- Integrity – a leader who can be trusted, will follow through on promises and show herself to be a real person who knows herself.

- Vision – a leader who knows where she is going and why; a leader who can paint an inspiring picture of possible futures for the tribe.

- Competence – a leader who has the gifts and intelligence necessary to understand the challenges facing the tribe and knows how to meet them.

- Confidence – a leader who can take decisions under all kinds of circumstances, and has the courage to stand by them.

These themes recur in the huge mountain of words written on leadership.

For the Greeks, the ideal was the philosopher-king – leaders needed to be smart and wise. The Romans, under the influence of Aristotle, embodied by Cicero, took a broader view: the leader embodying the idea of "virtue" – values that bind community.[7] A few hundred years later, in 15th century Italy, came a literate diplomat, Niccolò Machiavelli, who reminded us that leaders have to exercise control, through fear if necessary. Each of these accounts speaks to the tenor of their times: the Greeks striving for a perfect blend of knowledge and character; the Romans wanting leaders to cement their cohesion; Machiavelli urging a muscular pragmatism to replace the weak duplicity of the Florentine nobility he served and despised.[8]

So, when we read what people are saying about leadership today, what do we find? Answer: a great deal, but little about where we stand in history and why. Apart from these philosophical excursions, not much was really written on leadership until the 20th century, and since then no other topic has piled books and articles up higher. Yet the sum total is curiously dispiriting – plenty of schools of thought, but no unifying perspective on this topic – hence this book!

I'm not going to bore you with the short history of these writings over the last century, apart from picking out a few key ideas that have emerged:

1. **Leaders are different.** The people who emerge or are most picked to lead have distinctive drives and character profiles.[9] *Comment: Yes and no. Yes, leaders often are chosen because they are different. How they differ is not universal (see point 2).*

2. **Style is contingent.** Leadership styles have to be matched to situations, otherwise they won't work. Specifically, they have to get the right balance between focus on tasks and focus on people.[10]

Comment: True, but leadership is hard to put on and off like a suit of clothes, yet the point is valid. Leaders have to dress according to the weather, if they can! Also, there is more to the leader's situation than tasks and people, as we shall see.

3. **Leaders have to satisfy followers.** Leaders cannot lead in isolation, but have to respond appropriately to the needs of their people.[11]
   Comment: Also true, but which people? And don't the people change? This makes leadership a moving game.

4. **Leaders transform.** A chief function of leadership is to mobilize and motivate people to great achievements.[12]
   Comment: This is correct, but again there is a time for transformation and a time for consolidation. Leaders also have to do more mundane things to keep the system running. There is no one style for all seasons.

5. **Leaders are stewards.** Leaders take on responsibility for the tribe. It is their job to serve the community and embody its values.[13]
   Comment: This is indeed a valuable concept of leadership that has proved highly successful and has been appreciated – for example, in communal-type family firms – but again this model will not work at all times and in all places.

The reader will discern that my comments on all of these great ideas amount to a single thought: generalizations about leadership are all bounded by their context. Step into another world and something different is needed. The problem is that leadership theory has been following the herd – the main concerns of big US corporations – especially those that are prepared to pay top dollar for help with leadership development.[14] There is nothing wrong with this. Managers want to stay ahead of the game and in touch with the latest news from the front line. They read leadership hagiographies – but today's not yesterday's. The leadership lessons of Jack Welch are supplanted by those of Steve Jobs and those yet to come, no doubt, from Mark Zuckerberg or other *wunderkinder* of the digital age.

It is also limiting that a lot of research on leadership comes from laboratory studies of American college kids, acting out scenarios that simulate aspects of leadership – such as style, power and follower relationships.[15]

So let's go back to context.

THE RULE OF CULTURAL EVOLUTION

Our story is not just about leaders but entire social systems. The point here is that leadership, along with all the social forms that surround and define it, is a human cultural creation, and it was created to solve problems. The problem is how to live, whenever we are in time or wherever we are in geography.

At whatever juncture in history we stand, we face a set of challenges: some universal to human societies, others highly specific. Effective adaptation means adopting strategies that solve these and the problems we might expect to be just around the corner. Let's say we expect a good harvest this season, but fear that the rains might fail like they have done periodically in recent times. We shall have to encourage people to have appropriate expectations, to cooperate in the work that has to be done and to be able to deal with the unexpected difficulties that may occur. So we devise agreements, rules, conventions and command structures to ensure stuff gets done, along with incentives, networks, conventions and the like. These have to be flexed and sometimes to be overhauled radically to meet new challenges, but in so doing they have to obey a set of intimate and universal imperatives: human nature.[16]

Any social arrangements we invent – customs, cultures, systems – cannot afford to cross a line of improbability in the way they conceive of human nature. Any social system that is built upon a false view of human instincts, passions and ways of thinking will just get torn down, like the Berlin Wall, which similarly defended an empire of faulty reasoning and false ideology. Whatever model for living and working together we adopt, it has to be congruent with human nature, i.e. the essence of human motives and hardwired biases.[17]

Joseph Stalin, the man who built the Soviet Empire and whom we met in the last chapter, started his career as a street fighter cum dissident.[18] Expelled from the brutalizing environment of the Georgian seminary which radicalized him and many of his similarly expelled fellow trainees, he quickly found an ideology (bolshevism) and a network in tune with his cavalier, rebellious instincts. It was not long before he had set up business as a romantic highwayman and gangster, conducting daring raids and robberies as an armed horseman with a coterie of fellow bandits, bankrolling the exiled hero of the rebellion, Vladimir Lenin. Stalin's intelligence and magnetic personal power propelled him, over the years, into the leadership elite, and, after successive betrayals and factionalist conflict, he returned from two years of lonely and thoughtful exile in the desolation of a frozen Archangel labor camp to assume leadership of the Party. Thereafter, it was, tellingly, a pseudo-family affair, for his leading clique had, running through it, tribal strains of kinship and buddy bonds. Stalin systematically destroyed any actual or incipient rival networks with the potential for power – the kulak farmers, the military and the civil service – so that he, as the supreme mafia boss of the state, could have absolute control through his network of cronies.[19] A far cry from the dictatorship of the proletariat!

Communism survived for so long because it violated its own rules and allowed many ancient human instincts to flourish and habits to persist: dynastic succession, tribalism, favoritism, corruption and many extraordinarily inventive ways of gaming the system, which eventually collapsed under the weight of its own improbability. Actually, it was consumerism that destroyed the socialist empire.[20] The visibility of Western affluence was too much to bear for the hard-done-by Soviet Union's people.

So the rule of cultural evolution is to develop ways of life that are simultaneously adaptive to circumstances and congruent with human nature, and the history of our races tells just that story. We form different cultures according to whether we are island, mountain, river or plains dwelling people, under tropical skies or in the pale light of the Arctic steppes. Culture is part of human ecology, just as it is for the chimps, which scientists have found to evolve different forms of tool use, display rituals and patterns of domicile according to their context.[21] And here's the major twist for humans – the most important part of our context is each other. Our challenge is to adapt our systems to meet the needs of the human group and its circumstances.

Unlike any other species, our culture accumulates layer on layer on the adaptations of our forebears, until some warlord comes and tears it down and we start more or less afresh, finding new ways. The twist is this, though: unlike any other species, we can create frameworks of rules, norms and structures that change the rules of the adaptive game.[22] Suddenly, it no longer pays off to be the toughest guy in town, but instead it is better to be the best entertainer, toolmaker, teacher or whatever the present times prize.

Nelson Mandela was a leading member of a movement espousing and practicing armed insurrection against the dominant regime of apartheid in South Africa, an insurgency that grew over the 27 years of his imprisonment into a material threat to the state.[23] Mandela used this lever to bring the state's leadership to the negotiating table, and what he did on his release astonished the world. With the fiercest commitment, he set out a new model for the state based upon reconciliation and forgiveness – embodying a vision of a non-racist modern democracy in sub-Saharan Africa. Things would have gone very differently had the oppressed black majority exacted revenge on the white population.

Our two 26-year-olds – Hannibal and Elizabeth – changed history. Hannibal hastened the decline of the Roman Empire. Elizabeth ushered in a new model of monarchy of partnership with the people within an independent state, free from Catholic Rome, laying the foundations for much that followed in Britain, Europe and the world: mercantilism, the Industrial Revolution, colonialism and a residue of attitudes that persist to this day.[24]

The leader in history is part of the turning wheel that is called co-evolution.[25] She is partly produced by history and she is also the producer of history. Her time comes and goes; she is used and spat out. She makes and breaks old patterns and forges new ones. She is at the prow of history where the waves break, where the new course is charted. If war is coming, we will find a warrior. After, when we want peace and renewal, we will find a healer. We can get lucky, with a Nelson Mandela or an Elizabeth I; we can be unlucky, with an Adolf Hitler or a Pol Pot.

TRIBAL LEADERSHIP

We are the latest in a long line of hominid species – apes that walk on two legs – which arrived, as do many new species, under the evolutionary pressure of climate change. We know almost nothing about the social organization of the first of these hominids, the australopithecines of 4 million years ago, but it's a pretty sure thing that they were clan dwelling.[26] We know that they were the first primates to step out of the forests onto the newly opened vistas of the savanna, hunting in groups for big and small game as well as foraging for fruits, tubers, nuts and edible vegetation.

Homo sapiens continued this way of life for most of our history – around 95% of the estimated 200,000 years, and, in fact, the hunter-gatherer lifestyle persists to this day in remote pockets of the planet. The study of recent and surviving hunter-gatherer groups, and the historical record, allows us to reconstruct quite a lot about the way they lived and were led.[27] A pioneer of this research is Chris Boehm, a cultural anthropologist who cut his teeth in Gombe working with the legendary Jane Goodall studying primate societies before embarking on a hugely ambitious and definitive study of tribal societies.[28]

Here's what he found. The predominant pattern is one of democratic leadership. It is not always clear who are the leaders and who are the followers. In a hunting party it may not be decided who is to lead the hunt until the event is under way. There is no permanent hierarchy or dynastic succession. Leaders are those who are best fitted for the task of the moment. Jared Diamond, who has written about the prehistory of human cultural evolution and the advent of agrarian society, notes how stuck we are with our rigid conceptions of hierarchy and leadership and how we find it hard to think in any other way.[29] When Captain Cook landed in New Zealand and encountered the aboriginal peoples, his armed lieutenants, resplendent with their gold-braided epauletted uniform, confronted the assembled tribespeople and demanded "Take me to your leader." One can picture their puzzlement as they looked at each other quizzically, asking "Who shall we send?"

COOL AND THE GANG

A few years ago I went on a short field trip with two colleagues to spend time with a Maasai tribe in northern Kenya[30] – a pre-literate, non-monetized tribal group of pastoralists herding scrawny goats and cattle in a beautiful, but highly uncertain, environment under the shadow of Mount Kenya, where, from any year to the next, hardship threatens if the rains fail, as regularly happens. These are tough conditions and the culture that has evolved to maintain order and adaptability is intensively collectivist; rigidly stratified, by age and gender. Women, as in many tribal societies, do much of the day-to-day labor, while the focus of the social divisions, by age sets, is the men, who control decision-making. Males become warriors at puberty, and they remain such for around 14 years before graduating to become elders.[31]

We were only with them briefly, but it was my aim to ask them the kinds of questions I would if studying a family business, which, in a sense, they were. I interviewed the warriors, elders, women and children about their experience of life, labor and governance, through the translating skills of a Turkana journalist who joined us on the way. Quite early in our visit I met the magnificent Cool, a warrior chief of majestic bearing – tall, clean-limbed and smooth chested, with a strong-featured, lean-jawed head, his hair adorned with colored braids and plastic tulips. In addition to the customary *shuka*, the brightstriped Maasai red blanket worn as a robe by all males, his marks of distinction included various belts, bangles, necklaces and earrings. These are decorative expressions of individuality, yet also a sign of conformity. To the untrained eye, nothing in this costume marked him out as a leader.

I questioned him on the subject. "What does it take," I asked, "to be a really effective warrior chief?" His answer stunned me – only because I could not imagine receiving the same response from even the most "stewardly" of business leaders. He paused for thought and then replied, quietly but firmly in his majestic bass baritone, "Never demean anybody" – "never put anyone down" in street speak. Cool had arrived at his position by a protracted process of short-listing by elders before he was invited to take on the role. The criteria for selection, I was assured, did not involve looking the part, which Cool surely did, but rather the possession of emotional intelligence. For all the warriors' bluster and fantastical story-telling about their raids on their Samburu neighbors and lion hunts, the reality was a need to maintain social cohesion and gently douse the flames of any man-to-man conflicts, especially those where face-saving would be needed, such as when an elder wronged a warrior.

This mediation model of leadership is perfectly adapted to an intensively "collectivist" culture – the polar opposite of Western individualism[32] – whose chief purpose is to ensure a common fate for people through times of plenty and famine. Some individuals are slightly richer than others, in their possession of livestock and wives (a strong correlation with wealth – the only reason to have an extra wife is to do the extra herding and milking) – but all are bound within the same enclosed commonwealth of time-honored custom and practice. Within this world, personal differentiation is not encouraged, apart from choice of bodily decoration. At one point I asked the assembled elders what they would do if they found someone with an exceptional talent, say in tool-making or music. There was a pause, then one grizzled veteran spoke the answer of the group, "We don't want anyone with special talents."

Boehm's analysis[33] suggests there may be much more individual differentiation within tribes that have a more mobile and dynamic lifestyle, as in many hunter-gatherer societies, but they would be equally averse to dominant leadership. At first this seems curiously at odds with the fact that we humans, along with all other primate species, organize around male dominance hierarchies.[34] Boehm says that in pre-agrarian tribal societies, what he calls "reversed dominance hierarchy" operates. What this means in practice is that leaders are accepted but not allowed to get too big for their boots. He describes the various subtle and not so subtle means by which "upstartism" is checked – joshing humor, ridicule, indirect communication, the silent treatment, isolation and the ultimate sanction in any tribe, excommunication.

Let's come back to our world. At your local tennis club the same patterns may be observed. The Head Coach has certain rights, as does the Club Secretary, but members will quite gently let them know if they are overstepping a clear but invisible line of acceptable authority. Egalitarian forms of social organization can be found throughout our working institutions: project teams, partnerships, boards and the like, and the same tactics as Boehm's tribal put-downs can be observed exactly. It takes a particular type of gal or guy to be an effective leader in such structures, as we shall discover later.

THE ERAS OF LEADERSHIP

The hunter-gatherer model suited us for 95% of our existence, until, 10,000 years ago, global warming, rising sea levels and a heightened sense of population pressure created a set of conditions conducive to a huge innovation in our way of living.[35] In the classic *Guns, Germs and Steel*, Jared Diamond tells the story of the invention of agriculture.[36] Actually, proto-agriculture had long been a feature of hunter-gatherer existence. A clan would come back to spots where, in earlier seasons, edible annual plants had been seeded – but Diamond describes a step change, a coming together of uniquely propitious circumstances for the first agrarian settlements. This occurred in what he calls the fertile crescent of Mesopotamia, with terrain and favorable climate coinciding with the presence of naturally occurring plants and four animal species that proved susceptible to domestication.

The rest, as they say, is history, for the ability to store and accumulate the fruits of agriculture unleashed the dominance from the bonds of Boehm's reverse model. Now, the most ingenious, hard-working and determined individuals could command resources, which, in turn, meant the capacity to control men through rewards. Note that skill and brains are not the only ways to succeed – you can also kill to acquire, or just get lucky. The primate male dominance hierarchy can become a brutal and bloody battleground for supremacy.

One important transitional model is so-called "Big Man" leadership.[37] Hunter-gatherer peoples regulate and equalize food supply by powerful norms of altruistic sharing. If my group and I get lucky with a big kill, we will share with those who came back empty-handed. We will expect them to do the same. The Big Man in the tribe is the one who regularly over-achieves, is respected and revered for his mastery and for his values, for he selflessly shares his wealth, taking the last and least portion for himself. In many states, too many of them in Africa, we have seen the corrupted residue of this, where the leader claims to be the patriarch of his people and does his food sharing extravagantly and selectively to his tribal supporters, storing immense wealth for himself and his family, whilst brutally suppressing opposition to his rule.[38] They retain popularity by reaching over the heads of the educated elites to the rural poor, with whom they act out the ceremonials of Big Man largesse. Notable examples include Muammar Gaddafi, Robert Mugabe, Idi Amin, Jean-Bédel Bokassa and, most spectacularly – thanks to political manipulation and generous support from the West – Mobutu of the Congo, who took upon himself a bunch of forenames which translated as "the all-powerful warrior who, because of his endurance and inflexible will to win, will go from conquest to conquest leaving fire in his wake." In 1988 a British political party leader whose plane landed at the "wrong" airport in Zimbabwe was questioned by the authorities about his identity. His declaration that he was "Leader of the Opposition" promptly got him locked up![39]

The drive for power and dominance leaves many casualties among the weak and dispossessed. Many of the problems of modern society are what have been called disorders of rank.[40] Being of low status in a long hierarchy is bad news – impaired health, wealth and happiness all round.[41] People will strive to avoid such degradation at all costs. Social harmony is supplanted by social fear. Those who have, fear loss

47

and defend themselves; those who don't have, fear servitude and misfortune.[42] It is no accident that some of the world's wealthiest entrepreneurs, people like Andy Grove of Intel, Sergey Brin of Google and Jerry Yang of Yahoo, were themselves, or the children of, refugees, immigrants or from the social margins – imprinted with a need to succeed against the odds in a new world.[43] The Parsees who fled to India, Jews who escaped the Nazis and Asians expelled to the UK from Uganda have all added huge wealth to their new host countries.

Unfettered power coupled with ignorant and dependent populaces is a recipe for the despotic leadership model to prevail – warlords provide a protective shelter for dependent and powerless hordes. Periodic wars enable the exchange of ideas, methods, talented people and technologies.[44] You can see how, for millennia, this developmental pattern, despite its brutality, was an engine of growth, innovation and wealth.

We don't have time for a discourse on the great civilizations of the Sumerians, Mayans, Greeks and Romans, but they were islands of social experimentation – successful for their times, but floating in a sea of primitive warlordism – Dark Ages indeed. Social philosophies, such as Plato and Aristotle, form a key part of the co-evolutionary process – providing the emerging social order with a framework for leadership. Religion becomes a principal source of legitimacy, encouraging leaders to claim their divine rights to rule and sustain dynastic rule through their progeny (a well-established Darwinian preference for nepotism[45]). The arrival of the monasteries as places of industry, learning and faith provide the first models for business organization: managed systems for the production of knowledge, goods and services.[46]

All the while the formerly helpless and dependent people are getting smarter. Innovations come galloping in via trade and warfare, plus a demand for education to be able to call upon a less helpless and more knowledgeable populace. Education is a mixed blessing for leaders. It provides more support, but also an increasing requirement that they lead with followers' active consent. Before you know it, you have the Magna Carta, the establishment of governmental institutions and the countervailing powers of political parties, judiciary and representative associations. The balance of power shifts out from the center as landowners, industrialists and traders demand the organization of society be on terms that favor them, the creators of wealth.[47]

PATHS TO POWER

How do leaders get "selected" by the times they live in, or "self-select" – put themselves forward because they recognize this is their time? It is a haphazard business at the best of times, and we would be kidding ourselves if we supposed this to be a smooth, organic process. In fact it is very lumpy, with lots of casualties and failures on the way – people who assumed they were God's gift and turned out to be the devil's curse. There is a limited number of ways of getting leaders – five actually. They depend, of course, on context, and, thus, have been popular at different phases and times. In the contemporary world, all five prevail. Each has its constraints or preconditions, a narrative or a promise of what it will deliver, advantages and hazards or pitfalls, as Table 3.1 shows.

Table 3.1: Paths to power

Path to leadership	Preconditions	Narrative	Advantages	Pitfalls
Emergent	Egalitarian and fluid relationships	"I will do the job for you"	Flexibility; task effectiveness	Unreliability; "upstartism"
Hereditary	Legitimacy and group resources	"I embody all your interests"	Stability; order; stewardship	Incompetence; lack of commitment
Conquest	Power base and personal following	"I bring you strength and protection"	Survival of the fittest; resource acquisition	Treachery; defeat
Elected	Empowered followers and factions	"I will advance your interests"	Accountability; responsiveness; justice	Hypocrisy; sectarian conflict
Appointed	Rational order and accountability	"I will prove my competence"	Control; discipline; achievement	Unresponsive to followers; detachment

Emergent

In the hunting party, sports team, music group, project team, partner-ship or firm there may be no designated leaders, but there is leader-ship. It may consistently reside in the strongest player or the most commanding personality, yet, who leads, on either the task in hand or how the group is functioning, is likely to fluctuate according to what stage the group is at in its task or what kind of task it is engaged upon.[48] Emergence is a deeply attractive primal model – except perhaps to those who want to be kings – Boehm's "upstarts." One is reminded of the classic exchange between "upstart" Michael Jordan and Phil Jackson, coach of the Chicago Bulls basketball team; Jackson telling the players "There is no 'I' in team" and Jordan replying "Yeah, but there is in 'win'," The promise of the leader of the moment is operational – I will do the job for you. This is also the weakness of the model – it lacks consistency and vision, if that is what you want. When it comes to longer-term strategic questions, the team may struggle. Throughout history, however, there have been emergent leaders who have consolidated their positions. Nelson Mandela is a notable example. Duke Ellington, the great bandleader, was another, whom we shall profile later.

Hereditary

Monarchy is not a bad solution to the need for stable leadership, so long as the monarch has the right combination of wisdom, humility and strength to be the chief servant to the people. It is a position of trust and duty, and many a family firm has thrived with this kind of paternalism, or, more rarely, maternalism, in such leaders as Ratan Tata, Marilyn Carlson Nelson and William Gore. There is clearly a human appetite for hereditary leaders – look at the Gandhi dynasty of India or the Bushes and Kennedys in the USA. Dynasties require legitimacy. In the family firm it comes from ownership, though nepo-tism is often challenged by modern business values.[49] Monarchs have typically invoked a divine right, but a lot of blood has been spilt whilst claiming God's authority. The narrative of the selfless embodiment of all the people's interests is appealing, but easily corrupted into the worst kinds of Big Man leadership, and always vulnerable to the gene lottery – incompetent and uncommitted successors.

Conquest

The primitive world of leadership by dominance is a Darwinian struggle from which the commonwealth should ultimately benefit. Genghis Khan united the incoherent tribes of northeast Asia. Napoleon Bonaparte created a new order for Europe. The coup d'état follows the same logic. It is the way in which weak hereditary leaders are replaced by strong ones, and the people gain through the security of the chieftain's power and resources. In the boardroom, coups d'état have become quite common paths to succession. Look at Steve Jobs and Henry Ford, both ousted because they were seen as damaging to the health of their firms. The successor's narrative is one of reassurance about the new era she will usher in. However, the pitfalls are numerous: promises may not be kept and there is always the possibility of future rebellions. After all, if it happens once it can happen again. Unsettling!

Elected

In the absence of God or an army at your back, where better to get your legitimacy than from your followers, especially when they have the resources and sufficient voice to pull you down if you screw up? This is where leaders' narratives carry most weight. Here, the story has to carry them into power and sustain them. It is no wonder that politics is full of idealistic vision wrapped up in vague, slippery claims. You need a story that can be continually reworked to carry on convincing people, especially when reality changes. Political leaders are widely derided for this hypocrisy, even though, paradoxically, they are often talented, moral and belief-driven people. In democratic politics, the process became simplified by the innovation of political parties representing sets of interests. The risk is that leaders fail to unite and are seen as the captive of some sectarian group; the advantage is that they are accountable and have to answer the call of justice.

Something like an elective process also happens in disguised form in business. What appears to be a rational appointment is, in reality, the result of a boardroom vote, or the summation of "soundings" among followers. In some highly rational organizations, succession is according to a predetermined plan, but it is much more common for the very top-most appointments to be made by a more political process.[50]

Appointed

It seems the simplest and most rational way to create a leader. Some wise person or, better, a panel of experts, points and says, "that's the person who is fittest to lead this group at this time." This is done on a cool and impartial appraisal of the job to be done and the qualities of the person. At vast expense, armies of HR specialists are employed to oversee the process. The US military and British Civil Service developed some of the first sophisticated assessment regimes, and AT&T turned these into fully blown talent management systems.[51] IBM and legions of organizations have since followed this path. In Chapter 15 we shall examine how these systems have been perverted by deeper ancient instincts. For now, let us be content to note how appointment is often less rational and impartial at all levels, but especially the more senior you get. Emergent leaders get "appointed" to regularize their power – this happens a lot in politics. Family firms create rational systems to dignify the succession of relatives. Conquering warriors are promoted to official leadership roles. Elective and appointing processes get intertwined.

THE LESSON OF HISTORY FOR LEADERSHIP

Edith Cowan was the first female Member of Parliament in Australia in 1921.[52] Her life story had been a catalog of hardship, out of which came her burning passion for justice, especially about the rights of women – in her times an abused and taken-for-granted group, shorn of elementary rights. She took her country through a cultural transition. Would this revolution have happened anyway, without Edith Cowan? Was she just the tool of history, sitting on the cusp of change that was inevitable? It will always be the case that those with the most supercharged motivation will stand at the front while the forces of history push them from behind. Yes, of course change would have come to Australia without brave Edith Cowan, but maybe later and in a more painful way.

At the age of 18, Abraham Lincoln was sent down the great Ohio River with his friend Allen Gentry on a flatboat to the Mississippi Delta and the booming city of New Orleans, to trade Allen's dad's farming surplus, harvested under conditions of freedom and equality in the Mid-West.[53] The trip proved to be a shocking experience for Abe, who had been raised in a climate of vehement anti-slavery Baptism. He found the town filled with slave traders, and was especially outraged by witnessing the degradation of a lovely young Negro woman being prodded and pawed over like a beast at auction. Although subsequently in the Civil War Lincoln was more diplomatic and pragmatic rather than categorical and ideological in his stance towards the ending of slavery, it was an outcome he clearly cared about and helped to bring to completion. How long would this have taken without Lincoln?

Nelson Mandela ended something very close to a slave state persisting late into the 20th century, and did so in a way that has earned him more love and respect than any leader of modern times. Yet it was the Afrikaners who recognized the untenability of their position and the apartheid system they had created to enslave the native peoples of South Africa.[54] Mandela's timely release from 27 years of imprisonment and his powerful ideology of inclusion and forgiveness, rather than justice and retribution, gave birth to one of the most remarkable states of modern times, not untroubled today but with a more explicit dedication to human rights than almost any other.

Mandela's example is instructive. Leaders really do change the world in unique ways. The sub-Saharan region, and the world more widely, would have been radically different had an inter-racial bloodbath occurred. Australia and the USA would be different in ways we can only speculate on without the advent of Edith Cowan and

Abraham Lincoln. Who could deny that the world would be a very different place if Joseph Stalin, Adolf Hitler and Mohandas Gandhi had never been born? Leadership matters.[55]

So this is the mystery we shall be seeking to unfold through the remaining chapters of this book – how does this happen? Why does it happen the way it does? What can we do through leadership to direct history in better, rather than worse, ways?

Later I shall have something to say about the universals of leadership – what every leader needs to be and do, but here I have a much more difficult message. I shall call it the Leadership Formula:

> *The secret of leadership success is to be the right person, at the right place/time, doing the right things.*

History will help select the people who meet its demands and destroy those that stand in the way of its tides, but each of us can consider this question for ourselves. What do I need to be doing, at this place in time, to be having the best impact I can have on everything around me? This we shall explore through the SPQ framework – how leadership, as an adaptive social process, should, for the people who do it, be strategic.

IMPLICATIONS AND OBSERVATIONS FOR LEADERS AND ORGANIZATIONS

The lesson of history for leadership is that whatever worked yesterday won't necessarily work tomorrow. Leadership is context dependent. Leaders make history and are its victims if they cannot ride its waves. Strong leaders, who make history, force the world to bend to their will rather than by being versatile and accommodating it.[56] Some thoughts from the chapter:

- Pure dominance will not work, except under desperate circumstances. Leaders who would dominate need to consider what the currency of reputation is in their domain.

- Whatever model of leadership you want, expect people to want you to display what they consider to be integrity; some vision of possibilities; evidence of your competence; and to show you are confident of your purpose and decisions.

- Leadership is a distinct role with special responsibilities, but the precise nature of these depends upon the context.

- The job of leader is, at one level, to help institutions and organizations stand in a "correct" relationship between human nature – the needs of the people – and the times and circumstances they are living in.

- Remember, leaders can make the rules that make the game. This is potentially very powerful.

- One of the most effective models of leadership is a low-power, low-dominance model of fluid and flexible democratic guidance and action.

- How leaders get to their positions matters – it affects the risks and opportunities of leadership, and also the preconditions and narratives needed for success.

- Leaders need to take responsibility for helping members understand the nature of the reality around them and to help shape it.

- Leaders need to see their place in history – local and global – and be ready to communicate this as part of their narrative.

- This means reading the times of one's business – its journey to the present and its path into the future.

— 4 —

LEADERSHIP AS STRATEGY – SITUATIONS, PROCESSES AND QUALITIES (SPQ)

The reasonable man adapts himself to the world. The unreasonable man persists in trying to adapt the world to himself. Therefore, all progress depends on the unreasonable man.

George Bernard Shaw

THE IBM STORY

There are few companies that have had a more checkered or illustrious history than IBM. It grew as an equipment manufacturer out of the thrusting vision of Thomas Watson senior, who commanded the business with an iron fist, only handing it over shortly before his death, at the age of 82, to his son, Tom Watson Jr, as if it were a family firm, even though Watson entered the firm as a general manager, and together they never held more than 11% of the stock.[1] Both were smart, powerful men, driven by strict Presbyterian values. Watson senior was a tough guy who brutally sought to dominate his son. It was fortunate that Tom Jr was resilient and brilliantly able to build on the platform his father founded, restructuring the business around the nascent computing industry.

Watson Jr retired for health reasons in 1971, and after nearly 60 years of Watson leadership, there followed a succession of insider appointments. As the culture coalesced it earned the soubriquet "Big Blue," standing for the power, reach and uniformity of its growing army of blue-suited, white-shirted staff.[2] Under the leadership of John Akers, who took over as CEO in 1985, Big Blue grew in power and reputation, not least because of its end-to-end paternalistic care for its battalions. Meanwhile, all around the company, vast changes were taking place in the industry, amounting to commoditization of its product range. Suddenly the firm was out of touch and in trouble, clinging to the melting iceberg of dominance in mainframe computing.

For the first time the firm went outside to find a leader to rescue it. It spat out John Akers and found Lou Gerstner, who may be credited with one of the greatest turnarounds in corporate history, reinventing IBM as a software and services giant, which it remains to this day.[3] Akers, who had desperately decentralized Big Blue into a raft of Baby Blues, growing revenue whilst profits shrank, was a very different character to his successor. Akers was a salesperson who proudly promoted excellence at all levels, but was stuck with a resolutely inward vision. A former Navy fighter pilot, he was said to "lead" more than listen: continually exhorting his people.[4] Gerstner, a workaholic, visionary and "transformational leader," with a track record of focused achievement with Nabisco, Amex and McKinsey, came with the advantage of all outsiders – no fluid from the corporate culture flowing in his veins. He promptly reversed the decentralization plans, dismantling the bloated and arrogant bureaucracy that IBM had become, and proceeded to refocus the business on the commanding heights of the new emerging arena of IT services.

The point of this story is that great companies have to do two things to survive and prosper. First, they have to understand and move with the times, to ride the waves of change, to improvise solutions to newly emerging challenges – to be, in a word, agile.[5] The second thing they have to do is to shape their markets, awaken new tastes in their customers, bring visions of possible futures into people's minds, create new landscapes within which their business will be uniquely well equipped to prosper – to be, in another word, shapers.

ADAPTATION TO ECOLOGICAL CHANGE

This is the duality of leadership. Leaders need to understand their role sitting on the cusp of change. Change is unstoppable – adaptability is all.

In the wide context of evolution, adaptability is the challenge facing all species. There are four possible responses to an environmental shift, such as climate change.[6] The first and most common outcome is extinction, through inability to adapt. Second is what evolutionists call habitat-tracking. The species wanders off in search of fresh environments that resemble the vanished ones to which they were adapted. Third, the least likely outcome is good mutation – the species acquires new features that enable it to adapt to the changed environment. This is how new species emerge, as we described in the last chapter. Like all other species, we are improbable survivors of a ruthless process. But there is a fourth option that evolutionary scientists have only recently paid attention to – niche construction.[7] Ants, beavers and especially humans don't just select environments that suit their capabilities, they transform environments to supply their needs. Leaf-cutter ants create fungus gardens which they harvest; beavers dam rivers; the first humans practiced proto-agriculture to transform their environments.

There are close parallels in what happens to businesses facing radical change in their markets:

- **Extinction:** the disappearance of Woolworths, for example, a general store killed by the rise of the shopping mall.

- **Habitat-tracking:** the Swiss watch industry migrating to the new technology and retaining existing markets.

- **Mutation:** the transformation of a very small number of firms in the pocket calculator business which did not become extinct, like Texas Instruments, which morphed into the semiconductor business.

- **Niche construction:** Apple creating new markets around its innovative products.

Strategy professors like to portray these developments as the result of impersonal forces working on firms.[8] Yes, evolution is impersonal, but let us not rule out the human agent. It is hard to imagine how the personal entertainment market would have developed the way it did without the innovative leadership of Akio Morita of Sony,[9] or the PC market without Steve Jobs.

Leaders are the embodiment and the drivers of strategic options. Sometimes they are the captives of them, but their role is an indispensable part of the process. It is time to climb into the minds of some leaders to understand how this occurs.

THE LEADERSHIP FORMULA

Seasoned executives sent to business school to learn about leadership arrive with a healthy skepticism. What in heaven's name can this academically trained professor, who has way less business experience than me, teach me about the world I inhabit?[10] Am I going to be told lots of stories about great leaders and how to emulate them? Am I going to be given lots of psychometric tests and then be told what my leadership style is and what to do about it?

Well, yes, in all probability you are. Actually, some of these well-worn methods will have payoffs, but they are uneven. You may be entertained more than you are dazzled by insights. Most likely you'll go back to your business world to find it, like yourself, unchanged. But who knows? Maybe you will encounter a really great teacher. Here's the difference between a great, a good and a poor teacher:

- A great teacher *changes the way you see things.* The most profound insights alter your vision permanently. The world never looks the same again. To see is to be.

- A good teacher helps you envision more clearly or in different ways the world you will go back to after your training program, and perhaps changes the way you see yourself.

- A poor teacher shows you stuff – great leaders, war stories and the like – that just make you think, I wish I could do that.

As a teacher, one tries to inspire with ideas, but this is not guaranteed – unless you are a mesmeric orator or you have your audience well and truly tuned in. The trick of all influence is to make would-be learners receptive. As in so many things, readiness is all. What is needed is something that starts with them and their immediate situation, and then works outwards to the choices and opportunities they face as leaders.

This is what the SPQ framework seeks to do. It is simple, powerful, practical and strategic. It sprang out of my discontent with the stacks of leadership books and articles, especially the heroic leader war stories, all stuffed to the gills with shopping lists of desirable attributes, categorical recipes for effective action and tiresome, self-congratulatory yarns about achievements.

I introduced the Leadership Formula (see Figure 4.1) at the end of the last chapter. Its strength is that it is a frame into which you can input your own parameters to make it work.

> *The secret of leadership success is to be the right person, at the right place/ time, doing the right things.*

It's as simple as can be, isn't it? Well, yes and no, for this definition has sharp teeth and a sting in its tail. The teeth are the tough message – you'd better get it right or move out of the way for someone better. There's also a message of hope. Maybe you can wait, and you'll become

Figure 4.1:   The Leadership Formula

- To be the right person
- At the right time and place
- Doing the right things

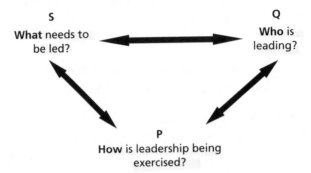

S
What needs to be led?

Q
Who is leading?

P
How is leadership being exercised?

Figure 4.2:   Questions raised by the Leadership Formula

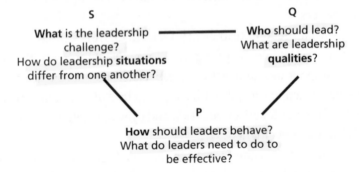

S
What is the leadership challenge?
How do leadership **situations** differ from one another?

Q
Who should lead?
What are leadership **qualities**?

P
How should leaders behave?
What do leaders need to do to be effective?

the right guy when the right time comes, like a broken clock that's right twice a day. Or maybe you can do it the hard way: figure out what needs to be done and just do it. Easy? That's the sting. There is also a promise. Change is possible because of what you do. This might be personal niche construction – you making your world. It may be by vision. Change the way you see the world and you will change the way you act. This, of course, is the great prize of education – to change the world by changing vision. Seeing is being.

There is no universal recipe to be found here; no list of attributes, just a puzzle to be unraveled (see Figure 4.2). The puzzle is adaptation. And the most effective adaptation is strategic: the *strategies* in the subtitle of this book. How many different ways can you achieve this – be the right person in the right place doing the right thing?

This formula, by the way, is not just for leaders, it is for anyone, since what it is asking is, how can I, being the person I am, adapt to a constantly changing world? This puzzle has absorbed me for much of my career, starting with work I did in the 1980s with Michael West about what happens to managers when they change jobs.[11] We found that various kinds of transformation, success and failure occurred. The act of moving to a new position is a challenge we all face, and, as we all know, sometimes it's great; sometimes it's painful; sometimes we screw up; sometimes we experience a profound discovery. In this and the next chapters I am going to show you how these outcomes occur, but they hinge on a duality.

The duality is captured in the Shaw quote at the start of this chapter.[12] Are we going to adapt, like reasonable men and women, or are we going to be unreasonable and persist in trying to change the world? The Leadership Formula captures the challenge that faces any of us when we change jobs. What should we do: adapt or innovate? Should we become more versatile and allow ourselves to learn and be molded by this new reality or should we seize the new world by the scruff of the neck and make it our own?

The key to leadership effectiveness is getting this right – when to bend; when to stand firm; when to shape; when to be shaped; and, of course, when to do nothing, and wait until the time is right for us.

THE ADAPTIVE LEADER

The extraordinary Steve Jobs, the energetic and demanding co-founder of Apple, built the business around his vision only to find that his way of leading it was causing increasing tensions with senior officers of the firm, who became exasperated and showed him the door. "The best thing that ever happened to me," averred Jobs in his famous commencement speech to the 2005 graduating class of MBAs at Stanford.[13] Why? Because it threw him into a space where, freed from the burdens of leadership, he could explore new ideas and issues. This led to a connection and deepening association with Pixar, culminating in his eventual reintegration into a bruised Apple, which he rejuvenated by streamlining its business model and launching a raft of products that were to define the marketplace for years to come. For Jobs, this sequence was one of personal transformation as well as the transformation of his business.

This duality of adaptation through innovation or personal adjustment is universal. It connects with the broader tide of ecological change in the history of our species. Later in this book I will show how this works at the micro level of psychological processing – as Tony Blair recounted at the start of this book on his reactions to the sudden news of a terrorist attack in his country's capital. Before we do this, we need to step back and look at the broader picture of the adaptive, and maladaptive, leader. This is what the SPQ model seeks to elucidate.

S: There are many types of situation. This is the "S" factor. Bush's and Blair's suddenly dawning consciousness of a changed state of the world are vivid instances of situational challenge. Leaders also get slower realizations of a changing leadership reality – sometimes, fatally, too slow – like Churchill failing to bring to peacetime leadership the force and effectiveness he had as a wartime leader.[14] Whenever we change jobs, we face the challenge of comprehending a new "S." Incoming leaders have to take care, for there may be many competing stories about what is going on in the organization. Which to believe? This is a critical moment – as it was for our two 26-year-olds, Hannibal and Elizabeth – stepping into situations of immediate challenge. What you see shapes what you do.

P: Leadership processes are what you do as a leader: actions, tactics and routines. Nothing may be the very thing to do.[15] Inaction may be the smartest strategy. Less is more. So what is a leadership behavior? Answer: anything is a leadership behavior. Lying on the floor fast asleep may be the most effective thing a stressed-out boss could do. Every leader faces the challenge of shot selection. Some leaders are naturally more gifted than others at playing different roles – Blair had this quality – but some of the best have a single, indelible style, like Lee Kuan Yew – founder of modern Singapore.[16]

Q: Leadership qualities are those indelible traits that we call character, plus a lot of other defining characteristics, like gender, age, resources and history, that make us who we are. There are many different ways of being a leader and many different types of leader. This area of the leadership literature is heavily populated.[17] There are reams of books and papers on leadership qualities: what works and why; what can and can't change; and what limits the likelihood of leadership success. More on this in the next chapter, but suffice it to say that one can discern three broad groupings of orientations to leadership:[18]

1. **Natural leaders:** people who, for whatever reason, have a deep drive to lead and the capacity to command; people who will move relatively freely between leadership situations, though not without conflict at times. Many of the named people in this book are of this type.

2. **Narrow-bandwidth leaders:** lots of people, and quite a few of the cases here, are willing and capable of leading but only in a quite circumscribed range of leadership situations.

3. **Non-leaders:** people who have no desire or interest in leading, or who have unshakeable reasons for not leading. They are a minority, but some of the most useful people on the planet – many artists, advisors, inventors and professionals – fall into this category.

THE SIX PRINCIPLES

Figures 4.1 and 4.2 show the SPQ factors as a system, seeking resolution in alignment. This is the leadership sweet spot. So many of the leaders we revere – Nelson Mandela, Aung San Suu Kyi, Duke Ellington, Ernest Shackleton and others in this book – are holding this alignment in different kinds of balance: striving, creating, envisioning, loving and earning our regard. Yet, in history and in business, the disasters seem rather to outnumber the heroes, so we need to see which SPQ strategies work and which do not. In the next chapters we shall be doing so through six principles:

Principle 1: Shaping

Principle 2: Discovery

Principle 3: Self-knowledge

Principle 4: Assimilation

Principle 5: Seeing

Principle 6: Selection

We shall unravel how these can be enchained into a leadership strategy in Chapter 8, but first let us examine the significance of the three main pillars of the model in turn – for it is essential that they are understood as primary sources of adaptive success and failure. In the next chapter, though, we look more closely at the elements of the framework, starting with the all-important questions around the "Q" factors – what choice do I have, being who I am, to lead in one way or another?

IMPLICATIONS AND OBSERVATIONS FOR LEADERS AND ORGANIZATIONS

This chapter has introduced the SPQ framework, which seeks to capture the adaptive challenge of leaders, faced with their knowledge of themselves, their experience of the world and the skills they want to deploy. It is a tricky dance to be performed to the music of their times.

- The Leadership Formula – to be the right person at the right place and time doing the right thing – is our definition of leadership effectiveness, and there are many paths to achieving this alignment.

- Broadly, this amounts to a balance of behaviors that work for the person and the situation; controlling the duality of adaptation vs. innovation or versatility vs. shaping.

- Faced with radical environmental change, leaders can play a significant part in taking their organizations in any of four ways: extinction, habitat-tracking, mutation or niche construction.

- Making followers receptive to change is a prerequisite for leading people successfully through these options.

- The key concept is alignment between the SPQ elements – but there are many different ways of being a leader; many different kinds of leadership situation; and an almost infinite range of leadership processes.

- Motivation to lead matters. There are three broad groupings of people: broad, narrow and no-bandwidth leaders.

— 5 —

WHO AM I? LEADERSHIP QUALITIES AND THE COMPASS QUESTION

Experience is not what happens to a man. It is what a man does with what happens to him.

Aldous Huxley

Barack Obama and Bill Clinton are both deeply reflective men. In his book, *Dreams from my Father*, Obama rakes through the undergrowth of memory and impression to answer deep questions about his purpose and identity.[1] Clinton also finds his values and mission in a fearless confrontation with memories of brutalizing encounters with his drunken stepfather.[2] Blair and Bush, whom we met earlier, had much more straightforward and privileged upbringings, and are given to less soul-searching – the complications for them are out there in the world more than in their Selves.

"Know thyself" was the cryptic injunction engraved on the portal of the temple at Delphi. That's all very well but:

- we may be severely limited in our powers of introspection;

- you can do too much navel gazing – it may make you unhappy;

Figure 5.1:   The SPQ framework: leadership qualities and the Compass Question

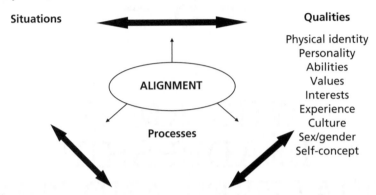

- some people find it harder than others and, when they do manage to do it, they don't seem able to do it very well.

That apart, when we look, what do we see? There is an exercise I use called the "Twenty Statements Test" which simply asks you to write on 20 numbered lines 20 answers to the question "Who am I?"[3] This proves to be interesting and revealing.

The most striking thing about this task is how enormously people vary in how easy they find it to do. Some get stuck at around 12 responses; others breeze through to 20 with descriptors to spare. For now, let us simply wonder at the huge colorful menagerie of human types that can be found to bear the title of leader. The leadership qualities listed in Figure 5.1 show there are so many ways to be a leader, and many ways to be a person, actually. They amount to potential answers to the Compass Question: what is the inner reference point or gravitational force that pulls a leader in one direction rather than another?

You are having lunch with a colleague. What do you see across the table? Go on, really look at her, from outside to inside and reflect on what you see and know, asking what makes her "different" or distinctive from you, or any other people you know:

1. **Physical:** She's taller than you, female, but with a distinctive build, hair and eye coloring. Hard to tell, but she may also have different energy levels and physical strength. There are,

no doubt, other physical differences that you can't see, some of which you'd need to know her really well to be aware of, such as allergies, tastes and biorhythms. And, yes, such factors can be critical for leadership. A reminder of the primitive susceptibilities of electorates is the fact that US presidents (and business leaders) are significantly taller than average.[4] Ronald Reagan is perhaps the epitome of a leader chosen for his physical bearing – the sonorous voice, folksy smile, big muscular frame. No matter if others wrote the words – he spoke them like a real leader.

There may be more overt physical requirements for leadership in certain specialized roles requiring attributes such as strength, speed, nice hair, but where such attributes are part of the job – nice hair is needed on the synchronized swim team – this is rarely a differentiator of the leader any more than the followers. We look for something a bit more substantial in our leaders. Yet, in sports there is a remarkably persistent foolishness that is practiced in choosing the best athlete to lead the team. It can ruin the person's game and end up not helping the team. You can get lucky. But it seems best to look for something else to define leadership.

There are many aspects of physicality. Energy is one of the most important – the ability to persist, endure, drive forward.[5] This was a gift of Ernest Shackleton, the explorer, a man who, in 1913–1914 led 28 men to survival over 21 months of the cruelest conditions a human can withstand.[6] Stranded on an Antarctic ice floe, he set out to save every life, and succeeded. In truth, there is no boundary between "physical" and mental qualities – they both swim in streams directed by hormones and DNA. Gender can be seen in this light. Feminists make much of women's inferior stature and strength. This can matter, but it is broader-based adaptations to their role in the human family that are related to leadership, not least a biological leaning toward different preferences.[7] Women's challenges in leadership are distinctive, and come from quite gender-specific sources, as we shall see.

2. **Personality:** So, looking once more at your lunch companion, how do you judge her character, and what exactly does this word mean? Psychologists define personality as "a disposition to behave in a particular way;" i.e. it's what you generally or regularly prefer to do rather than what's expected or demanded of you. The study of character has been going on since the time of Plato and before, but in the last century it has attracted a huge volume of attention in business and psychology, a lot of it quite technical, with much debate about whether there is a fundamental structure to human (and non-human!) personality (answer, probably yes).[8] People regularly ask whether leaders are "born" or "made."[9] Answer: both. We are all born with the rudiments of character pre-programmed into our DNA, so, yes, leaders are born – or rather it encodes the type of leader one might be. Leaders are also "made." Upbringing, schooling, critical relationships and formative experiences all play a part. There is a big literature showing how much leadership owes to personality. For many political leaders, and for plenty of business leaders – Jack Welch, Lee Iacocca, Rupert Murdoch, Larry Bossidy, Dick Fuld, Ratan Tata – it is their most distinguishing feature, and for every leader, personality is critical at some level for their performance.

Take the case of Carly Fiorina.[10] She learned her trade as a technologist in AT&T, deliberately choosing the most masculine areas of operations to assert her credentials. Subsequently, she moved to HP, where she rose to power largely through the strength of her personal convictions and ability to communicate them. So important is personality to leadership that it behooves one to ask the heretical question "can it ever *not* matter – or are there leaders without a 'personality'?"

This might not be such a dumb question as it appears. There do seem to be genuine differences in how "traited" some people are;[11] some are quite "untraited," lacking strong dispositions except for the commonplace essentials. Many actors have this kind of blurry identity. Such people are highly adaptable, but unlikely to innovate. We are back to the central duality of adaptation. Some seem able to switch their dispositions on and off – to act sociable at a party, but also appear just as at home in prolonged solitude, untroubled by urges to rush out and be with people.[12] Many of the least-known business leaders are like this. They are often very hard to read; lacking clearly defined personality profiles; able to switch their behavior quite abruptly as events or meetings unfold. They are enigmas to those who follow them, yet highly regarded as leaders who can steer them through minefields of politics and technological change.

3. **Aptitude and ability:** Many great leaders built their businesses around their talent. In the arts it is common, though ability cannot stand alone – it requires the support of character. Duke Ellington had a rare creative and technical talent, happily in train with a cool, committed, positive and charismatic personality.[13] Mark Zuckerberg, Soichiro Honda, Akio Morita, Bill Gates, Warren Buffett and Steve Jobs are all very different personalities whose careers were defined by their obsessive interests. Aptitude is the godfather of ability. Some of these people had parents who spotted and nurtured their aptitudes; others clawed out the space for themselves – the space needed to turn their aptitudes into abilities.

   But how sustainable is ability as a leadership quality? Clearly, none of these people have left their knowledge and skills in the background, but many leaders have to. It is a familiar sad story how would-be leaders, advanced on the basis of their technical abilities, lose their grip as these skills become less central and "soft" skills become more germane to their leadership role.[14] Failures to manage relationships, influence, communicate and make decisions can hide for a while behind a veneer of technical brilliance, but without support they risk downfall.[15] Gates, the über-nerd who built the mighty Microsoft, did so with the considerable help of the redoubtable organization-man Steve Ballmer.[16] Without him and other partners we might know little of his name today.

Probably the most important general purpose ability is intelligence, yet it turns out to be poorly correlated with leadership success.[17] It is more a threshold factor – you have to be smart enough for whatever you have to do. I have to say that most of the business leaders I know and admire are pretty smart people, and if they were less smart they would be worse leaders. Yet plenty of very smart leaders screw up horribly, and some genial idiots seem to do pretty well. There are two explanations. One: we are back to the Leadership Formula. Is this a situation where brains will help or hinder? You just have to be smart enough – how far above an IQ threshold you are will enhance your leadership capability in many, but not all, leadership roles. Second, in most business and political settings intelligence is a necessary but not a sufficient condition for effectiveness. In other words, you can't succeed without being smart enough, but being smart enough doesn't guarantee success. Kenneth Lay, the crook who commanded Enron, didn't fail because of lack of brains, but because he had no morals.[18]

4. **Values:** Every leader needs a value proposition, and for some their leadership can be defined as a moral commitment.[19] This is true of many politicians – Gandhi, Obama, Thatcher, Merkel – and quite a few business leaders, such as the legendary Max DuPree of Herman Miller,[20] the furniture manufacturers, Marilyn Carlson Nelson of the Carlson hotel and leisure group[21] and Sergey Brin of Google (slogan "Don't be evil").[22] Mo Ibrahim is an entrepreneur and philanthropist (whom we shall meet again in Chapter 12) – a founder of the cell phone industry in Africa who foreswore all corrupt and unethical practices in that most vulnerable of geographic regions.[23] For him, and many other businesspeople, if there is no social value at the end of their work, what's the point? This is a common

perspective among established family business leaders, such as Marilyn Carlson Nelson of the leisure and hotel group that includes Radisson and Park Plaza. Emblazoned across the business are the values of equal opportunities, integrity, courage, humility, relationships and respect.[24]

How readily can we discern the values of our lunch companion? Most leaders will claim to be value driven, but talk is cheap. To be confident about values, we need to see what people actually do – whether actions and choices match the talk. Even that is not so straightforward – bad people can do good things. Hitler was kind to children from time to time. But any discerning reader of corporate culture will quickly see that ethical beliefs and practices have to run through the veins of the organization at all its levels and be more than skin-deep.

The reality is that leaders differ enormously in the importance they attach to values.[25] All will claim the moral high ground but some are almost indifferent to the nature of the business they are leading – it is enough for them to be needed to do the leadership job. Others are clear on the matter: without a strong proposition that ties in with what they value – social justice, the environment, community improvement and the like – they can have no personal investment in their leadership role.

5. **Interests:** This is much easier territory. We can look across the table at our dining companion and ask her some simple questions, such as, "what do you like to do?" Vocational psychologists have kit bags full of questions to reveal the structure of our interests, to see which map onto job functions and work environments.[26] These are often clumped into broad categories, such as social, artistic or enterprising roles; or preferences for working in specific areas and functions such as finance, music, engineering, sales, education or charity.

The question here is how interested does a leader have to be in the domain she is supposed to lead? Do you have to love music to run an opera company? Probably yes, but you don't need to be a musician. Again, the Leadership Formula helps us to look at this strategically. Or rather it raises a question: when does it matter that a leader has a powerful interest in his domain and when does it not? And why is that?

Duke Ellington, George Patton and Soichiro Honda would have had precious little motivation to lead in areas other than music, military and engineering, but other leaders are much more flexible and unattached. Richard Branson, the British entrepreneur, started in music journalism, moved to producing and selling records, branched out to airlines, and has since overseen the Virgin empire move into everything from pet insurance to telephony.[27] Branson's interests are in relationships and activities rather than products or areas.

You may remember I earlier distinguished three broad leadership orientations: all-purpose, broad-bandwidth leaders (motivated to lead almost anything), narrow-bandwidth leaders (only lead when it really suits them) and non-leaders (will only lead when there is little choice). This is the dimension that is most influential for the second of these three groups, the situation-specific leaders. The logic also applies to the non-leaders, although there are lots of other reasons why some people hate to lead.

6. **Experience:** How much does experience matter? Alexander the Great started conquering the world at the age of 16.[28] You can make too much of track-record. The novice leader has all the advantages of youth: bravado, vision, energy, invention. If it's your first time, you have to invent. Yet, as has been said, "good judgment comes from experience, and experience comes from bad judgment." Hmm. The risks are evident, for which reason boards often elevate experience to be the top criterion[29] – selecting on the very attribute that will come anyway, for leadership, like any other function, can be learned, if not loved. You might or might not be born with favorable drives, values and aptitudes, but once you're pitched into a

leadership role you will discover, as many accidental or unexpected leaders, like J-P Mustier of Soc Gen, did, that it is a game with its own rules, boundaries and demands. You'd better get the hang of it pretty damn quick.

Poring over the CV of our lunch colleague will tell us what, precisely? So-called professional interviewers do this all the time, and consider themselves especially skilled at extracting insights about candidates on the basis of their questioning about experience. There is clearly an art to this. One common fault is to ask too many "why" questions and not enough "how" and "what" questions. Why questions will harvest heavily varnished chains of reasoning – stories really – about why certain things did or didn't happen.

At another level though, if you can detach yourself from their literal qualities, there is some mileage in decoding the "I" narrative – why we should listen to the stories leaders tell about their experience. We need to keep skeptical about the facts but pay attention to the stream of narrative. The Bush and Blair accounts are designed to be convincing – so they can feel true to themselves as much as to us. We have to get beyond their deliberate or unconscious truth bending.

When you hire someone for their experience, remember, you get the whole enchilada – a complex person, mental warts and all. Psychometric assessments of prospective CEOs might happen in some rarified circles, but what you usually get is a bunch of board members poring over a CV and airing their prejudices or grunting their assent. Relying on experience as your search criterion is, at best, hit and miss. You may get lucky; you may not.

7. **Culture:** Experience builds up layer by layer on two bedrocks. One is the DNA of individuality. This is the leader's personal dashboard of filters that sieves their experience and learning, much of it implanted before she had any choice. It steers her thought processes. The second bedrock is the leader's

awareness of the world around her and how this has been acquired.

Let us suppose your lunch guest has a different skin color to you and is plainly a non-native language speaker. Did it matter to Duke's leadership that he was an African-American, or to Barack Obama's that he emerged from American/African/Indonesian/Irish/Hawaiian cross-currents of birth and domicile? You bet! Did it matter that Steve Jobs's birth father was a Syrian national? Hardly. Less than the fact that his biological parent was a PhD. What part did Japanese culture play in the leadership style of Soichiro Honda, Akio Morita and Sakichi Toyoda? Their entrepreneurial skills, engineering excellence and inventive partnership were facilitated by the solid traditions of respect, tradition, integration, order and teamwork to be found in the philosophical traditions of Confucianism and Shintoism that stabilized the long-isolated cultures of the Far East.[30]

Culture is simultaneously skin-deep and profound. At the surface level it is apparel – a form of display. It is language and a tone – an expressive medium. More profoundly, it is the software of the mind's hardware; shaping what we pay attention to. Remember, seeing is being. It is formative. Culture is your toolkit for living. Sometimes these tools make a big difference to leaders and their achievements; sometimes not. We are back to the Leadership Formula: sometimes to be in the right place really matters; sometimes much less so. It depends on what the leader's challenge is, as we shall examine in the next chapter.

Culture is also a boundary. When you cross the boundary things look different, and that change of vision can be galvanizing. Indeed, you could say that just about every important development in arts, sciences and the economy came from a boundary being crossed – not just geographies but across domains of knowledge, thought and practice.[31] Sometimes it is a physicist wandering into biology; a painter traveling to see African art for the first time; an immigrant looking in wonder at the way his new host country does business. Benjamin Franklin, Pablo Picasso and Levi Strauss come to mind. Tycho Brahe's telescope transformed astronomy because it enabled Kepler to see with fresh eyes.[32] Leaders, like Jon Akers of IBM, get too stuck in familiar visions and need to be kicked out of them from time to time.[33]

8. **Sex/gender:** Your dinner companion is a woman. What difference does that make to anything? The terms sex and gender are used interchangeably but interesting things happen when you separate them. Consider Norah Vincent's fascinating role switch case study, described in her book *Self-Made Man*.[34] This is an eye-opening testimony by an American lesbian woman – endowed with an athletic frame, manly bearing and physiognomy to carry it off – who spent a year living a secret life as a man. After a painstaking make-over, she took a job as a regular guy in a factory, participating fully in their social life, including joining them after work at the local bowling club. She even dated women through the Internet.

    What I found totally compelling from my point of view as a male reader was her surprise at what she witnessed in the affiliative moments of men – stuff that many guys take for granted. She touchingly recalls her experience at the bowling club, where she anticipates she will have to play along with the guys trying to outdo each other. What she finds, and is unprepared for, is the intensely cooperative and mutually helpful ethos among the men. They all cheer like mad when one of their number gets three strikes in a row to earn a perfect score in the tenth and final frame. She comments disparagingly on the different ethos of female competitiveness as one that is more absorbed with image and acceptance, while she commends the men for the fatherly way they try to help each other to improve. Her view may be too jaundiced about her own sex, though she is right that women and men engage in different kinds of same-sex comparison. It is ironic and charming that she, for all her mannish athleticism, is still a woman when it comes to hurtling a 16lb pound bowling ball down an alley. Her male companions can't understand why she hits a performance plateau, and they all pitch in uselessly, like kindly elder brothers, trying to help her improve.

The difference between men and women in leadership touches on all the categories we have looked at. Women can be physically disadvantaged, but that is mostly irrelevant, as is ability. Character, culture, experience and values are all gender accented and more strongly typed.[35] But what Vincent observed tells a more subtle story. She witnessed the immense capacity for non-hierarchical matiness among men, even when they differ enormously. Napoleon mingled informally with his troops; Mandela was always close to his people. It is also remarkable how men can engage in a brutal encounter and shortly afterwards act is if it hadn't happened. This is a story about how dominance hierarchies operate, which we shall analyze in Chapter 15.

9. **Self-concept:** Let's do a thought experiment. We have two genetically identical leaders in exact copy parallel universes. The only difference between them is twin A thinks he is attractive, well-liked and a thoroughly good chap. Twin B has got the opposite idea about himself – he is self-critical, fault-finding and convinced that he is unattractive and ineffective. Self-belief is often identified as a highly desirable leadership characteristic, though too much of it can be a pain in the ass. But imagine what it would be like to have twin A vs. twin B as your boss. It would matter! Let's not now go into the question of how people come to be this way, except to say that the Self organizes itself around memory and belief in order to solve problems that confront the person, arising from inside and outside the Self.[36] Some of these are dark, psychic problems. Men like Stalin and Hitler who had early brutalizing experiences developed narratives of vengeance, glory, protection and domination. Their Selves were instruments of power. They chose to live stories that would bend the world to

their will. Millions died to protect their perspectives on the world.

The Self is a process – a story – that qualifies attributes and experience. How we conceive of ourselves matters a lot, and of all the nine dimensions we have reviewed, this is the only one that can change in an instant and without trauma. That is why the "I" is the centerpiece of this book.

Many leaders have moments that transform their lives. The change starts with an altered vision. The image may be of the world or of the Self, and usually both together. Steve Jobs seemed to find a new way of engaging creatively with the world after being fired by his own company. Gandhi started an entirely new narrative view of himself and his mission when ejected from his train seat in South Africa. His was a story of projection. Others are for protection.

Self-concept is also a hazardous territory for leaders whose beliefs about themselves get out of kilter with everyone else's. Henry Ford is a particularly tragic case.[37] A visionary entrepreneur, he didn't just invent the modern automobile, he created an entirely new model for business production and work organization. But the future he created overtook him. Ford increasingly became the prisoner of his past – imperiously maintaining an increasingly outworn business model, silencing dissenting voices, including crushing the initiative and ideas of his own son and grandson. The former died young, broken by his father; the latter led the rebellion that saw the great man ignominiously thrown off the board of the company he built.

The Self has to play a dangerous game for the major villains of business history – people like Kenneth Lay, Bernie Madoff, Robert Maxwell – who followed paths of power that put them beyond the law, all the time working hard to maintain a socially acceptable profile. I am afraid that business history is littered with a long line of fallen men and women who allowed credibility to get stretched to points of drastic improbability and failure.[38]

THE COMPASS QUESTION

So, let us review where we have got to. It is that there are many ways of being a leader and what matters in any given situation is not a simple process of determination but a dynamic process, for, one way or another, a leader has to find some kind of credible fit with the world. That's where we're going shortly.

But first, there is the Compass Question which we raised earlier. This question is: "what is my reference point for the most important choices I have to make?" Most of the time we just make choices – the compass works without our having to think about it.

Look at a person like Rosa Parks[39] – the black housewife who started the Civil Rights revolution in 1955 by refusing to give up her seat to a white passenger who demanded it by right. Consider Churchill – a man who switched party allegiances, often stood outside the establishment, but stepped forward with powerful conviction to lead his people in an unflinching and uncompromising fight to the death against Nazism.[40] See Steve Jobs coming back from exile to reshape the Apple Corporation with an entirely fresh vision and purpose. We are attached to the image of leaders who have certainty about their drivers, yet the reality for many may be a lot more uncertain. We might occasionally argue that leaders may sometimes function better by sailing along in blissful ignorance of their motives. Some will avoid the question because the answers don't come easily enough.

It is an axiom of this book that every leader needs a value proposition – they have to define what benefits their leadership will seek to bring to the commonwealth. Any of our nine compass questions may supply a central motif. Here are some examples:

1. I am physically powerful and can protect you.

2. I have an attractive personality and can forge strong bonds with stakeholders.

3. I have special talents that can bring benefits to you, my group.

4. I have clear and strong values that you and others can rally around.

5. I love and know this business intimately.

6. I have a long track record of experience and achievement that you can rely on.

7. I am one of you – I am the embodiment of our tribe.

8. I am a woman/man.

9. I know who I am – join me on my journey.

Most of these make sense. Number 8 is tricky. Elizabeth I, addressing the fleet at Tilbury Docks on August 19th 1588 on the eve of the arrival of the Spanish Armada (which her navy defeated), inspired her forces with the following words – cleverly using her gender as part of her inspiring conviction:[41]

> Let tyrants fear. I have always so behaved myself that, under God, I have placed my chiefest strength and safeguard in the loyal hearts and good-will of my subjects; and therefore I am come amongst you, as you see, at this time, not for my recreation and disport, but being resolved, in the midst and heat of the battle, to live and die amongst you all; to lay down for my God, and for my kingdom, and my people, my honour and my blood even, in the dust.
>
> I know I have the body but of a weak and feeble woman; but I have the heart and stomach of a king, and of a king of England too, and think foul scorn that *Parma* or *Spain*, or any prince of Europe, should dare to invade the borders of my realm; to which rather than any dishonour shall grow by me, I myself will take up arms, I myself will be your general, judge, and rewarder of every one of your virtues in the field.

Leaders will have personal propositions that combine several of the nine elements. This takes us into the issue of authenticity. Can we rely on leaders' accounts of themselves? Do they really know themselves? They think we follow them because of proposition X but in reality it may be quality Y. We may also come to conclude that our leaders are remarkably careless about the proposition – sometimes it is like they hardly can make the effort to speak to us, like Coriolanus, the general in Shakespeare's great play, who fatally disdained his followers.

The Compass Question matters to followers. They want to know what the deal is – what does it mean for them to be a leader's fellow traveler? If for no other reason, leaders need to think of the Compass Question from time to time, and how it is changing. This is important, since it is the failure to adapt one's proposition to changing times that is a prime cause of leadership "derailment," as failure is politely termed in the literature.[42] Too much authenticity is bad for you if you don't nurture your personal leadership proposition.

From here we move, in the next chapter, to the most critical question for leadership – what is the nature of the challenge? Is this a given? Can the leader write her own script or must she dance to the music of her times? What is the Law of the Situation?

IMPLICATIONS AND OBSERVATIONS FOR LEADERS AND ORGANIZATIONS

Leaders are differentiated from others by the responsibility they bear, but inside this casing they carry their own unique machinery of impulses, wants and biases that shapes their responses. The question that faces leaders is how to find the value these directive forces give them, and how to neutralize the ones that damage them and their purposes. Specifically:

- Leaders need to be very clear about their answer to the Compass Question – to know what aspects of their identities are crucial differentiators. This is not just a matter of PR – leaders need to be clear in their minds as to the basis of their value proposition for followers and associates.

- Leaders need to take care of their physical image and ensure that it tells the story they want about them. Sometimes you have to be dressed to lead and stand tall!

- Leaders shouldn't assume that their personality is their USP (unique selling point). It may be, but it may not. A leader's gift may be the adaptability that comes naturally from an absence of strong dispositions. But if your personality is your driver – watch out where it drives you.

- Leaders and followers often make too much of ability as a leadership quality. Leaders just have to be good enough. After that, stop worrying. The smartest guy in the room is often not the best leader.

- Many leaders proclaim the importance of their values, but it is a smaller number for whom values really are their chief driver.

- Specificity of interests separates the narrow- from the broad-bandwidth leader. The SPQ framework suggests that there are leadership situations that require narrow-bandwidth dedication and others that don't, though, as we shall see, the leader may shape the situation according to her interests.

- Experience is a lazy criterion for choosing leaders, though sometimes necessary. It makes people feel safe, which may be illusory. Experience does not eliminate risk.

- Culture matters as a medium for connection with followers, but crossing boundaries between subcultures is often a source of enrichment for leaders.

- Narratives of Self and identity matter – they foretell the future. This makes them both a source of danger and of promise.

– 6 –

THE "EYE" OF LEADERSHIP – THE LAW OF THE SITUATION

Reality leaves a lot to the imagination.

John Lennon

Here's a strange thing. A bunch of recent recruits to a company are promoted to their first positions bearing the title "manager." They then proceed to behave like total idiots – as if they have never been managed before.[1] Are they so besotted with the glory of their new titles that they have totally forgotten that only yesterday the boot was on the other foot? They knew what they liked and disliked about being managed, but mysteriously none of this memory or knowledge seems to have been carried the very short distance to their new roles. They prance around like little martinets, issuing orders as if from some cartoon version of a management soap opera. What is wrong with them? Are they so intoxicated with their new roles that all they can see is the brilliant imagery in their minds from watching too many bad movies about macho bosses? Are they so desperately nervous and afraid of not looking as authentic as their titles demand that they have to invent a performance that will convince on-looking superiors? Both are happening to a degree, but the extraordinary feature of this sorry saga is the fact that they seem to be in a state of willful, if not blissful, ignorance about the nature of the reality that surrounds them.

Mohandas Gandhi[2] – small, modest, bespectacled, in his best dark suit and tie notwithstanding the stuffiness of the South African railway carriage – is a newly qualified lawyer, coming to the sub-continent with pride in his newly minted qualifications from the great University of London, where he has recently trained. He is on a mission to advise on a local legal case involving one of his Indian fellow countrymen – only to advise, since, as an Indian, he is forbidden to practice in the South Africa of 1893. Glowing with the significance of his first assignment, he has bought a first class ticket and is sitting upright watching the scenery of the Transvaal pass before his eyes, when, without warning, he gets a rude awakening from his reverie. A hand on the shoulder; a sharp command; disbelief. "I have paid for a first class ticket but I am not allowed to sit here? How is this possible?" he asks gently. The response is brusque, racist and threatening. "Move, Coolie!" The demure and gentle Gandhi quietly but clearly affirms his rights. He is tossed off the train and sleeps the night on the station floor, lucky to be alive but burning with indignation.

It is, for sure, a moment of awakening. From this moment the world looked quite different to the little lawyer. It started a new life for him; fighting for the rights of his oppressed people, who were suffering indignity, discrimination and brutal usage as indentured labor – close to slavery – in this unreformed domain of Anglo-Dutch colonialism. The fight turned out to be with the local state government – the British were losing what little control they had of this outpost – which was turning the screws tighter to restrict the rights of its populous guests. For 20 years Gandhi fought, inventing the doctrine and practice of non-violent resistance and civil disobedience – *satyagraha* – that has become part of the armory of many protest and revolting groups ever since.

Seeing is being. As a pragmatist philosopher once put it: "If something is perceived as real, it is real in its consequences."[3] This has two important implications for leaders. One: regardless of how you see the world, you'd better be under no illusions about what your followers perceive, for it will shape their response to whatever you try to initiate. The other implication is a warning: don't take at face value what you see. Be ready to challenge it.

Gandhi woke up to a reality that was all around him but had not struck him until that Afrikaans rasped in his ear. No doubt for a man of his sensibilities it would not have been long before another trigger awoke him to his mission. What is important here is that it was a seismic shift in worldview that triggered the start of a compelling career of radical leadership.

JOB CHANGE AS WORLD CHANGE

We will never know what was going through the minds of our two 26-year-olds – Hannibal of Carthage and Elizabeth I. With 44-year-old Tony Blair we do have a record – his memoir – which is all about learning to lead and how he discovers how levers of power are more like tangled threads. Sometimes you carefully have to figure out which to tug; sometimes you have to take a blade and cut through them. Barack Obama was clearly on a steep learning curve when his first serious leadership role turned out to be President of the USA.

Coming into your first major leadership role is pretty well an automatic wake-up call that the world has changed for you. But what if you've just been raised a single step within a corporate hierarchy? The risk is either like the young managers we described earlier – you treat it as role play – or you act as if nothing has happened. And, actually, sometimes nothing has. A few years ago I was giving a speech on leadership to a large, newly promoted cohort in a European investment bank. The scene was a conference to equip these young men and women for their lives under their new titles of Associate Directors. They seemed to enjoy my presentation, and responded quite nicely in the group discussions, though it seemed to me in a somewhat polite and disengaged manner.

At the end there was the usual mingle of people chatting, when one of the young Associate Directors came up to me. "I think you've been misled somewhat," he said slightly shamefacedly. "We're not really leaders at all. This change means almost nothing at all. We're still the slaves of the real leaders, who are the Managing Directors; we've just been given fancy titles to keep us tethered to the firm." Not all job changes are the same, by any means.[4] Appearances can be deceptive, job descriptions downright lies and your assumptions false. Not surprisingly, you are likely to be rather more inquiring about a job shift to a new role in a new organization in a new business in a new location, than you are about a simple step up in your home corporation.

Here's an interesting phenomenon that I noticed from this work – people almost always agonize about exactly the wrong things, even when they've done extensive due diligence.[5] Most of their concern focuses on the question, "Will I be able to hack it – to perform in a way that convinces others; that lives up to expectations?" This pure self-centered anxiety is perfectly understandable, but quite wide of the mark. The people around them are (a) too self-absorbed to pay attention to some neurotic newcomer; (b) assume they were hired for a good reason; and (c) expect them to make mistakes and be a bit stupid, because that's what newcomers do. And in the end, people mostly do get it and figure out how to perform, so the anxiety was needless.

Only the chronic misfits fail to find their feet. Even the most stupid corporations screen out or flush out the dummies and misplaced people pretty early. So what should people worry about? Other people, of course. Our research showed that incoming executives enter their new worlds with a complacent optimism about the social environment. They believe that the grass is bound to be greener than the place they are leaving, and that they will have no trouble building fresh relationships easily.

The last point may be true for the confident and socially skilled leader. But even with a heap of post-decisional rationalization she may be forced to conclude that her performance anxieties were groundless, but she's entered a world where the top people have been over-promoted, where peers are watchful, envious and concealing, and subordinates quietly resentful. Worse, she may find that the chemistry with the person who appointed her doesn't live up to expectations.

This is a common saga in business relationships, such as the draining away of the high-trust partnership between Steve Jobs and John Scully.

According to his biographer,[6] Steve Jobs had something akin to a romance with John Scully, whom he had brought in to be CEO of Apple in 1983. They wreathed each other's talents in adulatory projections; made avowals of admiration and loyalty; and painted a glorified image of their future together; Jobs, an adopted child, seems to have repeatedly sought perfect father figures through his life. Scully was readily flattered out of the world of consumable products by the beckoning of this brave new technological world bursting into blossom in the fertile and febrile climate of Silicon Valley. But Jobs's dangerous gift was to create delusional fantasy worlds and get others to live in them – wittily dubbed his "reality distortion field" (a Star Trek concept) by a colleague. Reality broke through eventually – the destructive thrust of his management and decision-making style culminated in Jobs's exile from Apple.

WHERE ARE WE? WHAT IS A LEADERSHIP SITUATION?

There has been plenty written about "situational leadership" in the academic literature, though it is narrow and formalistic in the main. Mary Parker Follett was one of the first and greatest of that small breed, women writers on management, and was dubbed "the prophet of management" by the doyen of the genre, Peter Drucker. She asserted what she called "the Law of the Situation" (see Figure 6.1).[7] She says, rather startlingly, that no manager should accept on another manager's say-so what he or she should be doing. Rather than relying on what anyone else may tell you about the reality surrounding you, you must go figure it out for yourself.

But what you should pay attention to is a continuing challenge for managers at all levels. Where to start? Avoiding the impoverished models that the leadership literature focuses on, let us attempt to set out a more detailed and practical analysis for leaders. What should

Figure 6.1:   The SPQ framework: the Law of the Situation

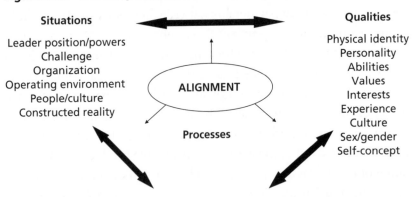

they look for in their leadership situation? Here's what we shall be looking at:

- Position and powers – not always what they seem, can the leader define them?

- Challenge – how are the leader's goals defined and by whom?

- Organization – are there "best" ways to organize; what should a leader do?

- External environment – in a changing world, where should leaders take the organization?

- People – how should the leader deal with people at various levels and sub-cultures?

- Constructed reality – what is the perceptual world of people around the leader and what should she do to inform or frame it?

Position/Powers

So, what is your new job title? Executive Director Special Projects. Wow! That sounds amazing. So what are "special projects?" Whom do I direct? What kind of resources will I have at my disposal? What's my freedom to hire and fire? Do I report to anyone? Does my title Executive Director actually mean anything? Sadly, it may not. I have bought automobiles from beardless youths in car showrooms whose business cards tell me they are Executive Directors. It's the oldest trick in the book. Lure someone to do the dirtiest jobs that no one else will touch – "Special Projects" – to operate with zero budgets, no powers or reports, to be directed on the whim of someone who invented the job for political purposes. At the same time I have met many men and women with modest titles – General Manager is a common example of the breed – who bear huge responsibilities for vast territories with virtually sole accountability.

Power is not a constant in leadership. We probably need to define power. This is tricky, because you really don't know you have it until you try to use it.[8] Certain things you do know. The title of your position carries with it certain rights and duties which others will be aware of. They may kowtow at the mere mention of General Director, and take it for granted that you, as boss, can order them to do certain things.

Here's a true story of the careless stupidity of power. A certain Chief Executive in banking, famous for his laser-like forensic powers and attention to detail and feared for his tendency to drill into people's weakness in public arenas (in the manner of Robert Maxwell, as we described him earlier), walks into one of the main offices in the metropolis and remarks, in an offhand manner, that the carpets are a shade wrong for the corporate blue. Without waiting for an order, a budget is assembled to re-carpet the entire office at great expense (though a fraction of the CEO's bonus). No doubt he was pleased, but this story is a salutary reminder for those who would don the raiment of leadership and fame – even casual expressions are taken very seriously.

Power also comes from your location in the system. Haldeman and Ehrlichman were dubbed the Berlin Wall for their capacity to block access to President Richard Nixon. This gave them power. In the comic movie and TV series *M.A.S.H.* about jock US doctors in the Korean War, the most powerful person is Radar – the meek, bespectacled radio operator, who commands the only link to the world beyond the camp.

Smart leaders take stock with cool realism about what their position actually does give them in terms of power. There are a number of simple questions to ask yourself: do the office and title bear particular weight and success, and, if so, how sustainably? Will the power fade after the first glow? Who are the friends and allies I can call on for support? Can I rely on them? What resources do I control that are scarce, important and valuable to others? Expertise often fits this bill. Yet, as we have seen, it can be a diminishing or unstable power base.[9] Steve Jobs and Soichiro Honda earned high regard for their expertise, but it was their ability to read the world in new ways and implement their vision that underpinned their leadership. Leaders need to be aware of material or psychological assumptions on which their position of power depends and be ready to build something more substantial to sustain their power base.

Challenge

In the TV series and movie *Mission Impossible*, each adventure starts with the team leader reading a self-destructing message – "Your mission, should you choose to accept it, is . . ." puff of smoke. A leader boldly marches forth to engage his destiny – Nelson Mandela and Aung San Suu Kyi did it in politics; Jack Welch and Lou Gerstner did it in business.

Of course, this vision has enduring appeal. So many movies and sagas depict the hero who comes, burning with righteous commitment and equipped with all the requisite skills to meet the challenge of the times. History, they say, is written by the victors, so you can see how such mythology is perpetuated by them and their supporters. But history is also littered with disasters – people who misread the challenge, fought the wrong battle. Enron didn't just fail because it was run by a crook, Kenneth Lay, but because it forgot it was an energy company and thought it was trading at the top of Wall Street.[10]

How do leaders define their challenge? In a crisis, one may have to act first and think later, but it is always worth reflecting, at some point, on the corny (and inaccurate) observation that the Chinese character for crisis combines the signs for danger and opportunity.[11] The point is that you always have a choice about life's challenges. If you are a novice leader there will be plenty of wise and friendly souls with images of the world to set before you. CEOs are appointed by boards, which often have quite precise goals in mind, and they have selected the leader to deal with these. For Lou Gerstner it was clearly "TURN-AROUND." Absolutely right!

The board of BP, which appointed the ill-fated Tony Hayward as CEO to succeed the visionary, cerebral but big-spending John Browne, was shouting "REDUCE COSTS." Right? Maybe, but not at the cost of risk exposure, as it turned out, for BP had become dogged by a sequence of safety issues not long before the catastrophic Deepwater Horizon offshore platform blowout in the Gulf of Mexico in 2010.[12] The catastrophe was compounded by Hayward appearing to fail to grasp the nature of the new challenge that confronted him and his organization. In a series of media gaffes, he referred initially to the spill as likely to have a "modest" environmental impact, and complained after the media storm had been raging for some weeks that he "wanted his life back" – a thoughtless comment, insensitive to the reality that 11 workers had lost their lives in the accident.[13] Hayward subsequently made matters worse by taking time out at the height of the crisis to jet back to England to watch his adult son compete in a yachting race. His defense was that he had not seen his son in three months.

Leaders need to remember the risks of the self-centered perspective, and the insights that can be gleaned by getting into a mental helicopter to rise above this view to understand the relativity of where people's views emanate from.[14] Every stakeholder has a point of view that identifies their position, and an accompanying wish list for the leader. The incoming leader needs to ask, listen, watch, wait and then . . . think for themselves.

When presented with someone or other's authoritative view, the correct response is: "Thank you for your thoughts and insights. Yes, I can see why you think this organization needs what you are saying, so I'm going to talk to people before I decide how to play this." Actually, this is pretty well what veteran management guru John Gabarro concluded in a classic *Harvard Business Review* article many years ago.[15] He drew a curve of leader activity on coming into the role, showing that at the start there tends to be a flurry of activity to fix all the obvious stuff that everyone agrees needs attention. Then follows a quiet period when the leader goes to ground, ferreting around in the guts of the organization, talking to stakeholders and reviewing the business environment. Then the leader comes back to the fore with a strategic intent to enact a new, farther-reaching program of reform – perhaps even moving the organization toward entirely new goals:

"The problem is not that our cost base is too high; it is that we are not connecting with our customers in the right way."

This was something like Lou Gerstner's approach on taking over at IBM[16] – some quick fixes and some slow fixes, but above all a challenge of presumptions. In India, Ratan Tata, as an insider at Tata Industries, a sprawling conglomerate in the 1970s, had more time to consider issues and options from his position as a director on the periphery of the group.[17] He saw the threat of disintegration of the group's centrifugally growing constituencies, and, on his appointment in 1981, he boldly, but diplomatically – using reason more than power – brought the businesses back under a unifying strategy and structure.

Organization

Tata recognized the interdependence of structure and strategy.[18] The study of organizational structure is grandly called "design" in the literature, as if firms were shaped by architects, when actually they are higgledy-piggledy concatenations of solutions to problems the business has faced since its inception. Processes often define structure. A particular technology or bureaucratic process is introduced that imposes its own logic on operating methods, which then have to be supported by management systems.[19] The leader's situation is defined by her position in this machinery.

Every "design" is intended to solve a particular problem or help the organization do certain things. Each design also has its dysfunctions – fresh problems it creates as unintended by-products. Companies reorganize to solve problems but sometimes this seems more like a talismanic activity – kidding the world (and themselves) that they are looking forward to tomorrow's solutions. In reality, restructuring may be just a power game – to stop certain functions or divisions becoming too powerful.[20] There are a lot of politics in design when you look into it. Structures are also climbing frames for careers.

Three principles govern design: integration, differentiation and adaptation.[21] You pull some things together; you split others apart. You set in motion processes and enabling processes that help people to make decisions, innovate and adjust to a changing world.

Structures are also arenas. In Chapter 15 I shall be returning to an important theme – how and why we allow our primeval preferences for arenas to display, contest, dominate and lead us to organize along particular hierarchical lines, when other ways might be much more effective and cooperative. Structure, in other words, is not always fit for purpose.[22]

Size matters. Dunbar's number (150) – widely cited as the "natural" size of the human clan after Robin Dunbar's discovery that primate group size was correlated with neo-cortical capacity[23] – can be seen as the network dimensions of the human brain – your 150 real friends on Facebook! Business units or functions on this scale are able to maintain a level of self-regulating informality, with the potential to self-govern.[24] Leadership is a quite different proposition in more monolithic structures. But when we look at firms we find structures within structures. The leader has to deal with some people in egalitarian and ad hoc groupings and others within much more formalistic machine-like structures. One can see a deal of uncertainty in how leaders move between these contexts and roles – clearly preferring some to others.

It's not just size – there's also complexity. It is quite a different matter to lead a simple structure, where you have widely separated islands of activity, like in some large retail and sales firms, than a complex structure, like NASA, where there is huge interdependency across a range of technologically sophisticated and information-rich activities. The former requires leaders who are closely aware of market response and the adjustments that need to be made to keep pace with what is happening at different locations and levels. The latter case requires leaders with intellect, skills and ability to empower, engage and link up the very smartest of people.

Creative industries offer special challenges, as do finance firms, educational establishments, competitive sports institutions, mechanized industrial firms, commercial and seasonal businesses such as tourism and agriculture, professional service firms, healthcare, government and so on. From a leadership perspective, each has a distinctive profile of issues, challenges and people.[25] The question is, how does organizational identity map on to leadership identity? Not a simple matter. It is not just a binary issue question of fit vs. misfit. The force of the SPQ model is that it explains adaptation as a dynamic process, as we shall discuss in Chapters 8 and 9. The leader has a key role in facilitating the adaptation of the organization to its challenges. Most of these challenges come from outside – the operating environment.

External Environment

The Native American hunter-gatherer tribes switched leaders at times of peace and war.[26] Winston Churchill – always a bold adventurer and something of an outsider – rose to prominence to be First Lord of the Admiralty in WWI, spent the inter-war years as a rebellious thorn in the side of political orthodoxy and the dominant elites, became one of the greatest wartime leaders in history through WWII, before descending into an abject and irrelevant figure in his last prominent role as a peacetime Prime Minister.[27] Like so many, he was not a man for all seasons.

Organizations and their leaders have to adapt to – or at least buffer and protect themselves from – the prevailing conditions external to the organization, tribe or state. These can be hostile vs. benign, volatile vs. stable, improving vs. deteriorating, competitive vs. uncompetitive, simple vs. complex and/or resource-rich vs. poor. Each can be met with a range of responses. The right one depends on what the leader and the organization are prepared to do or what they are capable of doing.

Two stories illustrate this. A relatively simple but challenging example is the heroic story of Ernest Shackleton, described by some writers as the greatest leader who ever lived.[28] There is a lot of hyperbole in the many writings on Shackleton, but his was a remarkable story. The other, who as far as I know has never figured in the canons of the leadership literature, is the great Duke Ellington, who undoubtedly was a chief of remarkable and varied gifts.

Shackleton's story is of 28 men setting off in a ship, the ironically named *Endurance*, on an expedition in 1913 to map the icecap of the Antarctic. What started as a straightforward expedition turned into a 21-month nightmare of isolation through the harshest climate on the planet, including one deepfreeze winter, 1200 miles from the nearest civilization. During this ordeal, the environment changed several times for Shackleton, each time requiring a different set of responses. First was the floating pack-ice enclosing and immobilizing his ship. Second was when the ice crushed the ship, requiring the men to abandon it and almost all their possessions and many of their supplies. Suddenly, their environment had become a lot leaner and a lot meaner. Third, he had to establish a survival platform for most of the men whilst he sailed off with five in search of rescue.

Shackleton's leadership genius resided in his ability to reconfigure and maintain a positive momentum in a situation that looked increasingly hopeless. He deployed a range of strategies and tactics to do this, for he readily apprehended that he would need to mobilize and sustain a powerful communal spirit among men on the edge of existence. He did this by making personal sacrifices obligatory and ceremonial – leading the way by solemnly throwing his gold sovereigns on to the snow, along with his father's bible from which he retained just the signed title page. Yet, he let the men keep their personal diaries, and one a heavy and cumbersome musical instrument – a banjo. Smart thinking – music is food to the spirit.

Shackleton gave command of the stores to the meanest man, ensuring that there was a regular flow of treats for the many celebrations he scheduled. He rode roughshod over the rigid Edwardian class distinctions between officers and men. Everyone had to do everything, with him leading the way by example. He strategically placed men in tents together to keep relationships in balance, and kept the most difficult men close to himself. In the end, he sailed 800 miles of stormy seas in a lifeboat with a handpicked selection of the men then climbed a mountain on South Georgia that no one had previously scaled, to present himself before the astonished gaze of Norwegians in a whaling station on the other side. It was not only remarkable that he saved every life, but the manner of his doing so, such that at least one of the survivors recollected afterwards that it had been "the best time of my life."

Duke Ellington's is a somewhat different story.[29] Born of a middle class Washington family – pampered and gifted – Duke ran away from the conservatoire to follow the jazz music he loved, pulled into the leadership of his nascent orchestra by the popular acclaim of his fellows after they threw out his predecessor for skimming the band's earnings. His band grew in size and maturity, but, most remarkably, survived as a big band for longer than any other in the highly volatile domain of popular music. By force of character and ceaseless innovation, Duke didn't just hold the band together over 40 years but retained the loyalty and affection of several key band members for almost equal duration.

What was notable here was the seismic shift in the environment that he and his orchestra survived. Due to unavailability of musicians after America entered the war, the fashion for big band jazz and swing music was replaced by the more mobile, dynamic and small-scale format of be-bop and chamber jazz.[30] Of the few survivors in this era, two stood out: Count Basie and the Duke. The important thing is that both leaders recognized that they had to re-engage and re-launch themselves to the new contemporary post-war audiences, which they did brilliantly. Basie followed a more conventional "habitat-tracking" route, while Ellington, especially in his remarkable partnership with Billy Strayhorn, creatively evolved his music, through his famous sacred concerts and series of composed thematic suites.

People

The most important part of the environment for leaders is other people. They don't just color the business landscape, they are the landscape. For a while in the 20th century we forgot this, when management and leadership was all about keeping the machines running. The paradox of the information age is that, although we can leave production more and more to the machines, we need to be much smarter about looking after who handles, coordinates and consumes the blizzards of data that suffuse the business world. In the webbed world of today's value chains, relationships matter. Leaders need emotional intelligence to resolve conflicts, relieve pressure, set the tone and keep connections healthy.[31] Systems are too vulnerable to emotional disturbance for such stuff to be left to chance.

The people make the place, it has been said,[32] and collectively characters coalesce into sub-cultures. Can leaders manage cultures, or do cultures manage leaders? Culture has been likened to a pickle jar.[33] Insider leaders tend to have been pickled by the culture to perpetuate it – the in-coming outsider has to move fast to make her mark; to change the culture before it pickles her too. More on this later, but it has always been true that leaders have to manage at several levels, often simultaneously:

Level 1: A small group of trusted intimates who are the leader's key instruments and informants.[34]

Level 2: The leader's network – key stakeholders, not more than 150 (Dunbar's number); enemies as well as friends. In some dynastic states, this could be a tribal sub-grouping – like the closest associates among Bashar Assad's Alawites of Syria – clinging together on their sectarian raft upon a hostile sea of enemies.[35]

Level 3: The people – the insider population of followers for whom this is their designated leader.

What is the state of mind of these groups – how much does this affect the leader or define her challenge? Here are some examples:

- a diversely skilled hunter-gatherer group with very clear ideas about the nature of their shared situation;

- fighters of uncertain allegiance, divided and ambiguous in goals and expectations, looking to be sure they are on the winning side;

- trained and experienced workers expecting clarity about their tasks and expected returns;

- once contented and now demoralized threatened office staff in a business trembling on the brink of extinction;

- low-level temporary employees, lacking in skills and motivation beyond whatever material inducements they can extract from the system;

- highly intelligent, self-motivated scientists with extreme needs for autonomy and a conviction that they are doing important work;

- a party of military and specialist personnel engaged on a scientific exploration who find themselves fighting for survival in a hostile environment;

- temperamental, diverse, creative and undisciplined artists and performers looking for chances to do their best work and win acclaim for it.

The last two represent the Shackleton and Ellington challenges. The rest represent historically and recently common forms of followership.

In terms of the people/culture dimension of leadership, a key consideration is what choices they have about where they are and their status as followers. This may be a simple matter of fact – if you were born into the tribe, the idea of quitting just doesn't enter your mind. This is your world and that's it. It may, at another extreme, be more of a psycho-economic calculus. What would it cost me to leave this firm? People who feel trapped in a situation represent a quite different challenge to the leader from those whose commitment is much more provisional, conditional and voluntary. If followers can freely walk across the road in search of a better leader, then we are in a radically different world from one where they feel power-less and captive.[36] Labor markets are not as free as they look, and lots of people are stuck with leaders they wouldn't choose on any day of the week.

It is to state the blindingly obvious that you have to switch your leadership style according to the state of mind and body of your followers, and perhaps less obvious that this is a circular process – what you do affects your followers.[37] An appropriate style when they are in one condition will cease to be effective if you maneuver them into a different state of mind by, for example, training them, raising their spirits or changing their view of the world. This was Jack Welch's insight – to keep moving his people at GE, and himself, to new levels of maturity as he transformed the business.[38] As we shall see, leaders often fail because they don't know how to step outside of the worlds for which they were the perfect leader and to move to a new level, taking their people with them.

Constructed Reality

Let us not divert into the murky waters of philosophical argument – well, not just now – but the nature of reality is something people can and will argue about.[39] Most of the time we don't have to; we know and agree when it's raining, though we could, if we wanted, dispute whether today is nicer than yesterday. Philosophers are helpful at this point, by noting how important the fact–value distinction is.[40] Whether something has happened is verifiable, but we can argue all day about its value.

But minds don't work like that. Fact and value get muddled up in mental space. With disciplined thought we can cool things down by separating them. This is often helpful, but requires an effort that a lot of leaders aren't prepared or able to take. We see the world through the ceaseless filter of our constantly changing sensory perception, including the thrum of our emotions. We differ enormously in how this works, and it is constantly changing. In financial markets, computers increasingly do the trading for us because, for them, the fact–value distinction is hardwired. For us, the muddle is hardwired.[41]

In this muddle, our beliefs play as big a part as what is observable and factual, for, after all, much of what we "see" of the world is hearsay – story-telling.[42] All fiction relies heavily on this interpretive subjectivity. The world is fictive in this sense – we have an internal model of the way things are, closely linked with beliefs about the way they should be, how they might be changing, what kinds of people are acting, and how we feel about it all – who are the good guys and who are the bad guys?[43]

Leaders need to command this narrative. This is a huge part of their mission, but this is contested territory. In leadership elections this is the battleground – whose story of the way-the-world-is will prevail? In business, leaders seek to define themselves as the solutions to problems as they have defined them. There is much more to say about this, for it is a key theme of this book.

A WORLD OF LOST LEADERSHIP – FINANCIAL SERVICES 2007–2012

There have been many financial "bubbles" in history – runaway demand and price inflation for some commodity. In 1630, Europe was gripped by one of the strangest – the Dutch tulip bubble.[44] The tulip is a pretty flower, botanically and esthetically distinctive, and in the 17th century it became a fad to possess and display its blooms, especially those with the "broken" color pattern. Unfortunately, this pattern was caused by a virus that delayed the development of a bulb – this biological irony widening the gap between demand and supply, fueling an ever-more feverish public appetite for this must-have fashion accessory. The tulip mania peaked in 1636 – by which time people were trading futures in tulip bulbs for thousands of guilders, with notional bulb holdings changing hands several times a day. The day the buyers refused to pay the inflated market price was the day the crash came.

Just under 400 years later, something similar happened with subprime mortgages, which spawned a vast array of consolidated financial packages of debt.[45] This turned out to go far beyond mortgages – the asset basis of all debt came sharply into focus as a mountain of speculative inflated value: the so-called "Credit Crunch" of 2007, the aftershocks of which are still shaking economies around the world, especially in the USA and Europe.

I worked with the leadership of more than one bank in the eye of the storm throughout this period and it is hard to overstate how fundamentally the leadership situation changed for these folks. The bubble contained huge volumes of what everyone believed was inviolate asset values. The platform that supported them, their lifestyle and their goals crumbled beneath their feet. The standard by which they measured their worth and the value of their business, shareholder value, was dissolving. In this new Arctic winter, people's reactions varied enormously. Some became bewildered, depressed, lost and embittered.[46] Others went into denial and carried on working as if this was a mere blip. But there was one very interesting group of improvisers and fixers who rejoiced – here was some chaos to get their teeth into. From a leadership point of view, at every level of our analysis the situation was transformed:

- Position and powers – radical decline in resources and rewards; complete inversion of assumed importance of different areas of business and trading; massive loss of liquidity.

- Challenge – complete reframing of goals of the business – a shift from bottom-line to so-called top-line, customers and the value of services delivered to them.

- Organization – whole divisions suddenly relegated to "non-core" status, and to be wound down; others losing swathes of people; reorganizing; submitting themselves to domination by new regulatory and risk-control imperatives.

- External environment – global scaling-down; reduced opportunities and volume of business.

- People – seriously impaired morale; disengaged people suffering major material loss.

- Constructed reality – the death of a universally accepted story about what bankers do and how they add value.

Working with leaders, it became clear to me that, for some, this was their leadership moment. This was a world where they could make a difference, help to restore battered morale and build a new vision for the industry. They were the exception, for most of the leadership consisted of people who thrived in the old, comfortable world of steady, unquestioning expansion.

We have not yet seen the emergence of the new model for the industry and its leadership. At the time of writing it is a work in progress, but for sure it is a significant leadership moment for those who can grasp it.

We conclude our tour of the elements of the SPQ framework in the next chapter when we look at leadership processes – what leaders actually do and what it takes to make actions strategic.

IMPLICATIONS AND OBSERVATIONS FOR LEADERS AND ORGANIZATIONS

Situations drive leadership. Context is the great shaper of leadership capability and action, and leaders have to grapple with reality at more than one level. The Law of the Situation asserts that they have to figure it out for themselves and then do the right thing. Too often, leaders operate lazily on presumption and habit. Key points:

- Leaders, whatever their level, need to see every job move, promotion and assignment as a world change – taking as little for granted as possible.

- There is a tendency to worry about oneself and one's performance when what the leader should be doing is looking at people and relationships, which is where the real challenge lies.

- Power is an abstract medium – it grows, wanes and transmutes. Leaders have to find it, work with it and build it. If it is put in your hands, watch out – it may run through your fingers.

- Whatever the leader is told by boards, bosses and analysts about the nature of their challenge, they should listen but then go figure it out for themselves.

- Structure is a tool for strategy. Leaders need to remember this and use it, and not let it use them.

- The external environment and its eruptions require creative and coherent responses with changes to strategy, structure and culture.

- Culture pickles people, including the leader. Leaders have to work hard to keep an inside–outside perspective.

- The leader should consider why her followers are there and what they perceive their choices to be. Locked-in people shouldn't be taken for granted. They can hurt the leader.

- Remember, the leader–follower relationship is dynamic and cyclical – leaders will have to adapt their style to cope with the effects, for good or ill, they have on followers.

- The fact–value distinction is often deeply muddled. Leaders need to keep clear in their minds the distinction, even when others don't.

— 7 —

THE ADAPTIVE LEADER – LEADERSHIP PROCESSES

Everyone thinks of changing the world, but no one thinks of changing himself.

Leo Tolstoy

THE OBAMA DILEMMA

I confess. I am British. I am happy about my origins, but without exception every writer on leadership needs to factor in his or her cultural biases. This matters now, particularly, since I want to talk about the US President, elected in 2008 and re-elected in 2012. In this regard, my origins dictate more a viewing position than a point of view. The outsider's view here is a mixed blessing – no axe to grind but a somewhat distant perspective. It is very early and perhaps unfair to comment on someone whose story is still unfolding, standing as we do at the start of the second presidential term after the mixed fortunes of the first. But it is important to do so, because his first term of office is perfectly illustrative of a partially misaligned leadership SPQ, which I shall illustrate briefly with three episodes.

First, I share with the whole planet the astonishment at how soon the US was able to shake a fist at its past and elect a black man to the most powerful job in the world – amazing given the recency of civil rights in the USA and the continued existence of racial division and tensions in American society. And looking at the "Q" factors, a truly remarkable man comes into view. Without regard to policies or ideologies it is rare to see a leader, a president indeed, so blessed with high intellect, oratorical gifts, literary skills, passionate commitment, moral sense and desire to serve his people.[1] In addition to his professorial stature he is physically the very model of a leader – tall, imposing, relaxed, charismatic in bearing, sonorous in voice, athletic and, above all, super-cool. He has another trait that distinguishes him from many of his calling – a thoughtful but deep introversion.[2]

Born of a Kenyan father and a white American mother, he is pretty hard to classify in the familiar lexicon of American racial politics. There is no slavery in his African ancestry – arguably the bane of US race relations – or indeed any other indignities beyond those of British colonial legacy in Kenya, which played a part in his father's educated perspective on the world. His parentage is ambiguous in terms of social class. His mother was a nomadic intellectual, and led him on an unusual peregrination to Indonesia before entrusting him to the care of undistinguished, kindly, instructive and decent middle class grandparents in Hawaii. This relocation also helped to displace him culturally to a position lacking any visible social affiliations that might brand him as a member of this or that tribe – apart from the Democratic Party, that is. His experience of leadership was limited, to say the least, having entered via a channel of political activism and the law.

The overarching "S" factor was his accession to office at a time of unprecedented challenge: at the very apogee of a great global financial crisis. The Bush presidency had terminated at a time of division and extreme difficulty in the US, with a sharply contracting economy and huge uncertainty. Arguably, Obama came to power at a time of crisis as a man in possession of two qualities that had the potential to heal a hurting and divided country: he had no race and no class.[3] In his inspiring speeches he was able to reach above the political divide, make his opponents look divisive and factional and speak to the people with a message of hope and self-belief – "Yes we can" – a redemptive message that, as psychologist Dan McAdams noted,[4] is a deep and enduring theme in the American psyche.

So, following the Leadership Formula, what does he do, what leadership processes does he enact, this interesting man who looks and sounds like he's the right person at the right time?

He does many things right and fights, and wins by the skin of his teeth, a great policy battle over healthcare, though not a final victory, for opposition to it was never quelled. If one asked even his supporters to judge on his first-term performance, the answer would be equivocating at best. Many have been disappointed – perhaps because their expectations were unreasonably high, as they were when Mandela became the first leader of the free South Africa. They, too, were disappointed but Mandela remained untainted. Obama has appeared at times factional, inconsistent, vacillating and unsure of himself, but interspersed with rousing speeches to supporters, and achieving presidential bearing in the Hurricane Sandy episode at the time of his re-election.

Three events from various junctures of his first term tell a story.

First was his response to the financial crisis. This was reasonably sure-footed in terms of actions. Sensibly, he surrounded himself by éminences grises, youthful experts and experienced politicians. As young family business leaders have told me, it is best to surround yourself by the very best talent. But you have to beware – before you know it, others are leading you. Bush – a man whose cowboy swagger made one wonder whether it was a smokescreen for deeper insecurities – surrendered the first-term narrative of his presidency to two very powerful aides – Rumsfeld and Cheney. Obama, who had a stronger narrative coming into office, also sought advice. In his case, from a large hand-picked team of specialists, seemingly to compensate for his lack of experience.

Yet, there was a missed opportunity. Although he delivered an ambitious recovery package, he never managed to build a consensus across party lines, appealing to a united constituency across a spectrum of his people.[5] Why? On the one hand, in the wings at his election victory stood a partisan rump of the Democratic Party, and opposite them, an aggrieved and intransigent Republican Party. He tried to broker a cross-party consensus on his economic stimulus plan but this was scotched by his opponents, so he fell back on his power base, which he could, since he held a majority in both houses. In effect, he allowed these interests to define the situation for him, rather than looking above and beyond to resonate with the American people as a leader above party. Remember, Obama had, in that moment of accession, the unusual credibility and power of a new president, plus a profile that suggested he could cross boundaries. You only win an election by traversing the rigid lines of stalwart party allegiance.

Obama grasped the leadership situation of a country in crisis, with a fast-shrinking GDP that required desperate remedies, but he appeared to lose his grasp of the wider contours of the leadership situation – i.e. to reach beyond the political and economic state of the union to the story of America and its people beyond. What became of the "we" in "yes we can"? Why did he not use the power of his moment to broker a bi-partisan new deal – detaching enough moderate elements of the Republicans to position himself as a one-nation president? This missed opportunity bequeathed him four years of increasingly bitter running battles with his opponents.

A second – two examples, rather – reflects on his public demeanor. Both examples reveal further curious blindness to his circumstances. One was his reported conduct on having, with powerful friends, a Capitol Hill private viewing of the Super Bowl.[6] Obama sat in the front row with a beer enjoying the match. How odd that this decent, retiring man failed to grasp what he was there for, and what his guests were there for – to groom each other (figuratively!) and bond. Right at the end of his term, an even more curious diffidence was striking during the first of the televised debates for the 2012 presidency. To a neutral outsider he looked like he didn't want to be there – humorless, formulaic, disengaged and somewhat passive – an introvert on a bad day.[7] Why did he not see what this situation demanded – upbeat, commanding and empathic – the kind of performance that his Democratic predecessor, Bill Clinton, could switch on in an instant? Because

Bill Clinton had the "Q" factors, both to summon readily the right response and to see the need in the first place. Obama succumbed to instinct.

The third example was his mid-term crisis moment of the Deepwater Horizon oil platform blowout in 2010. We have already seen how BP boss Tony Hayward appeared to fail to grasp the challenge – seeing it as a technical problem rather than a social drama, which led him to produce a stream of inept responses. Obama's public stance seemed to slide from one position to another – at its worst smacking of desperation, grandstanding and blaming, before recovering his poise as the solution emerged.[8] Clearly, Obama was floating and falling on the sea of publicity that engulfed this story. Yet, as a leader, he could have foreseen the inevitable end that would come, the plugging of the leak and how he might maximize his chances of coming out of it looking like a leader. His first-term presidency seemed to embody this pattern – chasing rather than shaping events, like a sports coach at the mercy of every short-run win, loss, transfer or management eruption.

What is a leader to do when beset with such a catastrophe? You have certain knowledge that it will be resolved, eventually, and that life will resume, more or less as normal. You have no idea when, and there is nothing you can do to affect the course of events. Yet your role is vital – to define the situation in ways that help people live with the uncertainty, engage in positive action and to be prepared to manage the aftermath. Both leaders in the oil spill – Obama and Hayward – failed to do this. Both viewed the situation as one of rational problem solving. Both understood that the people wanted justice and retribution, but neither understood the deeper need for a narrative of empathy.

Poor cerebral Obama seemed unable to evince the more raw emotional response, which he then appeared to manufacture. Hayward seemed to make light of the whole crisis in various ill-judged remarks. Both were criticized for not being angry enough, and then appearing to dissimulate, when the truth was they really did feel it more than they led people to believe. Intriguingly, the Obama coolness turned out to be a much more favorable attribute when there was no one to blame – the act of God that was Hurricane Sandy, which blasted the eastern seaboard and gave him a timely boost for his re-election.

So here is the Obama dilemma – people can be tossed into positions of great power from total obscurity and make an outstanding success of it. George Washington wasn't far from that in terms of his experience – but there are traps for the unwary. One is being captured by the opinions and experience of people clustered around the throne. One way to capture the Law of the Situation is to make sure you hear more than a single set of voices. One of the US's most successful presidents, Teddy Roosevelt, a New Yorker who reinvented himself as a Midwestern cowboy, had a strategy for doing this.[9] He deliberately appointed to key advisory positions aides who held radically different views of the situation, so he would be forced to come to his own conclusion. How unlike the yes-men and women who, since, have crowded round the White House door.

WHAT DO LEADERS DO, ANYWAY?

The SPQ framework helps us take apart three elements of strategic adaptive leadership: being (Qualities), seeing (Situations) and doing (Processes).[10]

> **Being:** You are who you are, and, yes, with disciplined training, self-management (more on that later) and a little help from your friends, you can acquire new skills and ways of being, but it is a hard road to change your instincts and impulses.[11] Perhaps it is easier to change how you think and feel about yourself, the story of you that you tell to yourself – the "I" of leadership – but that's a lot less easy than one might suppose.[12] Novice leaders like Obama and Blair find their journeys change their vision of themselves, quite quickly in the first 100 days when they are playing themselves in, but, as we have warned, there are inertial forces as well. First, you are who you are – the face staring back at you in the mirror is unavoidably yours. Second, people will persist in seeing you their own way regardless of how you try to rewrite your identity. Any way you

look at it, there's not much wiggle room in being who you are, though in Chapters 13 and 14 we'll go into this in much more detail, because it is so critical to leadership success.

Seeing: Leadership situations can be battlegrounds for competing versions of reality; you can tell all the stories you like, people continue to be unconvinced and cling to their version of the truth, either because it fits their experience or because it fits their needs. The ability to change people's vision is one of the defining features of "charisma,"[13] by the way, and is something we shall dwell on in the next chapter.

Doing: Isn't this what leadership is really all about? We all know the clichés – actions speak louder than words; you have to walk the talk. What's the point of "being the right person at the right place and time" if you don't do the right thing? Of course, this is true, but we should beware. The "action man" leader can be a pain in the ass – wheel-spinning to create nothing more constructive than heat and clouds of dust. Nicolas Sarkozy – lately president of the French Republic – quickly earned himself the label of being a "hyperactive" leader.[14] And little good it did him – he failed to get re-elected and withdrew from front-line politics. It is a matter of engaging in the right actions, and sometimes the right actions are words. As a leader you have to pick your battles, pick your words, pick your images and weld them into something that people can recognize, believe in and follow.

As we look at the SPQ framework, a number of things jump out from this:

- Leaders' situations are always disequilibrating. If the leader ever believes she has found the alignment of being the right person in the right situation doing the right thing, it won't be long before the earth shifts under her feet and some new equilibrium must be found.

- The change can come from within the Self – a leader can change her mind; her way of thinking and feeling. Anyone can have a Damascene moment of truth about themselves, but change more often comes from the situation. What made Jack Welch such an interesting leader was that he enacted change cyclically in reforming GE. He found his experience of the new organization he had created changed his way of thinking, triggering a fresh wave of innovative leadership.

- Situations are not usually in states of constant flux, but rather what evolutionists call "punctuated equilibrium."[15] Environments reach a relatively stable state and then some event or process (bad harvest; corporate takeover; new technology) comes to upset the apple-cart. All the pieces fly up in the air and then settle down into a new equilibrium. This cycle may be a lot shorter in some environments than others – e.g. consulting firm vs. law firm. Some firms inhabit radically more turbulent environments than others.

- Adaptation to a changing world can be purely psychological – you change your view of the world, or your view of yourself as an actor in it, but do nothing differently.[16] This somewhat passive accommodation of life is clearly what happened to Gandhi several times in what he called his youthful "experiments with the truth" (such as meat-eating, which he hated).[17] It is possible for leaders to find peace of mind or some other adaptive benefit from shifts of perspective, but clearly if the leader is to take charge of adaptive change, then Route 1 has got to be action. Gandhi's story illustrates this perfectly, for he did spring into action of historic proportions after his South African moment of truth, because the experience triggered a changed view of the world and of himself.

THE SAVING GIFT: PROCESSES

If the story of adaptation were simply one of people stuck with unchangeable identities, confronting immoveable situations, then life would be an unhappy affair of search and disappointment. We would struggle around the world, hoping to find islands of contentment.

Figure 7.1:   Leadership processes: the art of adaptation

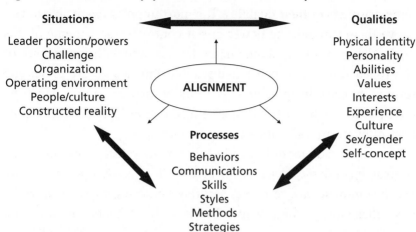

Luckily, human adaptability means we are capable of acting in lots of different ways (see Figure 7.1). We cannot change the weather. We cannot change our physical susceptibility to extremes of hot and cold. But we can change our apparel. As my wife is fond of remarking, there is no such thing as bad weather, just bad clothing.

Let's delve a bit deeper. As we have seen, leaders differ, as we all do, in drives and tastes. The taciturn boss of few words may feel very uncomfortable in after-work schmoozing. One African leader I know – a brilliant, cool, rational man who transited from boyhood in the north Kenyan bush herding goats and cows to become the leader of a major international corporation – confessed how much he hated such events. "What I like to do at weekends," he confided, "is to go back to my people and herd cattle." Yet, he had learned – and it was not easy for him – how to unbend, talk small-talk and mix in sociably. Another Canadian business leader I know is relentlessly voluble, cheery, dominant and always ready to assume command. Even when he's silent you can see people reluctant to forge out into the verbal space that he so fully occupies. He has learned how to keep his silence, but it requires more controlled measures to dampen his impact – like rotating the chairing of meetings among other group members, delegating and making polite excuses when people want to draw him into all their ex-work social gatherings. Duke Ellington – an intensely social being – always preserved a degree of distance with the band.[18]

117

My point is that leaders – or any of us for that matter – don't have to be prisoners of their qualities. The most impressive are able to rise above them through the power of self-control – a key theme of this book. Nelson Mandela, a man naturally endowed with a demeanor of controlled reserve, turned self-discipline into a fine art under the severest tutelage imaginable – 27 years of incarceration – which he then put to use by instructing an entire nation in a miracle of self-control by means of Truth and Reconciliation.[19]

Yet, it is a sad fact of leadership that many refuse to exercise self-control, *because they don't see the need to*. That is what power can do. If you command vast resources securely, you can get away with ruthless inflexibility – for a while. The tragedy of history is often the human cost incurred while despots and dictators are belatedly and painfully removed. This has been the story of the Arab Spring, where, from 2011, a succession of autocrats belatedly awoke to the voice of their people, coalesced for the first time into a force of resistance by mobile telephony, the Internet and social networks.

Yet, there are also flexible ways of being despotic. Jo Stalin could be charming and romantic, and strategically flexible in dealing with threats and enemies, though mainly careless of others' opinions. Many leaders fail because they are too much themselves, making no effort to moderate their instinctive style. Business founders and family patriarchs seem especially prone to such surfeits of authenticity – look at Henry Ford's fatal inflexibility in how he conducted both business and personal relationships.[20]

On the other side, versatility can be a handicap – if that means oversensitivity to context, seeking to satisfy all sides or moving between positions according to which way the wind blows. This is just to underline the SPQ logic that any quality is a liability if you can't vary it, and that extends to flexibility as a disposition. Leaders who bend with every breeze are as bad as those who are rigid and dogmatic. We are back to the Leadership Formula. Sometimes the right thing to be is flexible[21] and sometimes it is smart to be immoveable and obdurate. You just have to know when to be what – in sports, it's called shot selection.

Ultimately, it is leadership processes that are the salvation of leaders. Never mind one's personal qualities – instincts, habits, values, interests and abilities – the question is, can the leader generate the right response to meet the challenge of the moment?[22] If they can't, can they swallow this realization and get someone else into the front line to do what they don't have the stomach or skills for? This is a key point we shall come back to in Chapter 11. Either way, leadership processes are the salvation of leadership because, in theory at least, *a leader can always find the right response.* Limitations of skill and physical disability are irrelevant to the most important leadership behaviors, which are mainly acts of communication or, at worst, feats of endurance. The question is, does the leader possess the awareness and can she summon the willpower to see what is necessary to do, and then do it?

It is no accident that the leaders of the digital age include a lot of young men and a sprinkling of women who are highly intelligent, self-willed, independent minded, non-materialist, casual and democratic technical wizards – people like Eric Schmidt, Marissa Mayer and Mark Zuckerberg.[23] They have the "Q"s to match the "S"s of their businesses – Google, Yahoo and Facebook. In the case of Google, it was two such 25-year-old bright sparks, Larry Page and Sergey Brin, who founded the company in 1998 and realized, three years later, that they needed some experience at the helm. So they hired the 46-year-old electrical engineer Eric Schmidt, CEO of Novell at the time, to run Google.[24] The three gelled quickly, for Schmidt was a very bright, mild, low-key personality, but a seasoned business pragmatist who knew how to get things done. Together, they grew the company to its vast and powerful dimensions.

THE VERSATILITY STRUGGLE

We are all a lot less flexible than we could be. It is instinctive to find economical and efficient solutions to dealing with what life throws at us, so we put together a repertoire of routines and behaviors that suit our "Q" factors and serve most of the "S" factors that we meet. As we get older we make a virtue of them and call them "character." You can see many grey-haired leaders basking with pride in their limitations and absurdly being supported by underlings. Everyone can feel comfortable around their predictability. People don't like it, and may even diminish their respect for you, if you act out of character.[25]

Steve Jobs – whose adventurous inclinations led him to experimentation with psychedelic drugs, a key factor in his development – was forever mercurial and experimental, without losing his "character." The inflexibility of many leaders is pure self-indulgence, reinforced by the uncritical support of lackeys, plus an accumulated belief system that the past holds the lessons for the future. They call it strategy, but really it's just self-regard + inertia. Jobs, on the other hand, suffered from the opposite pathology – spinning from one action to another without being strategic. However, his eventual triumph at the reborn Apple in the last years of his life was entirely strategic; a vision of end-to-end product relationships around a shared proprietary hub, driven by principles of beauteous design and user-friendliness. Yet, earlier in his career especially, Jobs's behavior also ricocheted off ideas like a pinball.[26]

Effective leadership processes have three levels: acts, tactics and strategies.

> **Acts:** The leader is quick to recognize when some new response is required – this is improvisation. Duke Ellington, a professional improviser in music, was likewise in management; constantly inventive, finding new ways of dealing with the troublesome people that inhabit the world of jazz production, distribution and consumption.[27] Ernest Shackleton, hero of the Antarctic, showed he was willing and able to do anything he required of his men, constantly inventing new diversions and actions to keep people motivated and happy under conditions of extraordinary privation and unpredictability.[28]

> **Tactics:** Tactics are to acts as phrases are to words – they bundle ideas and actions. Leaders are often at their most tactical in meetings – for example, knowing when to interject for maximum effect. One of the most common and powerful

tactical forms is what cognitive scientists call "heuristics" – commonly known as rules of thumb.[29] These are operational principles to govern thought and action. Leaders have libraries of heuristics, often in the form of "if – then" principles, such as "keep your friends close but your enemies closer." Machiavelli's treatise on leadership is a compendium of such heuristics.[30] Of course, the trick is knowing when to apply them, but you can see how many a smooth operator can appear no more than a slick trickster if that's all they've got – a bunch of routines for dealing with a bunch of situations. Ellington and Shackleton were tactical masters. Everything they did was nuanced and sequenced to meet a specific goal.

Strategies: Forty years ago, management guru Henry Mintzberg published his groundbreaking analysis of managerial work – an intimate ethnographic observation of what executives actually do, rather than what the textbooks at the time depicted, in which he noted how their daily life was a blizzard of improvised action, dealing with unscheduled meetings and unexpected events.[31] But Mintzberg shrewdly noted that some are able, by shot selection, to shape this blizzard into a coherent, purposeful shape. Others just churn – frustrated and frantic, driven by events. The wheel is turning but the hamster is dead!

Shackleton and Ellington were strategic, in that each had an over-arching goal and purpose which all their actions served; which gave direction to their choices and supplied meaning for their reflections. For Ellington it was his grand vision of music, connection and spirituality. For Shackleton it was simpler – his singular goal to save all his men.

THE DUKE ELLINGTON METHOD

It was said by one of his band that "everyone loved Duke, he was on everybody's side."[32, 33] This is a statement to ponder and wonder at, not least because of the vicissitudes of running a 16 or so piece jazz orchestra. Of all the difficult people in the world to organize and lead, jazz musicians must come near the top of the list – feckless, drug and alcohol abusers, unreliable, undisciplined, anti-authority, you name it.

One of his long-standing tenor players – Ben Webster – was distinguished by his magical ability to produce a lush, almost sentimental, subtle and beguiling sound from his horn. However, off the bandstand, he was such a roughhouse that he earned the nickname "Animal." Not a man to get the wrong side of. But Ellington was an impervious charmer – a man of grace, elegance and unruffled good humor. He knew how to turn away wrath, as the Good Book recommends, to the extent that, as legend has it, when Oscar Pettiford, a bass player given to emotional firestorms, started screaming grievances in Duke's face, the great man simply fell asleep.[34] A superb instance of the right behavior for the moment.

As a motivator, Duke was a great strategist as well as a tactician. One of his most winning techniques was to have numbers especially tailored to showcase the talents of particular instrumentalists. Everyone got their place in the sun – very addictive. Moreover, he had a great contrarian strategy for dealing with the bad boys who showed up late or, worse, under the influence. He would not only feature them, but allow their solo spots to extend beyond the point of creative comfort. It was one such a mammoth solo that Ellington used to turn around the band's fortunes at its nadir in 1956, when, at the Newport Jazz Festival, Nelson-like he turned a blind eye to frantic instructions to close his set and make way for the "bigger" acts that were supposed to follow. Instead, he launched the band into a 12-bar blues, "Diminuendo and Crescendo in Blue," in which the prolific genius of tenor man Paul Gonsalves turned in an unprecedented 27 choruses of his solo, lifting the crowd to heights of ecstatic appreciation unseen for years at the festival, and reviving the band's reputation overnight.[35] (Check out the recording, it's awesome!)

In the next chapter we put the SPQ model to work, for the Leadership Formula impels a number of dynamics as people and situations change. The art of leadership is to find new, adaptive equilibria and there are many ways of achieving this. Together they amount to strategic leadership.

IMPLICATIONS AND OBSERVATIONS FOR LEADERS AND ORGANIZATIONS

In theory, anyone can do almost anything. With the will, opportunity, right tools and practice, leaders can be truly versatile and adjust their style to match the needs of the situation. In theory, that is! We turn out to be a lot less versatile than we could be, and are often driven by events and habits rather than learning new behaviors and bundling them into strategies. Key points:

- In their scanning of the environment, leaders need to make sure that they keep their focus flexible – it's important to pay attention to the right part of the horizon.

- Flurries of activity do not constitute leadership – sometimes less is more.

- Action comes from both habit and choice. Leaders should not be forever deciding, but unthinking habit is the ruin of many a leader.

- Leaders don't have to be the prisoners of their "Q" factors – flexible behavior can be a leader's salvation.

- Leaders need to remember that we are all less flexible than we believe we are.

- Skilled behavior needs to link to a purpose, tactics and part of a wider perspective on the leadership journey – that is strategy.

- Leaders make their luck; as Pasteur said, "Chance favors the prepared mind."

— 8 —

DYNAMIC LEADERSHIP – SHAPING AND DISCOVERY

The best form of saying is being.

Che Guevara

Strategic leadership means figuring out how to lead *in* the world and *out* of your Self. Many different worlds; many possible Selves. If there was a single solution to the challenge, it would be operational, not strategic. So now we are going to look at the options and sequences through which leaders can bring outstanding value to the systems for which they are responsible.

So far, we have looked at Qualities, Situations and Processes separately, asking three big questions:

- **Qualities:** What is your compass? What is the basis for your leadership proposition?

- **Situations:** How are you seeing your leadership situation? What might you be missing, and what might you benefit from seeing differently?

Figure 8.1: SPQ as strategy: the six paths to alignment

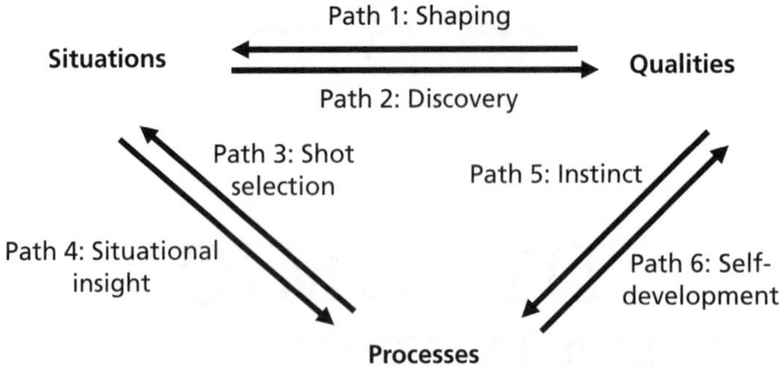

* **Processes:** When you look at what you do, how much is in the habit/comfort zone and how much is truly strategic – reaching out towards a purpose and goal?

The deceptive simplicity of the SPQ model gets more complicated once we start to unpick it and look at the adaptive options it opens up. As Figure 8.1 shows, there are six paths, which, combined, constitute strategic leadership.

PATH 1: SHAPING AND SELECTING[1]

It's a familiar pattern – an incoming CEO brings with her a bunch of trusted cronies, especially a strong finance guy and maybe a few others critical to past success.[2] This is pretty rational. Earlier we used the metaphor of organizational culture as a kind of pickling medium, and noted that many leaders strive to re-engineer the culture to make it their own before it pickles them.

Al "Chainsaw" Dunlap did this malevolently. Entering Sunbeam with his long-standing sidekick, Russell Kersh, a former financial analyst, he publicly attacked and humiliated every member of the board, firing several of them, in his high-profile mission of extreme culture change.[3] The end to his story was his own demise as CEO and the wholesale destruction of what he had dedicated his ruthless methods to: shareholder value. Lee Iacocca turned Chrysler around by firing 33 of 35 VPs, slashing costs and taking a $1 dollar salary for himself plus stock options.[4] Less dramatic and just as effective, Lou Gerstner, on entering IBM, decimated top management and hand-picked appointments for a smaller, more cohesive board. Significantly, one of the first of his team was communications executive, David Kalis, whose brief was to run PR defense for Gerstner as he embarked on his radical strategic transformation of Big Blue.[5]

This is a time-honored tradition. Alexander the Great didn't engage in a lot of post-merger integration activity with the tribes he conquered. If you march in as an all-conquering hero, you adopt their best inventions, steal the local women and generally impose your own order on the assumption that it is superior to what came before. However, the wise leader goes through the pockets of his defeated enemies before he throws their bodies off the bridge. Some local habits, customs and faiths inevitably get a foothold in the invading culture. People "go native." Good ideas have viral qualities.

So, what can a leader actually shape (see Figure 8.2)? Looking at our "S" list – position/powers; challenge; organization; environment; people/culture; constructed reality – quite a lot. Strategic adaptive leadership comes from:

- **Position/powers:** A CEO may change reporting lines to bring potential sources of challenge under direct control; move to restructure the remuneration systems to serve the strategic vision more directly; change decision-making routines and approvals to retain control. Leaders can act to build new power bases through a variety of tactics and measures.

Figure 8.2: SPQ strategic dynamic #1 – shaping and selecting

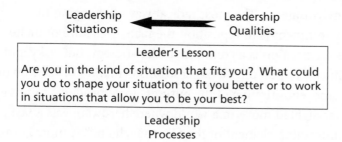

Leadership Situations ← Leadership Qualities

Leader's Lesson
Are you in the kind of situation that fits you? What could you do to shape your situation to fit you better or to work in situations that allow you to be your best?

Leadership Processes

- **Challenge:** We have already taken to heart Mary Parker Follett's injunction that managers should figure out the challenge for themselves,[6] though that is not always a walk in the park. For Shackleton, it was simple for him to redefine his challenge in a 180 degree turn to become "SAVE ALL LIVES." Lou Gerstner, like many imported leaders, was sanctioned to enact a turnaround challenge. Aung San Suu Kyi, heroine of Burma, patiently and intelligently defined her challenge as sticking to a message of speaking quiet and simple truth on behalf of her dispossessed compatriots, whilst awaiting the inevitable crumbling of the military's nerve.[7] Defining the challenge is probably the most central and essential element of leadership shaping, and it often requires the rejection of conventional wisdom.

- **Organization:** Incoming business leaders love to restructure. It is one of the ways they reinforce their power base. It is also an article of faith in the field of strategic management that structure follows strategy.[8] So, cunningly, the leader says this is how we have to be to do what I want us to do. Gerstner's primary moves were to recentralize Big Blue. Jobs, on returning to Apple, set about radically simplifying the product range and integrating around a single platform. Ratan Tata, on taking over the running of the Indian conglomerate empire, started from a weak powerbase – surrounded on all sides by princelings with unfettered command over their family fiefdoms.[9] As he succeeded in imposing a federal order over the business, so grew his power and his reputation as a benevolent but firm and wise ruler.

- **Environment:** The most radical way of changing the environment is to reposition the firm. This kind of niche reconstruction is a common leader strategy, but risky and difficult to pull off. Gerstner's transformation of IBM involved a major repositioning of the business from products to services – a far-sighted move in a world where hardware was a fast-diminishing element of the IT value chain.[10] A more common story of corporate transformation comes from the companies which start in one world and end up in one that is totally different. Actually, this is very common. Many businesses start with a money-making idea that provides a raft of cash to do something bolder and quite different. Thus it was for Samsung, the giant electronics *chaebol*, which started life in 1938 as a family owned and run noodle business before smartly transforming itself via a bunch of successive approximations into what it is today – the world's biggest technology firm.[11] In fact, the corporate world is full of such cases. It is much more challenging to shift the mature business into new markets. Look at Time-Warner's fatal attempt to get into the ISP market by acquiring AOL,[12] or Seagram the drinks giant's impulsive diversion into the movies, surrendering all its shareholder value in its disastrous takeover of Universal Studios.[13]

In earlier chapters we talked about the role of leaders in changing, or following, the tides of history. This they do by repositioning institutions and, ultimately, if they can get their hands on the right levers, cultures. If the climate changes, the tribe can either habitat track – go off in search of the old familiar environment elsewhere – or adapt. And, as we noted, there is the possibility of niche construction – changing the landscape by working on it. Visionaries like Steve Jobs redefine the environment for everyone – through the iPod and iTunes he changed the music industry forever. Would it have turned out the same way had he never lived? Some aspects of marketing and functionality would be here as now, but much else would not. It is fair to say that Jobs was one of a handful of business leaders to move society in a new direction through his innovations.

Not all leaders of change are lone visionaries. Jobs had his buddies – first and best the techy genius that was Steve Wozniak.[14] Jobs and Wozniak fooled around with kit in their garage. So did Steve Hewlett and Dave Packard, Mark Zuckerberg and his pals, the gang at Google and others of the 21st century digital Generation Y. These young blades were at the apex of the tide of transformation. In the last chapter we shall come back to the question of how much we can hope to be in any degree of control of our own destinies through our leaders.

When it comes to repositioning, the road is strewn with failures and many near-death experiences. Look at HP, a fine technology company that lost its way in the journey from genius in printer production to sixth in the world in PC production.[15] The lost horizons of HP have been accentuated in recent years by outsiders expected to work repositioning miracles. Others have disappeared, if not from memory, like DEC computers, Marconi electronics and General Foods.[16]

• **People/Culture:** The most critical aspect of the leadership situation is its human face. The leader–follower relationship is one of the most documented themes in the leadership literature. It is, in academic jargon, an exchange relationship.[17] It is all about expectations, giving and reciprocating, earning trust, building harmony, serving people's needs and interests. You can find plenty written about how to do this in many excellent books, so I shan't retread this ground.[18] Rather, I want us to take a step back and look at how this relationship changes historically.

We have noted how leaders get "pickled" by the culture, and the leaders will attempt to shape the culture to one that fits their purpose. This is a topic that has been much written about in many guises. It can be seen as the process by which leaders sell a vision and embed their values in a business.[19] It is equally a more intimate influence tactic – especially how leaders recruit true believers to their cause. Jesus of Nazareth could be seen as an ultimate example of both – capturing the hearts and minds of his disciples and then leading them away from their families and communities towards his new realm of faith. More commonplace examples abound in business and politics – such as the IBM case, and Margaret Thatcher capturing and refocusing an initially skeptical Conservative Party and steering it to a new ideological position.[20]

- **Constructed reality:** We have already said a lot about this, but it is worth briefly noting that the leader can attempt (and sometimes succeed) to shape the way their people see the world, respond to its laws and structures, interpret its environment and conceive of themselves. To be able to cast such spells over an organization is the fate of few.[21] The great faiths of the world are visions binding institutions, cultures and systems of law and governance into a complete ideological reality. We are back to culture and its evolution. No human's consciousness is free of belief systems – we are a believing animal. This is the domain of the Self, which we come to later in this book.

It is vital that leaders grasp this point – the belief systems out there are really important, even when they are fantastical and absurd. Seeing is being.[22] People's identities and capabilities are defined by their beliefs about reality. In my book *Managing the Human Animal* I wrote about the importance of gossip in organizations – as a form of network intelligence that everyone uses.[23] Leaders need to remember: nose in, fingers out. Keep your ear to the ground but hold your vision and intelligence at a higher level. The ability to be appropriately skeptical is important – listen and stand above.

PATH 2: DISCOVERY

Restructuring a business – refocusing, shedding lines, adding new functions – is a common way for leaders to claim their territory.[24] But what happens if you, as a leader, find yourself in a strange land? The people might look familiar but their ways are alien to you. They take for granted what you would question, and pay undue attention to what you would not bother with. The sky might look the same but the landscape has changed. This is what culture shock feels like. The response of some expats on their first posting to foreign parts is to find other expats with whom they can interact, maintaining as closely as possible the life they had back home.

Some years ago a Japanese student and I did a study of Japanese financial services expats on long assignments in London.[25] The chief and clearest finding was that the ones who struggled most to adjust and perform were those who stuck to the warm embrace of the familiar – the very welcoming large Japanese diaspora in London. The happiest and best-performing individuals were the fellows who went native: finding a social life with new British friends and embedding themselves in the host community.

A similar dilemma faces leaders, separating those relentless shapers and habitat trackers who minimize the need for change to be accommodated mentally. They find and build niches in which they can practice leadership the way they like it. This is what Al Dunlap did – ruthless pruning to boost shareholder value, which had disastrous consequences for Sunbeam.

But what if you surrender yourself to novelty? You move from a well-known and practiced world into one where your previous skills and knowledge have little relevance; where you are bereft of your network of nurtured relationships. You are going to have to adapt by adopting new behaviors, forming new relationships and, in all likelihood, adjusting your beliefs. As work on adjusting to transitions shows, during the Encounter phase – the first weeks on the job – you find yourself just reacting to all kinds of unfamiliar stimuli.[26] But you don't just discover a new world; you re-discover yourself, and perhaps some quite new insights.

In this way, leadership situations "play" leadership qualities like the wind plays chimes. We only learn through experience – even about ourselves (see Figure 8.3). Novelist E. M. Forster once said, "How do I know what I think until I hear what I say?" Let us rework that slightly – "How do I know who I am until I see what I do?" Our self-knowledge is incomplete, or, to put it another way, the Self is a perpetual work in progress.[27] More concretely, you have to taste celery, caviar and kidneys to discover whether they are to your taste. How do we know how we feel about leading until we've led some people?

Figure 8.3: SPQ strategic dynamic #2 – discovery

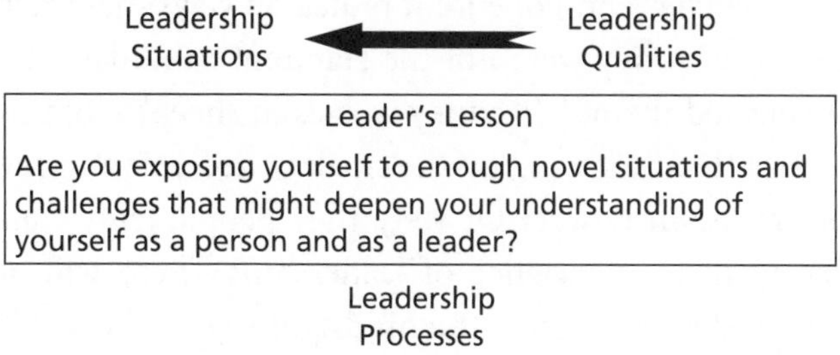

Leadership   Leadership
Situations ◄══════════ Qualities

Leader's Lesson
Are you exposing yourself to enough novel situations and challenges that might deepen your understanding of yourself as a person and as a leader?

Leadership
Processes

The principle of discovery was eloquently articulated in relation to leadership by Howard Gardner in his fine book, *Leading Minds*.[28] Among his leadership stories is the arresting saga of Pope John XXIII, elected to the papacy after a series of 12 deadlocked ballots and picked as the safe compromise candidate. This seemingly mild, jolly, plump old Cardinal, nearing the end of his earthly ministry, was the perfect stop-gap – a little breathing space while the next generation prepared itself for accession. But this narrative did not play out as the scheming kingmakers of the Vatican planned. John turned out to be a visionary and a radical, shocking his colleagues with the temerity of his mission, which was no less than wholesale reform of the papacy. This he enacted in 1962 with Vatican II, which boldly ushered in a new era of freedom, modernity and ecumenism. Having set in motion that grand task that he felt his faith had called him to, he died.

Margaret Thatcher, the Western world's first elected female leader, was similarly alighted upon as a compromise candidate to lead the British Conservative Party during a period of great economic turmoil in 1979.[29] She too surprised those who didn't know her by revealing a strident radicalism and commitment to reform. She scared the hell out of the old patrician Tories of her party, pronouncing them "wet" and then surrounded herself with men (no women) she considered to be suitably "dry," i.e. prepared to share her relentlessly austere Hayekian economic vision. Leading Britain into the Falklands War years later confirmed her credentials as an emergent warrior chieftain. She was little loved, yet has come to be increasingly respected for her leadership legacy – one of that special breed of leaders who creates a genuine break with the past and resets the political agenda.

So, here's the question – what was the nature of the "discovery" here? Were Thatcher and Pope John radical in ways that their electors didn't see? Clearly they were not the standout candidates to most of those who elected them. Were they wolves in sheep's clothing; biding their time and then throwing off the cloak of deception to reveal their true intent to attain power? Or were they people truly transformed personally by their experience of leadership? There will always be proponents of the first view – the hindsight sages who say, "I always saw it in him/her." For sure, in both cases the nascent leader was visible, but more as a hint than a promise.

The truth is that all our visible qualities were once no more than suggestions. You just have to go back far enough and then watch how they were refined through experience and practice to the point where they became visible, robust and unsinkable. The science of behavior genetics tells how this becomes a positive loop.[30] The infant's budding instincts lead it, by trial and error, to discover preferences that parents then notice and nurture. The teenager experiments with a bounded range of possible Selves, and, through a mixture of luck, feedback and selection, figures out what works and adopts it as a strategy – just like evolution really.

Thatcher, as a young, new leader, was still learning and reinforcing her profile. Pope John had had longer, and was able to spring forth more fully formed as the leader he was waiting to be. We should also bear in mind that this analysis implies even the leader themselves might not spot their own potential until it is awakened. It is worth reflecting on how leaders learn to lead. This is a question I regularly ask of them. Two answers come back more than any other:

1. There was some exemplar or role model who inspired them; often an early mentor.

2. They were given early responsibility for a project or a posting that showed them a new world of possibility.

Discovery by observing someone else requires hard work for the reflective Self. Discovery from observing one's own actions is a direct route to insight.

Either way, it is more than trial and error – it is a re-framing of the Self in the world. It feels new. Discovery feels good . . . usually. It may come immediately or after a time delay. We've all had analogous experiences in areas other than leadership, from cookery, to sports, to home improvements – the inner voice that awakens, surprised, and says, "I never knew it would be like this." It may extend further. "Maybe I'm not what I thought I was." We are keyboards played by life. The world stimulates and excites us and we note our new reactions.

Look at Warren Buffett.[31] His parents clearly watched in wonder as his instinct for numbers manifested itself in the child – endlessly playing with the statistical properties of car number plates and moving on to the mountains of tickertape from his father's stockbroking business. Buffett's numerical and entrepreneurial instincts evolved in tandem, with a lot of shaping – building business enterprises that embodied his philosophy of investment, hand-in-glove with his gargantuan appetite for self-instruction. Buffett seemed to discover quite early that he had no particular liking for leadership – making money was his game, based upon a deep conviction about his ability to apprehend true value in what businesses are and do.

His diffidence about leadership was revealed when he found himself thrust into the role of white knight to rescue one of his ailing investments, the mighty Salomon Brothers, which had befallen a nearly fatally compromising scandal over the misuse of information by leading executives, and a subsequent cover-up.[32] The Sage of Omaha, with typical clarity, quickly established a framework for exemplary action and then scuttled back to the Mid-West, leaving the day-to-day business of leadership to those with an appetite for it.

Plenty of people who crave status and recognition climb the ladder only to discover that their elevated roles include the uncongenial requirement of leadership: that they have to take responsibility for other people, some of them quite complex and difficult characters, when they would rather just carry on being technicians and specialists. Then they seek refuge in the task rather than the human aspects of their roles. Of course, this is terribly damaging to companies, and it is the direct result (as I shall argue in Chapter 15) of the insistent organizational design norm of the linear pyramidal hierarchy, where status and leadership are joined at the hip.

The banking crisis of 2008 involved a great deal of this kind of mismanagement, especially of traders. Many banks promoted traders to management positions who turned out to be reluctant leaders, continuing to run their own trading book on the side and only paying attention to the traders under their care when there was an obvious problem, such as major losses.[33] This was not helped by the introvert instincts of traders, who tend not to share their reflections and anxieties. Under such circumstances, in a high-risk environment, management by exception just doesn't work.

The malaise ran deep in financial services, where they lacked any kind of credible model of leadership and management, over-reliant on the generous rising tide of bull markets, a tide that raises all boats. For the harbor masters of finance overseeing this bounty, it sustained a leadership myth that they were gifted and fully deserved plaudits and vast bonuses.[34] This leadership illusion has been shattered. Now, discovery of a new reality-based model of leadership has become an industry priority.

Discovery is a time-limited phenomenon – as, indeed, are all the SPQ dynamics. It is how the six paths are sequenced into a story that gives them both a strategic and a lifespan character. The leadership journey may take you through all points of the compass: morphing between shaping, discovery and the other elements.

This is a voyage for many leaders – they shape a world and then learn things about themselves from living in the world they have created. Another journey is the leader who adapts to some new situation and then figures out how to shape it to their will. The first voyage is the classic path of the entrepreneur; the latter the experience of the migrant leader. Both happen often, and each can be both hazardous and rewarding.

But let us now explore the other paths in the SPQ model – those that underpin effectiveness. In the next chapter we examine a key process that underlies adaptation – the ability to read the environment and produce appropriate responses.

IMPLICATIONS AND OBSERVATIONS FOR LEADERS AND ORGANIZATIONS

Intelligent leadership holds and varies the balance between the duality of shaping innovation vs. adaptive flexibility. The balance depends on the leader's drives, which are both enabling and inhibiting, and on how irresistible the forces are surrounding the leadership situation. Some key points:

- To shape their environment, leaders often need to have a strong team standing at their back.

- There are plenty of levers for leaders to lay their hands on in the leadership situation – shoring up powers, defining the challenge, structuring, filtering the environment, picking the people and shaping beliefs and perceptions.

- Experience teaches leadership. Leaders need to test themselves to know themselves. This insight needs to be applied in raising the next generation of leaders in a business.

- It is easy to miss the lessons of discovery if people are lured by rewards into conventional and unchallenging paths.

— 9 —

READING THE
WORLD – A
LEADERSHIP
CONUNDRUM

We don't see things as they are; we see them as we are.

Anaïs Nin

The pragmatist dictum, "If something is perceived as real, it is real in its consequences" might seem to imply that all a leader has to do to be effective is to shape the perceptions of people around her; that is, until reality comes up and bites her in the tail. Hitler is perhaps the most notable example in history of this delusion – he shaped the consciousness of his people into a compelling collective delusion.[1] Such was his magnetism that those closest to him clung on to it, as to a hunk of driftwood in a chaotic torrent, even as it bore them to destruction.

The conundrum is how much to take reality as an external given or something to be imagined, created and controlled. We have dwelt quite a lot on the latter, so let's go back to one admirable role model: the Versatile Leader.[2]

This is the sage who reads the winds of change with super-sensory perception. Like the cattle before the storm, the fox before snow, the snake before rain, he knows when to build, when to run, when to fight and when to shelter. Some politicians possess instincts – how to remain on the right side, when to shift with the tides of history and stay on the winning side. Advisors to capricious rulers have this capacity. The court jester, the vizier to the sultan, the "chef de cabinet," the chancellor to the king, the COO to the CEO; to survive, all have to master the art of changing their tune when there is a leadership succession or when the king gets some big new idea.

The first, and perhaps the greatest, diarist of history, Samuel Pepys, had, as his day job in 17th century England, running the navy.[3] This was a pretty important position for an island people, and Pepys deployed his prodigious intelligence to create a new model for organizing the service that played no small part in the future ascendant power of his nation. Yet, all the while, he was having to perform an elaborate dance of rhetoric to keep his head on his shoulders as England lurched from monarchy (Charles I, beheaded) to parliamentary rule (Oliver Cromwell) and back to monarchy (Charles II). Each successive administration had to be embraced and its predecessor renounced, as well as expunging all evidence of his own role as a fervent public supporter of the previous status quo. In the last of these three regimes, Pepys was hauled up before the courts and, by the skin of his teeth, through his powers of oratory and the support of his dwindled network of old mates, he was able to save his neck and drift into an honorable retirement.

PATH 3: SHOT SELECTION

The best advisors excel in the art of shot selection (Figure 9.1), like a seasoned caddy managing the judgment of a gifted golfer. I am not a golfer but I reckon the first time I set foot on a course some kind person might say, "When you start, and want to hit the ball as far as possible off the tee, you need to use this big, knobbly club." I slice the ball and it goes flying into the undergrowth. My trusted advisor gives me a rueful and knowing smile. "You'd better use this one now," she says, handing me what looks like an enlarged cooking utensil. So it

Figure 9.1: SPQ strategic dynamic #3 – shot selection

Leadership   Leadership
Situations   Qualities

Leadership
Processes

Leader's Lesson
What behaviors and tactics might you need to be generating
to be more effective in neglected or difficult areas of your
current leader role?

goes on until eventually I get to the green, where, with a stick I recognize as a putter, I spend a happy ten minutes and five shots to get
the ball in the hole. For sure I am like a stupid king with a smart
chancellor who's not allowed to touch the ball. When I'm playing
tennis, it's a different matter. I'm in charge. The ball comes to me. Do
I advance and volley, step back and drive the ball, run round and play
a forehand, take it early with a slice or late and lob? So many choices.
I look over the net – where is my opponent standing? What's the wind
doing? What is his weakness – forehand or backhand? What's my
weakness? I think I'll just stick to what is safest for me – one of the
less challenging shots. I lose the point. Should have been bolder.

Let's break this down into its components:

1. Read the situation.

2. Consider the range of options.

3. Pick an option.

4. Execute.

Hmm. Is this what leaders do? Is it even what they should do? What
are the complications? Convoluted cogitation is all very well at a chess
table, though even there time is not unlimited, but is it appropriate in
the middle of a tennis match or a boardroom meeting where I am
supposed to be the leader? No way. This is the point where we say, "to
hell with it, let's go with good old gut feeling."

Since effectiveness through versatility is all about shot selection, it follows that the successful versatile leader has great instincts. And how, in God's name, do you get those? Remember British Prime Minister Tony Blair at the start of this book, learning the news of the London terrorist bombings. His call to himself to "be a leader" meant, in effect, "You know what to do. Do it." I shall have a lot more to say in Chapter 10 about the mental process of knowing which instincts to trust and which not to, but it is clear that many great leaders do exactly this – trust their gut. But their instincts do not rest on thin air. Underlying them is a wealth of what psychologists call "tacit knowledge" – stuff you know that is uncodified and, at a certain level, unconscious.[4] You get this stuff by osmosis – it enters your system as a by-product of experience.

This can be relentlessly schooled,[5] as it was for Mozart in music, Tiger Woods in golf, Andre Agassi in tennis and Hannibal in warfare. For lesser mortals, such as you and me, our learning follows our preferences as much as our schooling. We naturally pay attention to the stuff that captures our attention – apart from shocks and alarms that everyone notices, we are attuned to our unique profile of interests and needs. Warren Buffett became a whiz at financial data analysis and intuitive stock-picking from years of childhood number play and relentless self-instruction. Naturally, and wisely, apart from his reluctant excursions into conventional leadership, Buffett shaped a world around himself (Path 1) that enabled his repertoire of shots to be exactly what his self-created world needed.

So it is that every leader needs a repertoire. People become reliant on their trademark tricks, rhetorical flourishes and tactical ploys. Sensible leaders play to their strengths, but to do this can also be our Achilles' heel, via over-reliance on the known, lack of imagination and insufficient courage to step out of the comfort zone. Worst of all are leaders who build frameworks that only exist to give the leader a stage to play on.

As we noted in Chapter 2, and as any poker player or competitive sports player will tell you, it is risky to become predictable. Once people can read and anticipate the leader's moves, she can be outmaneuvered. There are times when the most powerful strategy is to be unpredictable, as we saw earlier with newspaper magnate, Robert Maxwell.

PATH 4: INSIGHT

Relying on leadership instincts has been a recipe for success for many a heroic leader – Steve Jobs, Warren Buffett, Florence Nightingale, Nelson Mandela, Mother Teresa, even Joseph Stalin all followed their feelings to different kinds of pre-eminence. But then so did a bunch of failures: Bernie Madoff, Adolf Hitler, Robert Maxwell, Jimmy Cayne, Fred Goodwin, Dick Fuld. It is a sad fact – exemplified by the SPQ framework – that leaders following their instincts will succeed until they fail; which they will, inevitably, if they don't adapt.[6] It's just a matter of time, and how long depends on how much the world changes in ways that leave them stranded with the wrong instincts and interests. One of the smartest things Mandela did was to quit while he was ahead – having built the vision of the new South Africa, he handed over power to the technocrat Thabo Mbeki just when the country had moved from needing a compelling vision to needing sound finances.[7]

Thatcher, on the other hand, found she excelled as the strong leader with radical solutions to social and economic problems, but continued trying to transform her country long after it had grown tired of transformation. The Tony Blair case is an interesting one. As he describes in *A Journey*, he started as an ingénue leader, yet deployed his leadership instinctive skills to good effect. He was deeply conscious of his need to learn and raise his level of awareness, and the early part of the book documents the strategies he enacted to truly understand how the wheels of the political machine turn. What makes his memoir especially interesting as a leadership testament is that it records his growing confidence in his insight into the world – his ability to read situations.

"Situation sensing," as it has been called,[8] is not pure instinct, but instinct plus effort of will and carefully judged calculus. Blair became a controversial figure in his home country – admired for his leaderly bearing and oratory but criticized for his seeming stubborn adherence to his beliefs, as if they were held on the basis of faith before reason. Certainly, Blair was a man of deep religious conviction, which was a platform of security for his will and intent, but as you read his testament you come to see that his belief in the rightness of his actions was based upon his faith in his ability to use his reason to read his leadership situation. The book shows him to be relentlessly analytical about every situation he confronts, and to have a growing faith in the correctness of his analysis. This leads him to his interesting, but paradoxical, declaration that he was never fitter to lead than when he quit.

Let us return to the philosophical problem we have mentioned more than once – about perception and reality. Philosophers worry rather fruitlessly about whether the color red you see is the same as the one I see,[9] or whether all our experience is illusory – I am dreaming I am writing this book, you are dreaming you are reading it. The respectable compromise that most of us and a good few philosophers would accept is that (a) yes, there is a real world out there; (b) yes, we do perceive genuinely occurring phenomena in it; (c) there is much we do not see at all; (d) we are inherently limited in our capacity to see and understand the world because of biological limitations in our senses, organs, information processing and intelligence and (e) beliefs color and sometimes shape perceptions of reality.[10]

The sounds and sights of the world are digitalized and reconstructed by our brains. There are lots of simple visual illusions which prove that we are not designed to see what is there, but *what we need to see*. Evolution didn't bother to give us infra-red vision because we are diurnal creatures and do quite well with our visible range of light frequencies, and, moreover, we have seldom been threatened by space aliens who use such frequencies. Evolution gave us some neat tricks, though, including the constancy effect, whereby distant objects are magnified in our vision (the reason why long shots on TV from one end of a football field make the far end seem unnaturally small and distant).[11]

So, we live in a world of appearances and, as thinking creatures, also in a world of beliefs. It was from Hannibal's belief that the Romans

144

would never expect him to attack from the mountains that he concocted his audacious plan to descend from them riding elephants.
Hannibal is a supreme example of a leader who understood the Law
of the Situation. His string of victories against the Romans, Gauls and
other tribes owed greatly to his assiduous study of terrain before a
battle – one of the first great generals to make this a central theme in
his art of war.[12]

Reliance on beliefs is a fool's game. Leaders' beliefs can often fuse
quite dangerously with perceptions, as with Hitler, but his triumph
and folly was to convince so many others to share his deeply irrational
beliefs. Many social scientists lay great store by the fact that we live in
a world of social constructions.[13] Culture suffuses us, and co-evolved
with us.[14] The world we live in today is very different to the one our
forefathers inhabited. We have quite different sensibilities and sensi-
tivities. It is a common problem for old leaders to lose touch with the
latest currents in their culture. For sure it happened to John Akers,
Richard Nixon, Hosni Mubarak and Charles I of England (it cost him
his head), and it is a recurrent theme in family firms. Old leaders are
often venerated, but woe betide the leader who drifts into a position
that prevents her from being connected to the vital concerns of key
stakeholders – especially customers, employees and suppliers.

Henry Ford is a supreme example – the greatest pioneer of the
industrial age, inventing new technologies, ways of organizing and
how to connect a brand to legions of new consumers in a transforming
world.[15] But his dominance defeated him. He believed that the world
whose taste in automobiles he had created was a fixed landscape that
only he truly understood. As consumer tastes rapidly started to change
in the early decades of the 20th century, his son Edsel was in the
forefront of those urging Henry to diversify the product range. Henry
stuck rigidly to his view about what the American consumer wanted,
and ridiculed Edsel's innovative ideas. Such was his punitive onslaught
on his son that it effectively destroyed him – Edsel drank himself to
death. Henry's jealous ire was subsequently unleashed on his grandson, Henry Jr, for his temerity to seek influence in the company.
But Henry Jr was made of sterner stuff than Edsel and rose above
the humiliations heaped upon him, eventually leading a boardroom

revolt that led to the ignominious ejection of his venerable grandfather from the business he created.

So let's not fall into the myth of social constructivism – that is, any version of reality will work so long as everyone believes it is true, whatever the "it" is. One is reminded of the Hans Christian Andersen story of the *Emperor's New Clothes*. Unfortunately, management is full of naked kings parading before people too insecure and fearful of having their own stupidity unmasked by calling out "BUT HE'S GOT NO CLOTHES ON." But it is the limitation in what people know and what they are prepared to say that is the biggest barrier to the leader's insight.

Here, we run into one of the great and terrible wonders of human evolution – our love of each other, our desire to cooperate and the inexorable process by which we desire to reach agreement about . . . well, just about anything.[16] One of the earliest classic experiments in social psychology witnessed a parade of unsuspecting subjects perceiving an object of fixed length to be longer (or shorter) than it was in actuality, because a bunch of strangers in the group (paid stooges) said it was.[17]

So here's what happens to an incoming leader. She brings a small entourage perhaps; people she has worked with in the past, whom she trusts. A lot of this is based upon a common worldview they have built up over previous assignments. Maybe she comes alone. She will soon find herself surrounded by well-wishers. The cocktail party syndrome now goes into overdrive – people quickly figure out (a) whether she is going to share their worldview; (b) what her worldview is; and (c) how much adjustment will have to be made to close the gap between worldviews. If she comes from inside the company then the battle is effectively over. Everyone knows who her allies and rivals have been and what scores may have to be settled.

This is how the cultural pickling process works. It is in the nature of culture at any level that we take for granted the medium in which we swim. There is an Australian joke that goes:

Two young fish are swaggering along the Great Barrier Reef when a big old fish looms into view coming their way. As he passes them, he says, with his gruff, friendly Aussie accent: "Hello boys; how's the water?" They mumble politely in response and continue on their way. As the old-timer disappears behind them, one of the young fish turns to his companion and asks, "What's water?"

Like these fish, we fail to appreciate how much we take for granted the cultural pickle we swim around in.

So how do leaders gain deep insights? Napoleon sleeping, wrapped in a blanket on the battlefield alongside his men; Gates inviting emails from the ranks of his global Microsoft empire;[18] company patriarch Raymond Ackerman continually touring the stores of his South African Pick n Pay grocery chain;[19] and numerous hands-on business leaders the world over walking the job in an unscheduled, intimate manner, chatting to their people – it's called Management By Wandering Around (MBWA), and it is one of the most essential and under-used leadership processes.

One company I worked with had its global operations Head Office in a central European location. A new CEO was brought in by an acquiring company to oversee the relocation of the HO to a Middle Eastern location. The CEO was a smoker, and, as was the European habit, smokers congregated around a side entrance to the building at various times of day, he among them. They never asked him and he never told them who he was. He just hung out and gossiped with them – acquiring the kind of intelligence that is rarely accessible to leaders. Needless to say, when the penny dropped and they figured out who the chatty stranger was, they were not too pleased. It is a sad commentary on the alienation between hierarchical levels in much of the business world that modern performance management systems and organizational design conspire to separate leaders from their people and the truths they have to tell.

So leaders need ways of getting under the wire; to penetrate the defenses and delusions that thickly sprout around all the interstices of power in organizations (see Figure 9.2). As we have noted, many of these come from the desire of people to have the good regard of their boss, to keep her confident in her beliefs and for them to be on her side – the winning side. The best bosses teach their people that

147

Figure 9.2:   SPQ strategic dynamic #4 – insight

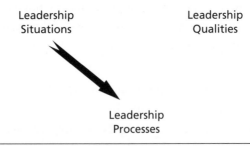

Leadership   Leadership
Situations   Qualities

Leadership
Processes

| Leader's Lesson |
| Are you getting enough of the right sort of data to enable you to analyze your situation deeply enough, and to be aware of the effects of your own strategies? |

they really do love the truth and are not afraid of it, even when it may reflect badly on them, but many doubletalk, like the remark of the legendary movie mogul, Sam Goldwyn, who reputedly said:

"I don't want any yes men around me. I want people to tell me the truth, even if costs them their jobs."

Or, to put it another way, "Tell your boss the truth and the truth will set you free."

Joking apart, it is the most difficult and important challenge of leadership to answer these questions:

- What kind of world am I in?

- What, in this world, should I be paying attention to?

- What do I need to discover that might be important and lurking under the surface or around the corner?

- Who are the people who are most critical to my fate as a leader? Are they the people I think they are, or who are closest and most familiar?

- How do I know for sure what they are thinking and feeling? How much can I trust my instincts about them?

- How is my world changing? What new sources of intelligence should I be paying attention to?

- How much of my world is an extension of my will, persuasive powers and taken-for-granted sub-culture?

- What are the risks of what lies beyond in a reality that I, as the leader, cannot shape?

Leaders need a mental model that encompasses the factors listed in the "S" box of the SPQ framework. Too often they have too narrow and impoverished a view of the world. Whatever is on their minds is what is in their face. Too many are at the mercy of the analysts, soothsayers, key staff, media, trusted advisors and experts, all of whom see the world through their own tinted spectacles and from their own highly partial perspectives. If the leader is passive, she will be swept on the tides of change and the opinions of others, as happens with weak and insecure leaders. The world of politics has a way of throwing novice leaders into the arena. They get elected because *other people believe in them*. That is pretty seductive and compelling. It is also pretty dangerous – it can become a delusionary bubble.

In the next chapter we come back to leadership qualities, to view them as instincts and motivations that lead us toward different leadership models, and the question of how they can change or be modified by experience.

IMPLICATIONS AND OBSERVATIONS FOR LEADERS AND ORGANIZATIONS

Leaders need to be competent, but having skills is useless if you don't follow the Leadership Formula and do the right thing at the right time – shot selection. But shot selection requires insight – or out-sight, perhaps – to read the world correctly. This is one of the most important challenges for leaders. Key points from the chapter:

- Perception controls behavior – seeing is doing – but you can just lead by managing the media.

(Continued)

149

- Leaders need good instincts for shot selection, good investigative practices and good advice. None of these can be taken for granted.

- Leaders are always at risk of sticking excessively to the shots they know and like.

- Leaders also get easily swept along in torrents of belief, by the faithful who surround them.

- Leaders need to practice MBWA – walk the job, sniff the air, look for insight in unexpected quarters to get out from under the fog of local opinion and belief.

- Read the hearts and minds of people – not just those close to you and easily accessible, but also your critics. As the saying goes, keep your friends close but your enemies closer.

— 10 —

BORN TO LEAD?
LEADERS LOST
AND FOUND

Leadership and learning are indispensable to each other.
John Fitzgerald Kennedy

LEE KUAN YEW – LEADER EXTRAORDINAIRE

Sir Stamford Raffles was a typical romantic figure of the Age of Enlightenment[1] – born on a boat to an indebted sea captain, he took a job with the British East India Company and found himself in the humid settlements of Malaysia. In the midst of colonial rivalry between the British and the Dutch, Raffles became an adept negotiator and was appointed Governor of Malacca, where he ended the slave trade and introduced a measure of self-government. After a spell back home in England, he returned to the region and, using a mixture of charm and power, negotiated the possession of the strategically important island of Singapore to the East India Company, which subsequently became a regional hub for the burgeoning trade across the Indian Ocean.

Raffles established a modern infrastructure and governance, including strong support for business.

Singapore thrived and became militarily strategic in WWII, when it fell briefly to Japanese invaders. Following liberation, the colony moved steadily towards autonomous self-government until it was absorbed into a fully self-governing state of Malaysia, from which it secured its independence in 1965. It is currently in the top rank of nations in per capita GDP – above the US and every country in Europe except Luxembourg – and this it owes to one of the most talented leaders of modern times, the remarkable Lee Kuan Yew.[2]

Ethnically Chinese, but born into a middle class Anglophone family, he revealed his intellectual gifts early – effortlessly top of the class – and studied law at Cambridge during the war years. Returning to Singapore in 1951, he immediately immersed himself in politics, helping to lead the push to independence in 1959. He became the first Prime Minister of the island for three decades, including the fateful separation from Malaysia in 1965 – overseeing the astonishing growth to the front rank of states of a small island, devoid of natural resources. Lee's approach to government could be described as tough love – for the island became, and remains today, governed by an iron discipline over many aspects of daily life. This is a reflection of his own belief that control of one's temper is essential in a good leader. On being asked about whether it was his destiny to be a great leader, Lee could only affirm that he assumed it was in his DNA. He always knew he had strong power over people, rejecting any kind of ideology to guide him but believing that to rule wisely you have to rule strongly. Lee's total self-confidence provided a mix of authoritarianism and inspiration that has served the economic and social interests of his people well, though at some cost to the rights we in the West take for granted.

THE EMERGENT LEADER[3]

It would be nice if the Leadership Formula ensured that, cometh the hour cometh the man; that there was some natural self-selective process which ensured that for every crisis the right person would step on to the stage and lead the way. This hope is a narrative embedded in our minds by millennia of heroic sagas, as we noted at the start of this book. Many leaders trade on this narrative, claiming to be the man or woman of the hour. Rationally, we know too much about history to cling to such naïve optimism, but our instincts persistently dupe us into hope for a new hero.[4] Indeed, the emergence of leaders is an instinctive process of selection and self-selection. Tough guys who would be passed over in times of peace come to the fore when war looms. Yet, the selection is not inevitable and unerring. The sad fact is that the visible qualities that fit someone to lead need to be accompanied by the right invisible qualities. Leaders' flaws, obsessions, foibles and limitations do not get eliminated by recognition of their talents.

The stage play *The Admirable Crichton*, by J. M. Barrie[5] (the author of *Peter Pan*), is a comedy of class manners, depicting an aristocratic family who are shipwrecked along with their butler, Crichton, on a tropical island. Their incompetence at the practicalities of survival is quickly laid bare, so the resourceful Crichton takes over – building a secure and well-ordered existence for them. This leadership is rewarded by a complete reversal of the previous class order. Crichton is now waited upon and respectfully called "the Guv." At length they are rescued, but by the time their saviors have set foot on the island, Crichton has resumed his former garb and role of their honest butler.

This little saga has two implications. One is that structures often inhibit the emergence of leadership talent, but at the same time it is a parable telling us that leaders can be found in the most unlikely of places. One might even go further and conclude that we are all born to lead – we just don't know it half the time. Indeed, the logic of my argument so far is that there is a leadership moment waiting for you somewhere in the universe. However, it is also the case that you may never find it, or it may never find you. And if you do, there is no guarantee you will want it or be any good at it. That is because effective leadership depends on having (a) the motivation to take on the responsibilities of the role and (b) personal qualities that match the demands of the situation.

Table 10.1: Fitness to lead

Motivation to lead	Leadership qualities	
	High fit with demands	Low fit with demands
High	Q1. Motivated leader	Q2. Unfit leader
Low	Q3. Reluctant leader	Q4. Motivated follower

Look at Table 10.1. When we look around us it is clear that these four types are not equally common. Happily, motive to lead and ability to lead are often correlated. That means there should be more good, driven bosses and contentedly willing followers (Q1 and Q4) than unfit or reluctant leaders (Q2 and Q3). A lot of those who want to lead do so because they sense in themselves leadership capabilities, including many accidental leaders who have been pitched into a leadership role and discover not only that they have a taste for it but also that they are quite good at it. Some of these are broad-bandwidth leaders – souls who thirst for the opportunity to take responsibility for people, tasks and decisions. They love to lead and they don't care too much where they do it, though they will strenuously avoid those situations where they could put their reputation as leaders at risk.

Lee Kuan Yew, and no doubt Raffles before him, and many prominent men and women in history, have found such a leadership vocation. Sure, the Leadership Formula blessed Yew – he arrived at just the right time – but one suspects he would have been a leader of men pretty well wherever he went. These are those assured leaders we find in Quadrant 1. But in this quadrant we also find the Admirable Crichton, who, unlike Yew, is what I called earlier a "narrow-bandwidth leader" – one of the legions of people out there who might be great leaders if the circumstances were right for them. There are many people who have little interest per se in leadership – they don't mind rewards, accolades, status and prestige, but they figure that they'd prefer to get these by being great at what they do rather than by leading.[6] They will be drawn into leadership only if it connects with their interests, values and expertise.

These are people who exist contentedly in Q4 as acquiescent followers until they are called forth. There are some who make the journey from Q4 to Q1 via Q3: the reluctant leader who discovers she loves leading. It might take a delegation of imploring colleagues to come knocking on her door, arguing her special fitness to lead them in their hour of need, which is exactly what happened to Duke Ellington. This scenario is played out in many professions. In academia it is hard to find volunteers to be head of department, and in many professional service firms many potential leaders are reluctant to trade the client work they love for dealing with the management problems they hate. These are the folks in Q3 in Table 10.1. And if you induce people with flattery and bribes, the risk is you get a Q2 group of unfit but willing leaders. This was a key element in the toxic mix that poisoned banking and many other high-reward industries – too many unmotivated and incompetent leaders.

So who is in Q4? It is a mix, but it contains a lot of people who are happy for someone else to take the strain of leading while they get on with their work. Some of these, as we have said, can be dragged happily into Q3; and others dangerously lured into Q2. But Quadrant 4 also contains what I have called "zero-bandwidth leaders" – people who have no interest whatsoever in leading, no talent for it and no intention of succumbing to any inducements. Why not? Because they have examined themselves and come to the completely reasonable conclusion that leading would be deeply unrewarding for them. They understand all too well that leading means taking responsibility for people who will jump all over you in a frenzy of criticism if you screw up; and who expect you, without thanks, to run defense for them, enabling them, undisturbed, to attend to their clients/design new products/solve technical problems/do creative work etc. They may take satirical business cartoonist Scott Adams's view that "leadership is Nature's way of removing morons from the productive flow."

A more charitable view says that people who love the dirty work of leadership should be rewarded; the people who hate it should be protected; and the rest sign up to lead when they are needed. Gore-Tex – the specialist fabric producer – has institutionalized this model. In its adventurous culture, everyone in the company is designated an

Associate; you only get to be called a leader for as long as you have voluntary followers.[7]

So this innocent little matrix suggests we face a big problem in organizations today. There is a bunch of people who should be leaders but don't want to be, and a bunch who are leaders but really are unfit for it. The size of these groups is a worry. If the reluctant leader group is too big, it is because leadership roles have become too uncongenial and dangerous. If the unfit leader group is too big, it is because we have allowed the rewards and inducements of leadership to become disproportionate.

PATH 5: INSTINCT/SELF-KNOWLEDGE

The Delphic injunction "know thyself" contains two challenges for modern leaders. The first is that they should beware of overreaching themselves with egoism – it suggests that knowing yourself is more than a matter of simply believing in your own stories, having faith in your own intelligence and abilities and holding a positive appraisal of your own personality. Wisdom is understanding how it all works together – the ability to decode the way we shade the truth to get what we want, and how we are liable to tolerate and explain away our weaknesses (see Figure 10.1). The second meaning is that one needs to understand the deeper unconscious motives that pull the strings of

Figure 10.1: SPQ strategic dynamic #5 – instinct

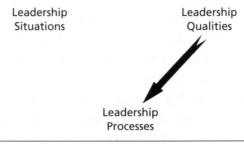

Leadership
Situations

Leadership
Qualities

Leadership
Processes

Leader's Lesson
Are you risking derailment through giving free rein to your instincts? How aware are you of weaknesses that might be leadership risk factors for you?

our surface desires. These are far from simple challenges – perhaps the most difficult we face. It is commonplace in the modern world to assume that if we get our heart's desire we will achieve happiness. This propels us into the jaws of a consumption trap:[8] the prospect of empty disappointment that all the unwrapped toys have solved none of the problems of the human heart.

There are many deeply unhappy people living highly successful lives. They got all the money, power and adulation they could possibly desire, but the inner itch remains unscratched; the heartache persists; the void remains unfilled. Among these are the unfit leaders who have kidded themselves that this is what they want, under the lure of extravagant rewards, loud encouragement and the cowardice of others. Then, when confronted by the realities of the role, they run away from all the most uncongenial yet important aspects of it, burying them-selves in piles of minutiae; playing control games whilst avoiding the meat and drink of leadership – which is how to set direction, align resources and structures and motivate people.[9] "Fit" leaders actually enjoy taking responsibility for the mass of uncertainty that people bring into every encounter. They understand that it is more valuable to spend time helping the difficult people than schmoozing with the easy ones. They take joy in solving people problems. They get turned on by the knowledge that they have unlocked the potential of their people.

At its simplest, the benefit of self-knowledge is the same as a marks-man understanding the bias in his gun – he can correct his aim to hit the target. Even if a leader cannot alter her genetically anchored traits, she can alter her behavior. Steve Jobs was forever wrestling back and forth with his impulses and reactions. Many leaders just surrender to their instincts.

This is the weakness of authenticity – a much-lauded concept in the leadership literature. It is one thing to face up to your weaknesses and fearlessly accept and compensate for them, but there is a thin line that separates this honorable stance from the pure self-indulgence of the leader who gives free rein to all his basest impulses in the name of "to thine own self be true." It is an equal and opposite failing to turn a deaf ear to the call of one's identity.

POOR JACQUES

Jacques's story is a dramatic and sad example. I was working with the top managers of a French multinational company and, although they get one-to-one coaching, I try to get a little time with each of them, to go through some of the data we have put together about who they are and how they perform. I looked at the names crossed off my list to see whom I had yet to speak to, and spotted Jacques's name at the same instant as I saw him by the coffee machine in the lounge. "Hi," I said, "would you like to have a few minutes to go through your data?" He was a compact, neat man, very nicely coiffured and unusually smartly dressed for such a program, where most of the guys tend to wear polo shirts and jeans. He darted me a look and said, very politely, "Yes, of course. Please just give me a few minutes." He disappeared and did not return to the lounge.

I approached him again at another break. This time the evasion was more obvious, but in the interim I'd had more time to look closely at his data and I could see why he might be avoiding me. His was not a straightforward profile – in fact, it looked to be quite a troubled one. Here was a man, designated CEO of a major East European operation, whose profile was that of an extremely anxious, vulnerable and introverted person, with no apparent desire to have leadership responsibility. My chats with participants are voluntary, but I sensed this one should not slip away. "Let's sit down now, if only for a few minutes," I said, indicating the adjacent empty dining room.

He followed me in and we sat down. I started to ask him what his reactions to the profile were. He looked up at me. "This tells me I am not a leader," he said. I reminded him that the data are not infallible, and they do no more than sum up the person's own responses to some focused questions and compare them with norms. What mattered, I said, was his reality. "Why do you say you are not a leader? What do you see? There are many ways of being a leader." He looked up at me again. This time, astonished, I could see tears welling up in his eyes. "Look at me," he said, "I am in this foreign country. I know hardly anyone. I am in charge of several hundred people. All the time I have to be the boss, and it is an act. I hate it." Now he was sobbing, "I feel I am living a false existence."

"Who knows that you feel like this?" I asked. "Do you talk about this to anyone at all? Does your wife know how you feel?" He shook his head, still sobbing. My concern increased. It seems I had pressed a button that connected with a huge discontinuity lying just beneath the surface of this poor man's mind; one that he had allowed to become overgrown with a dense tangle of obligations. Indeed, cultivation of this concealment had become his secret vocation. I could see what he was saying was true. No amount of work by me or my coaches seemed likely to repackage this man's instincts into a positive orientation to his leadership role.

I tried a different tack. "What do you really enjoy in your life?" I asked. This proved to be quite easy for him, and his mood slowly started to brighten. Before long he had elaborated a picture of his passions for the arts, discovery, teamwork with like-minded people and reflective occupations. "Take possession of your life," I urged him. "You only have one life. It is wonderful and rich and you deserve to enjoy it." I continued, "What opportunities are there for you back in Paris that could allow you to do what you really like?" As we talked, it became clear he was on a cusp and this interlude of free reflection had become a catalyst for him to seek and find a new resolution of the Leadership Formula. It transpired he could find a position at the company's Paris HQ in a strategic advisory team with no line responsibility and a lot of autonomy. Previously, such a move would have seemed like an admission of defeat, but with the help of the coaches he began to plot a new career direction toward a more aligned existence.

The story is worrying, for who knows how many people are enduring their working lives unhappily, haunted by the feeling that there is something wrong with them because they don't feel the way they should? A role has been handed to them as a fait accompli, or sold to them, in which process they have been willing conspirators in their own oppression. It's called "living a lie." We do not wish to admit to ourselves that we have made bad choices, and that reality won't conform to what we hoped for. Too often, we accept a position because someone else wants us to. "You're just the person we need," they say. "It'll be great for you." The flattery; the elevation; to be really wanted – it's irresistible. But there is always time to stop and think, and to search one's heart. This is the real meaning of authenticity.

PATH 6: SELF-CONTROL AND SELF-DEVELOPMENT

Admiral James Stockdale deserves the accolade of one of the bravest men ever to have lived. At the height of the Vietnam War, for seven years he was held captive in the notorious Hoa Lo – Hell's hole – also known as "the Hanoi Hilton."[10] For four years of his residency of this unspeakable establishment he was in solitary confinement, and throughout his incarceration he was afflicted with the most unimaginable assaults on his being: torture, beatings and interrogations. Such was his determination to concede nothing to his captors that he deliberately disfigured himself to avoid being paraded as a propaganda tool. Jim Collins, in his wise book, *Good to Great*,[11] names a paradox after Stockdale that states (a) have faith in your eventual deliverance, but (b) confront the most brutal truths of your reality. Collins is impressed by the Admiral's answer to his question about who did *not* survive this ordeal, which was that the first to crack were the optimists; those who believed they would be out by Christmas.

Yet it wasn't pessimism that enabled Stockdale to survive or even hope, but a more calculated trick of the mind, which he credited to the Greek Stoic philosopher Epictetus. The Stoics believed we are victims of capricious fate, so should accept what happens to us dispassionately and take responsibility for our own actions and responses.[12] It is a philosophy of detachment and supreme self-control. Stockdale turned this into something like a yogic detachment of mind from experience.

Knowing one's weaknesses is one thing – controlling them is something else entirely. This most difficult of all the paths is required at times to complete the loop of SPQ alignment – doing the right thing.

Figure 10.2: SPQ strategic dynamic #6 – self-development

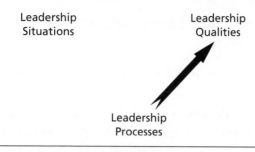

Leadership
Situations

Leadership
Qualities

Leadership
Processes

| Leader's Lesson |
| Are you learning new tactics and practicing new behaviors that will enhance your leadership capability and versatility? |

It is not enough to read the world or read oneself with insight – one then has to act and in ways that do not come easily and naturally (see Figure 10.2). True, some people are more versatile than others, but we all cling to comfortable habits that we have practiced for years. The path of instinct from Q to P is just that. We are like Rogers and Hart's *The Lady is a Tramp* who "never bothers with people she hates." Leaders cannot afford to take this stance.

As we have noted, you can be too versatile, especially if the leader lacks strong drivers and has no clear and consistent compass. It matters less for non-leaders who can happily live the life of the butterfly or hobo – moving through the avenues of life more as a spectator than an actor. This won't do for a leader, yet, as we have also seen, too much rigidity comes from too strong a compass. So, here's the dilemma for a leader. If she needs to change the world or to adapt herself to the world in some way by delivering actions from outside her repertoire and she has a strong compass that fits the world as it is, what is she to do?

Remember the four major options mentioned earlier as evolutionary options for species facing environmental change?

1. Persist with what used to work, and fail (become extinct).

2. Quit and find a new situation that resembles the one where you have been successful (habitat tracking).

3. Evolve – develop new behaviors, strategies and tactics.

4. Construct a niche – build a world around you that works for you and your pals.

As we noted earlier, the last two of these options are challenging, but do happen.

Let us be clear. Personal change IS possible. If you lose the use of your right hand, you will learn to use the left. It only seems costly and painful, like all radical new learning, until you become proficient. People who lose their jobs often develop new skills and interests. Leaders can become good at things they find uncongenial. It's just hard, disciplined work, and, as we also have noted, people with power have the luxury of being able to avoid such disciplines.

But there is a fifth path: get someone else to do the dirty or difficult work. This is much easier, but not without risks. As we shall see in the next chapter, this is actually one of the effective leader's most accessible strategies – to surround oneself with complementary talents to do what is needed.

IMPLICATIONS AND OBSERVATIONS FOR LEADERS AND ORGANIZATIONS

One of the most commonly asked questions in management is, "are leaders born or made?" As I hope is clear by now, the answer is yes! They are both born and made. It's in your DNA who you are, but that still leaves you with a lot of choice, and whether you are fit to lead is context dependent. That being said, leadership is a discipline, and even if you have the motivation, you'd better learn the right moves. Some key points:

- Some of the best leaders "emerge" but this process needs help and support from the organization in the form of role models and assignments.

- Organizations also need to watch out for unfit leaders who have been lured by the prize of status and reward.

- Also watch out for the reluctant leader, induced by obligation. They may turn out just fine, but support is needed.

- Don't make it a sin not to want to be a leader. We need people to do lots of other really valuable things without the burden of responsibilities they neither want nor like.

- Don't give automatic trust to people eager to lead. There's more to fitness than motivation.

- Help narrow-bandwidth leaders find their place in the sun, but beware of overextension. They are not leaders for all seasons.

- There's a narrow boundary between "authenticity" and "self-indulgence." Leaders need help to be themselves and simultaneously to control themselves.

- You can change your "Q" factors, but it's a hard road and a slow one, though often very necessary.

— 11 —

WHO'S YOUR BUDDY? CRITICAL LEADER RELATIONSHIPS

The best way to find out if you can trust somebody is to trust them.

Ernest Hemingway

LOVE, ACTUALLY?

Duke Ellington and Billy Strayhorn were pretty special together; so were Michael Eisner and Frank Wells;[1] Akio Morita and Masaru Ibuka; Bill Gates and Steve Ballmer; and Steve Jobs and John Scully. All of these were powerful relationships that meant a lot to their protagonists. Each was unique and delivered special value – the elusive quality of "synergy," when the whole is greater than the sum of the parts – and their organizations reaped the considerable benefits. Duke Ellington produced a continuous stream of exhilaratingly original music and kept his fine orchestra together. Eisner and Wells presided over a flowering of profitable creativity and growth in the movies over more than a decade. Morita and Ibuka transformed consumer electronics;[2] Gates and Ballmer, through their blend of technical insight and focused energy, brought personal computing within the reach of a mass market, and, in the process, built a world-beating corporation of enormous power.[3]

The odd couple out of this array is, as ever, the one containing Steve Jobs, whose almost embarrassing infatuation with John Scully produced no more than a momentary flare in Jobs's traverse across the skies, for the relationship, if you accept the rather convincing account of his biographer, was deeply delusional. At the height of their mutual infatuation, each projected on to the other the qualities they sought to perfect themselves. Jobs, for sure, needed people he could look up to, as well as others he could direct at will.

Despite his charisma, many friends and intimates, he was the ultimate loner – caring little for the opinions of others and always bending the world to his unquenchable will. Yet, there were people who stood up to his emotional tantrums and caprice and gave him solid feedback; people who stood up for their ideas against his mercurial assaults. It is a by-product of the highest reaches of charisma that acolytes will cluster distractingly around you,[4] and it was fortunate for history that Jobs ferociously rebarbative style winnowed them to a few key players who could give him what he really needed. Lesser talents use people more consistently.

Well, let me qualify that. For some leaders their partnerships with "significant others" is an indelible thread running through their leadership stories. Obama has his Michelle;[5] Tony Blair his Cherie; and many business leaders their long-suffering spouses to fulfill the role of key confidant(e). They can be a source of strength, but it can severely test the relationship.

RICH PICKINGS

We can call these Critical Leader Relationships – CLRs – and they exert an often hidden and generally overlooked influence on organizations. They have profound significance in their potential impact on leader effectiveness. At their deepest they have a unique ability to enter the territory of the Self – the control room of leadership. We shall be diving into this territory to look at the battles that have to be fought in the leader's mind in the next two chapters, but, anticipating some of the key themes, CLRs can operate on three key areas.

First, they help to supply muscle and nuance to the exercise of willpower – the power behind the throne sometimes, as in Shakespeare's dark drama where Lady Macbeth steadies her husband's nerve and resolve to murder his way to the throne.

Second, they supply an enriched portrait of the world. This is especially important in highly complex environments where two pairs of eyes that are capable of sharing data can lead to superior intelligence and strategy.

Third, they tell you the truth in ways you can accept. This is the court jester syndrome – the partner who is able to sneak under your defenses and, by gentle mockery or persuasion, help you review your goals and motives. The same person may also be the one to raise your awareness of your blindspots and prick your delusions about your character.

It is said that the victorious Roman tribunes would enter the city with a slave at their ear saying "momento mori" – remember you are only a mortal man. So aware were they of the benefits of shared responsibility, as well of the political risks that could come from allowing too much power to accrete to a single individual, that they instituted a rule of dual Consulship, and duplication in other key roles,[6] that endured for 400 years until the Roman Empire morphed into the imperial singularity that Julius Caesar cultivated, a hubris that put the skids under Rome's status as a superpower.

More locally in time and space, Goldman Sachs,[7] from close to the time of its founding, established co-headship to drive its lauded one-firm culture. The tandems of John Weinberg and John Whitehead, Stephen Friedman and Robert Rubin grew the firm through its years of pre-eminence. This model was indispensable to the highly integrated team culture and dedicated commitment to customers. We shall not digress on GS's post-IPO decline into a mire of double-dealing and shoddy customer care, except to note that its former excellence owed a good deal to its origins as a family firm – Goldman and his son-in-law Sachs.

In the world of family firms there is a mixed history of partnership.[8] Many have been wrecked by the narcissism, arbitrary decision-making and leadership hubris of founders and successors, acting without restraint from anyone. Yet, in family firms, and many of the best in their sectors, competitive advantage is secured through their most inimitable asset – their family culture, at the center of which sits a nexus of powerful relationships. These have a special character. On the one hand is diversity. Sometimes this is quite centrifugal – the family that struggles to see eye to eye about anything. On the other hand is the centripetal force of love and commitment. This powerful combination of binding and differentiating forces is what makes family firms so special, enduring, difficult and inimitable, achieving competitive advantage through their paradoxical cultures.[9] Some of the mightiest companies in the world are driven by such dynamics: Samsung in Korea; Wal-Mart in the USA; Fiat in Italy; Mittal in India; Swatch in Switzerland; and legions of firms throughout Asia and Latin America.[10] Friends do it too – look at Hewlett and Packard; Jobs and Wozniak at Apple; Gates and Allen at Microsoft; Brin and Page at Google.

Such combinations stretch response capability. As the SPQ model shows, leadership is seriously demanding, yet the load can be shared. More than one person can drive leadership processes. This is true, but genuine double acts, or even more rarely treble acts, remain a rarity.[11] Most firms are headed by a singularity, supported by teams of various hues. And, as we go through the ranks of the hierarchy, many middle-ranking managers are leading in quite a lonely way – the burden of adaptation falls on them alone. This brings us back to our starting question – who helps the leader? Who's there to tell her the truth; support her in her loneliness; give her fresh and different eyes and ears? This seems to be an important empirical question about leadership that hardly anyone has talked about. Just how lonely are leaders at all levels of organizations? Do they really have confidant(e)s to whom they can bare their souls? How many have casual supporters and advisors who fail to level with them?

Many leaders will point to their top team and claim this is the source of their leadership support and advice.[12] Yes, a talented top team is a source of competitive advantage, but what is the leader's relationship to the team? An executive team is partly a toolkit and partly a feature of the leadership landscape. Support for the deepest needs of the leader is likely to come from specific relationships rather than from the shifting alliances of the top team.

WHAT AND WHY?

Over the past decade I have looked into the question of what are the "critical relationships" that leaders have – the CLRs as we have termed them. We define them as in Figure 11.1, and they involve people who help the leaders with their most difficult decisions.

The questions are these:

• Who has them?

• Who does not?

• What are the benefits to be gained from a CLR?

• Who believes they have CLRs but actually makes inadequate use of them?

• What sort of person creates a good CLR, and how can you best use them to get these benefits?

Quite apart from the data I have gathered on this topic, just asking these questions of executives really does stop them in their tracks.

Figure 11.1: Sharing the burden: critical leader relationships

Definition
"A working relationship that provides help and support on a regular basis for the most important decisions a leader has to make."

Forms:
    Upward – e.g. Chairman
    Downward – e.g. MD, CFO, COO
    Lateral – e.g. co-leader
    External – e.g. spouse, personal coach, advisor

Why? Because most have only given the issue passing thought. CLRs are very much taken for granted by leaders, yet, once they start to think about them analytically, they are quick to recognize unused potential and power to help them meet their leadership challenges. Most leaders have sporadic or fleeting intimacy with colleagues, and a sizeable minority have no one at all they could call a confidant(e). Indeed, the "trusted advisors" offered by audit and consulting firms may be the closest they get.[13] There's nothing wrong with these apart from their ulterior transactional motive. This can muddy the water.

Let's revisit the benefits, and look at some examples from history and what the research shows. Here's the list:

1. **Help:** concrete assistance with the multiple tasks of leadership; an extra pair of hands.[14] Gates and Ballmer at Microsoft were a winning team on the strength of their division of labor in running one of the most complex corporations ever to exist – Gates the thought leader, technical chief, boffin and front man; Ballmer the cheerleader, boss, organizer and point man for corporate strategy.

2. **Insight:** the gift of extra eyes and ears; seeing more of the leader's known world, yielding a different take on it or giving a view from a different angle. Warren Buffett used his partner Charlie Munger in this way; an extra brain to find new avenues for their innovative practice.[15]

3. **Challenge:** the court jester function; the person who is bold enough to question the leader's taken-for-granted view of themselves, their goals and their worldview. Michael Eisner's COO Frank Wells was the trusted ally who could stand up to Eisner's towering ego and pull it back to areas of greater realism and control.[16]

4. **Feedback:** the person who can tell the leader the truth (another jester!); about their impacts, intended and unintended, on the world and its people. Family partners are often quick – sometimes too quick – to do this.

5. **Ideas:** new perspectives and tools to help the leader think about the what, how and why of actions, and extend them in new, productive directions. Steve Jobs, as we have observed, was a mercurial and inconstant partner, but he was always on the hunt for fresh ideas that he could reframe, reintegrate and fly with. A major element in his success was his ability to attract and feed off creative intellects.

6. **Support:** comfort during stress, buffering under pressure, reassurance in the face of difficulty and belief in the face of challenge.[17] This is what every human in a difficult place could ask of their most trusted ally. Margaret Thatcher freely admitted that the loyal, steadying and tolerant presence of her husband Denis was a constant bulwark against an often very unfriendly and untrustworthy world.[18]

Look again at this list. What a fantastic menu of outcomes! What leader would not want this bag of goodies? Curiously, there do exist individuals (mainly men) who are so autonomous, self-driven, aloof and insulated that they get none of the above. How can someone lead from such a position? The pattern of many so-called charismatic leaders is to reach over the heads of subordinates to assume a god-like elevation to adoring followers.[19] It is scarcely sustainable because it is disconnected and therefore insusceptible to external correction. The big bad beasts of history – Stalin, Hitler, Pol Pot – may have come close, but actually they so selectively secured inputs from partners, in climates devoid of trust and intimacy, that the most they could make of their CLRs was for them to be extensions of their will. This contains little of any kind of corrective that could aid them.

HOW?

So what does a leader have to do to get these benefits? My investigations reveal that most leaders have confidant(e)s, but their conversations are sporadic, unplanned and vary in focus and depth. They deliver benefits irregularly.

This is hardly surprising. Most of us seek out people when we've got a problem, going to who's at hand rather than who would best deliver what you need. Spouses, partners and close relatives are favorite targets – on account of their proximity and trust – but what do you get from them? Some deeply intimate couples have far-reaching conversations about every aspect of their lives and experiences – tightly bound together in a state of extreme mutual dependency – but even these have limits. For most leaders their partner is a selective support.[20] Yet, if you have no one at work or friends outside who can you go to for a shoulder to cry on, or for fresh ideas? In looking for such support there is a lot of misfiring.

Jill tells John about a problem with a colleague at work. John responds readily, "I'll tell you what I think is happening and what you should do about it." This will not do if what Jill really wants is a bit of listening, understanding and empathy. John's attempts to analyze and prescribe may breach a credibility gap – insufficient insight into Jill's context – and speak more about the world in John's head than in Jill's life. Trained coaches and counselors get round these problems by simple strategies that anyone can master. At the heart of them is what psychologists call "mindfulness"[21] – to be fully present, engaged and focused on what the other is feeling and thinking; the unspoken and implied as much as the stated.

Here's another common hazard. Bob tells Bella about a difficult boss he has. He is getting into full flight, expressing how oppressed and unfairly treated he is when Bella chimes in, "Yeah, I had a boss like that . . ." and then proceeds to elaborate at some length the story of her own hierarchical oppression. This may actually be pretty harmless and help Bob to put the problem into proportion, but it hardly helps at a more practical level of him figuring out what to do.

Inadequate, insensitive, unhelpful, poorly informed and ill-judged responses are very common. So much so that many people are pretty limited in what they share and with whom they share. Leaders, especially, may fear exposure. Giving a confidence and not getting any in return creates dissonance; the leader will feel put at risk and vulnerable.[22] Worse, kiss and tell is a threat.

WHO?

We are all a little wary of whom we bare our souls to, and in the minds of many executives in low-trust environments sits the idea (consistent with what evolutionary biologists note in other social mammals) that the higher you ascend the ladder of success, the more you have to watch your back and be circumspect in what you reveal.

One in ten CEOs in my sample confessed that they lacked any kind of CLR. A larger number avoid confiding with anyone inside their organization – they have no boss to turn to, and all other relationships lack sufficient trust.

The only place to go is *Out*. Interestingly, this turns out to be where many of the most productive CLR partners reside: such people as former bosses, buddies and trusted advisors. Outsiders may lack company insights and contextual knowledge, but they are often the best fitted to tell hard truths, tolerate and accept strong emotions and to confront the leader with a contrarian view.

Yet, within the organization, potentially three-way relationships are to be found: up, down and lateral.

Up: Many a CEO has a close bond with the Chairman of the board. Interestingly, in family firms, many a highly successful partnership is to be found between a non-family CEO and a family non-executive Chairman, or the reverse arrangement of family Chair and non-family chief executive.[23] Having a CLR with your boss may not always be a brilliant idea, especially if the give and take are grossly unequal – you give and the boss takes. To avoid these difficulties, mentoring has been adopted to support rising executives in many firms over the past few decades. These quasi uncle/auntie, nephew/niece or grandparent models sometimes work fine; sometimes not. This will always be the case with "arranged" relationships. Spontaneous mutual selection might be the ideal but is haphazard and constrained in many organizations.

Down: The power dynamic is perhaps easier down than up. After all, the leader has a choice among the many smiling faces looking up at her. Powerful leaders, as we have seen, may be accompanied by a traveling entourage, but only one or two of these people are likely to fit the bill. Top finance guys usually like to have the backup of an ops person; marketers want the finance director. It depends on your environment – for a media mogul it might be a legal person (overdependence on this function was a fatal flaw in Rupert Murdoch's NewsCorp in 2011/12 when it was engulfed in a phone-hacking scandal[24]). The role of personal assistant can be critical. Indeed, it has been suggested that it takes a particular skill profile to be a great #2 in business.[25] Possibly. Managing the powerful is an art, but we need to remember the SPQ logic that compels us to perceive that a critical part of the #2's situation is the #1. The need cannot be judged independently of the boss or the context they share. Yet, when the #1 falls under a bus, does it make sense for the #2 to step into her shoes? In politics this has happened from time to time, with mixed results: Johnson after Kennedy was a success;[26] Brown after Blair an abject failure.[27] In business it often works, as we saw with the J-P Mustier example from Société Générale, pitched into the top job after the sudden death of his predecessor. This variability in outcomes is largely because #2s are chosen not because of their #2-like qualities but because they are part of a succession plan and seen as leaders in waiting. Whether it works or not depends on the factors we have discussed in previous chapters.

Lateral: These have flourished in the flat world of high-tech and information industries, where hierarchy gets in the way; but the democratic instincts of someone like Eric Schmidt at Google have proved harder to sustain when businesses become more corporate. In the traditional bureaucracies it is in the middle ranks where one would hope to find CLRs with peers flourishing. Alas, here they are among the least common. The barrier, as middle managers will tell you, is trust and the politics of competition.[28] It is an extraordinary and sad testament to the pervasiveness of the dominance hierarchy (which we shall examine in Chapter 15) that cohorts are induced to see themselves as in competition, even when this is manifestly against the best interests of the business.

Yet, we all have friends, don't we, whom we regard as equals? These are relationships uncontaminated by formal distinctions of power or status, though within them there are always invisible boundaries, risks, presumptions and games of mutual regard that can suddenly be revealed as fracture points. The ideal CLR partner might be the pal with whom you regularly play squash or have lunch, and in the sociable intervals outside ball-hitting or eating you could actually talk about stuff that really matters to you both. The question here is with whom does this work best, and what do you have to do to make it deliver what you need?

THE PERFECT CLR IS WITH . . .

. . . someone who is similar enough to you for you to be able to generate trust and understanding; and different enough to bring something fresh to your thoughts, feelings and actions.

Sounds like the recipe for a happy marriage.[29] Actually, we are dealing with something pretty universal in human relationships. Marriage, after all, is just one way of learning about how humans can give and be given value by each other.

The prior question to answer is: what does the leader need? Which of our list of benefits is most critical for any particular leader? For the person under enormous stress and danger (e.g. military commanders), emotional *support* and material *help* are likely to be priorities. For the person leading operations of great complexity (e.g. technical leaders), *help*, *ideas* and *insight* will matter most. For the person dealing with human complexities, alliances and cultural divisions (e.g. political leaders), *feedback* and *insight* will be at a premium. And for the person leading innovation and change (e.g. leaders in media, consultancy and the arts), *challenge* will be a prime need.

What people need is highly individualized. Some people need more emotional affirmation than others. Others provide their own challenge and don't want more of this from their friends. Steve Jobs was famously needy and demanding in equal measure. Personal feedback was hardly what he craved, but he valued most of the other benefits we have identified, requiring people to fight through the thickets of his convoluted psyche to get through to him.

Research indicates that the six benefits come unevenly from people in different positions. The best upward CLR partners deliver plenty of challenge, insight and ideas, but are often weaker on feedback, support and help. Downward CLR partners are stronger on feedback, help and ideas, if handled right. Peers should be strong on the contrasting benefits of challenge and support, but it is the outsiders who are most comprehensive in what they offer. Despite lacking detailed knowledge of the business they seem to be able to deliver across the full range and at great intensity.

Perhaps it is as a result of freedom from organizational constraints, and the greater degree to which the leader can schedule both the timing and content of interactions, without the contaminating distractions from all the other things we talk to colleagues about. But, ultimately, what matters most is how you behave when you and your CLR partner are together.

Finding a CLR partner is inevitably haphazard, though it is worth searching through the deck of one's current relationships to see which might offer some possible deepening of connection. The full-blown CLR model we have considered here requires, as noted, the right amount of similarity and the right amount of difference – both needed for complementarity to be exploited.

As a general rule, the more sensitive and deep you want to go, the more trust you will need between you. Trust rests on a platform of understanding and surety, such as only comes from people who are not a million miles from your world of experience. There is little point in a middle-aged man and a teenage girl trying to forge a deep connection, even if there may be much they could learn from each other.

Yet, "reverse mentoring" – young entrants mentoring senior bosses – was used by Jack Welch at GE to bring the leaders up to the mark on new technology; it has also been used in PwC, the audit and advisory firm.[30] But even crossing a gender divide may present a challenge for some people. Men have heart-to-hearts with their male pals in a way they may be unable to with their wives, and, understandably, many women seek out other women in male-dominated corporate environments for advice or succor.

Yet, the more "extension" you want – by that I mean, challenge, surprise and novel insights; the things that turn complementarity into synergy – the more you need people whose ways of thinking, feeling and acting are quite different to your own. These are born of personality, experience and instinct. Only you can know what will work for the goals that you aspire to.

- Emotional support, for example, requires a CLR partner with whom you have empathic connections.

- Challenge requires people who are robust enough emotionally and intellectually to stand up to you.

- Insight requires someone whose experience and position gives them a different vantage point.

- Feedback requires someone with observational gifts who has been in a position to witness your intended and unintended impacts.

- Ideas require people with the requisite intellectual attributes, plus the ability to communicate in ways that you will be receptive to.

- Help comes from people with complementary assets and skills, plus the personal chemistry for you to be able to accept their cooperation.

These are just starting conditions. Any conversation can wander off into mists of irrelevance. You need the right connection for the right conversation.

THE RIGHT CONVERSATION

As we saw earlier, it is easy to screw up intimate conversations. People fail to hear what their partner is asking for; they don't grasp the message beneath the words; they get distracted by their own agendas.

When I talk to executives about setting rules for the conduct of CLRs – such elements as norms of practice, behavioral disciplines and shared understandings – they see the point, but many rebel against the idea of any kind of formality. The thought of scheduling and formalizing what should be spontaneous, organic and informal seems forced, contradictory or, worse, a bureaucratic offence against Nature. You can understand the feeling, but much the same objection could be raised about plain good manners. Whether we like it or not, all our social interactions are regulated by implicit conventions and unspoken rules. Moreover, we can all think of times when a bit more regulation would have improved a conversation we've had. Let's agree that writing down rules of conduct and sticking them on the wall is not what this is about (though some families do just that, and find it helpful). Rather, it is a set of implicit understandings and practices.

Where to start? Perhaps it is in the mechanics of meeting – where and when and how often should you connect? To function effectively, CLRs need some kind of schedule. One-shot encounters can be powerful, but here we are talking about making benefits part of the fabric of one's life as a leader. For specific challenges – role transitions especially – a short series of conversations might suffice, but for the leader's more continuous development, something more regular and long term will be needed.

So, rule #1 is: Agree to meet again – put something in the diary and protect it.

Do you know why you are meeting? If you have been having helpful, informal conversations, take the initiative: "I find talking to you really helpful. I get fresh perspectives from our conversations. Maybe you do too. Perhaps we could do this again, and give ourselves a decent slug of time to really talk and listen to each other?"

So, rule #2 is: Make the intention and goal explicit.

It is best if the benefits are shared and it is not all one-way traffic –
unless it is a professional coaching or counseling relationship. With
anyone else, the encounter will get to deeper levels and be mutually
reinforcing if both parties get benefits. That means some implicit or
even explicit agreement about reciprocation and time-sharing.

Rule #3 is, therefore: Take it in turns to talk and listen; either within
a single session or over time.

What does this mean – talking and listening? There are many ways
to do this – some more powerful, penetrating and meaningful than
others. Many good, practical books have been written on this, all
containing much the same advice and techniques. These amount to
what we can call "co-coaching."[31] The key elements are these. First
is to recognize which role you are in at any given time: coach or
"coachee." If you are the coachee, be prepared to talk, share, reveal and
respond. If you are the coach, you need to practice the art of questioning and what in coaching jargon is called "active listening," which
means mindfulness – staying in the moment – absorbing all the
nuances and then checking understanding by replaying to the coachee:
"So what you are saying is . . ."[32]

Many coaches use what is called the GROW technique:[33]

- **Goals:** what is the person trying to achieve, and how are they
  thinking of the scale, scope and specificity of the challenge?
  Are they thinking of it in ways that are too narrow and limited,
  or that make it impossibly hard to deal with?

- **Reality:** what is happening inside and around this challenge,
  in terms of history, actors, context, processes and constraints?
  What are the key players thinking and doing?

- **Options:** what different courses of action does the person have
  in mind? Could this set be expanded or focused better? Can
  you help the person to think out of the box a little?

- **Willingness:** what psychological and material resources are
  required to move forward on this issue? How ready and
  committed is the coachee to do what it takes and follow
  through?

Coaching in this model is the relentless asking of smart questions. It is not an expert–novice or parent–child model where one person comes to the other for answers. That creates dependency and disempowers. The methodology is facilitative and empowering, based upon the presumption that people will grow in confidence and capability the more they find their own answers to their problems and challenges. This is not incompatible with being helped. Coaching is one of the most empowering techniques in a leader's repertoire.

This should not turn conversations into stultified, scripted affairs; it is done in a spirit of assisted inquiry – questioning that is capable of being warm, supportive, challenging, thoughtful and creative by turns. To return to the "I" of leadership, a leader's CLR partner needs to bear in mind what kind of forest she is entering. If she is to help the leader clear a path to action or new ways of thinking, she needs to understand at quite a profound level – intuitively as much as analytically – what the leader's own story is. That is the art of decentering – seeing the world from another person's perspective – a tricky business we shall discuss in Chapter 15.

But first a final word on the CLR compact. A few things need to be remembered and perhaps made explicit around rules of conduct. They are these:

1. It is a high-trust relationship which needs to be protected. Hence, a rule of absolute confidentiality has to be held as paramount.

2. It is a process whose contents we, the parties, control. It has boundaries. If there's stuff we don't want to talk about (personal relationships perhaps), then it is fine to put them off limits, but within the allowed boundaries, maximum openness should be the norm.

3. It is a tool to hand. We should have a shared understanding that we can call upon each other as and when a need arises.

4. It is not a marriage – you can walk away after a little or a long while. Because it is organic, it can outgrow its usefulness and

needs to be understood as such. There should be no blame and no rancor if we stop talking as we used to.

Leaders have to do many things: observe, think, analyze and act, and not necessarily in that order! Much of the heavy lifting consists of acts of communication. There are stories to tell, speeches to be made and people to persuade. But there are also a host of much smaller and deeper conversations to be had. Too often, we drift in and out of these without much thought. That's fine much of the time, though when you're a leader even a purposeless conversation should be had on purpose. Every conversation is an opportunity. The importance of the CLR idea is that leaders can give and receive benefits from conducting them in a more mindful manner. Key points are summarized in Figure 11.2.

So, let us review where this leaves us. It seems that the SPQ model paints a demanding picture for leadership – the constant adaptation and innovation, and even knowing when to do nothing is pretty taxing. Luckily, we are not alone. Through CLRs, leaders can garner strength and support. It has been one of the curses of the corporate hierarchy that it leaves leaders in not-so-splendid isolation, with too few intimates they can really trust and talk to.

But if we dig deeper into what is going on here, it is clear that we can go in two directions for insight. One is into the wider context of a life as a strategy. What we have seen in the SPQ chapters is that

Figure 11.2: Making CLRs work as a key to leadership effectiveness

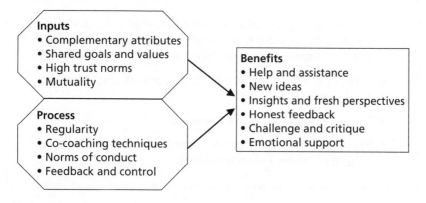

Inputs
• Complementary attributes
• Shared goals and values
• High trust norms
• Mutuality

Process
• Regularity
• Co-coaching techniques
• Norms of conduct
• Feedback and control

Benefits
• Help and assistance
• New ideas
• Insights and fresh perspectives
• Honest feedback
• Challenge and critique
• Emotional support

leaders have to make choices – about what to see, what to be, what to do and, in this chapter, who to partner with or whom to allow to help them. The other direction is inward toward the mental processes that allow leaders to make such choices. None of us is free, for the Self, as one sage put it, is where all of the significant battles are waged.[34]

In the next chapters we travel in both directions. First, we shall move outwards to the context of the leader's life, where we find we are not as free as we think we are, yet, we persistently miss out on chances to be free that are under our noses. Second, we shall plunge back into the mind of the leader, to see how, moment by moment, choices are made or missed.

IMPLICATIONS AND OBSERVATIONS FOR LEADERS AND ORGANIZATIONS

Leadership seemed a lot simpler in the almost bygone era of "command and control." New complexities of business and commerce, the impossibility of relying on old-fashioned authority and the requirement of consent from multiple interests all mean leaders have to be many things simultaneously. This is well-nigh impossible, so leaders need partners to help shoulder the burden and truth-tellers to help steady the leader's grasp on reality. This is what Critical Leader Relationships do. Key points are:

- The more of a shaper a leader is, i.e. the stronger their leadership proposition, the less versatile they are likely to be, and the greater the need for partners to counterbalance their gifts and biases.

- Successful partnership requires skillful accommodation of someone with radically different qualities, so also a lot of goodwill, on both sides.

- CLRs are distinct from other relationships in their depth and impact. They have the potential to deliver priceless benefits and give leaders a deal of protection from what they don't see, know or understand.

- To get these benefits requires questioning and listening skills – such as are practiced in coaching.

- CLRs work best when they are reciprocal.

- Trust is essential, which requires a shared framework of norms, informal disciplines and understandings.

– 12 –

DESTINY, DRAMA AND DELIBERATION – THE LIVES OF LEADERS

The unexamined life is not worth living.

Socrates

ANDRE'S STORY

From the first sensation of his crushing handshake, the vision of his imposing frame and the handsome, confident and strong African-American face, you know Andre Norman is a force of nature – a man not to be messed with. Yet, he also strikes you as a kindly giant and a man who does not price his words cheaply. He impresses as a warm-hearted and positive spirit. You would feel confident about putting yourself in this man's trust.[1]

I met Andre when I was co-leading an executive development program for a group of mainly European executives.[2] We were on a "discovery" tour of the criminal justice system of Boston, Massachu-setts. His role was to be our lead guide, a man who had seen the system from all sides, but now from the vantage point of his position as a community leader in the roughest part of the city. This was a role about which he was a zealous evangelist, plunging his strong arms into the vortex of gang, drug and street culture and pulling out to safety what young black souls he could lay hold of and keep a grip of. He was especially well qualified to do this, for descent into these depths had been the story of his childhood. As he recounted to me, he was one of six kids, illiterate to the age of 9 and psychologically abandoned by his father. His salvation came in the form of a female teacher from a third grade class who spotted his native intelligence and showed him the fulfillment that comes from learning. When he reached high school level, she presented him with an extraordinary opportunity, to become his school's first ever exchange student on a sponsored trip to Europe.

Overcoming the improbability of such a trip at the last minute, and after some agonizing and family maneuvering, he agreed. It proved to be life-changing; not immediately, but on a long delayed time fuse. The trip left deep in Andre's mind the indelible image of other possible lives, societies, worlds apart from his own. Returned to the vortex he found its embrace irresistible. Where else can a young man in these circumstances find pride except in the gang? Being smart and tough, Andre slipped inexorably into a life of crime – his specialty was robbing drug dealers – before collecting his inevitable first term of confinement in a juvenile institution. Before long he had graduated to State prison where he defined his status as #10,000 in the pecking order of the incarcerated. As he "progressed" through to Federal prisons, by the relentless deployment of his dominant intellect, fear-lessness and physical toughness, he had progressed by his reckoning to #3 in the entire system. A position of pride? Andre set to thinking, and became increasingly perplexed. Into his mind a persistent image kept resurfacing of that time in his childhood where he had glimpsed the vivid possibilities of other worlds. A decision began to formulate in his mind. "I want out. If I reach the top of this system I'll be #1 of nowhere. Where can I go from there?"

Education had to be the way. He started to teach himself law and enrolled for counseling – a daring step in prison, since this was normally only taken up by sex offenders or crazies. "I used to think

184

hurting people was fun," he said, "now I realized I was the smartest person in prison and there was a way out." After eight years in therapy he got early parole and, in 1999, after a total of 14 years in prison, he walked free to start his new life.

DESTINY, DRAMA AND DELIBERATION – HOW LIVES ARE MADE

For each of us the equation is different. For some, Destiny rules – life follows a predictable course. Some leaders seem to be the victims of their inheritance and never break free. There are leaders – perhaps George Bush might be seen as one of them, or any other dynastic leaders – who seem to tread a path that has been laid out for them. In many cultures, leadership rolls along well-worn tracks. Woe betide the scion who seeks to throw off the mantel and live a chosen life. Yet, if we are to believe the testimony of Bush in his memoir, he did a great deal of deliberating – pausing, reflecting and then making game-changing choices.[3]

But what triggers choice? Of course, it can be anything – your state of readiness to choose is what matters.

The most notable case, enshrined in the faith of the millions, is the story of the prince who had everything a heart could desire, shielded by his doting parents from knowledge of human suffering. But his perfect contentment troubled him, and he picked himself up and left his family and the protection of the palace compound to explore the wilderness beyond and bear witness to the ills of the world.[4] Prince Siddhartha Gautama was his name. Astonished, dismayed and pondering, he squatted under the Bodhi tree and deliberated long and hard. After 49 days of meditation, his mind apprehended the blissful state of transcendental enlightenment, Nirvana, which led him on his new path of spiritual leadership for his people. The Buddha had arrived, thanks to a particularly sublime form of deliberation.

For over a decade I have run a Biography class for mid-career executives and professionals who are mostly in transition between life and career stages.[5] In this course they look outward at the lives of

185

others and inward to their own, seeking to understand the forces that have shaped their paths, and to help them find the best ways to make choices about their future lives. Most of them – especially the Anglo-Saxon types – tend to dislike the notion of Destiny intensely. It suggests your life is "written," bequeathing you the role as no more than a helpless, though perhaps fascinated, observer of its unfolding path from birth to the grave. They prefer the view that in every moment we can change our fate by a single decision. There is a middle course. Yes, our lives do change at a stroke, and are often guided by our preferences and choices, yet our options – the number of lives we can live – are limited. We cannot change the world or the times we were born in. We cannot change our DNA.[6]

So is Destiny something to be found or transcended? Many people spend years of experience in search of what is right for them – the pursuit of the Compass Question. Quite right too; as the Leadership Formula dictates, alignment (doing what satisfies you) is most people's legitimate and ultimate goal. Yet many people – often the same people – are seeking to escape the Destiny that life has laid out for them – social origins, role models and the norms of one's culture. One thinks of people like Andy Grove, and many other migrants, who determinedly made a break with their origins.[7] Many a family firm has found the scion of the clan rejecting the path laid out for him.

Destiny played a strong part in Andre's life. He was born a black man in a predominantly white man's world – come, like his brethren, from the stock of Africans transported, enslaved and then released into the life of urban struggle that characterized the great industrial conurbations of northern US cities. He was born at a particular point in history – a post civil rights era where education was providing opportunities for the young but under the threat of a burgeoning drug and gang culture. None of these things could Andre change; nor his family milieu; his parentage or the influences to which he was exposed. Also given were the most salient aspects of his personal identity: his powerful physicality, dominant nature and, most of all, his considerable intellect.

Drama is what lifespan developmental psychologists call "non-normative life events"[8] which is pretty well everything that happens to us that is not culturally scheduled. Marriage is normative but whom you marry is non-normative. Who this person turns out to be may be a surprise not long after the honeymoon! Even if you have done extensive research before making some life choices, what they trigger may play into your life in unpredicted ways. Drama in some lives resembles the apocryphal story, "for the sake of a horseshoe nail the kingdom was lost" (horse goes lame; messenger fails to deliver message; army defeated in battle; kingdom is lost). It is a fact that many of the most important turning points in life come unbidden and are scarcely recognized as pivotal moments when they occur. We make a seemingly innocent choice (go left rather than right) or we stumble across something that proves to be life-changing. Drama can come in moments of small simplicity as well as high theater.

Yet, the pull of Destiny may be stronger than we like to admit. We follow the track and meander through its many diversions but still end up in the same place we would have reached by taking other paths. Wherever we are, our drives and instincts pull us back to a limited range of personal destinations. In his novel, *Armadillo*,[9] William Boyd invents a splendid new word, *zemblanity*, to capture the irony of human self-determination, which he defines as the opposite of *serendipity*. Serendipity means good stuff that happens to us by accident. Zemblanity is bad stuff that happens to us because we make it happen – the dark compulsion to screw up in the same old ways.

One could say it was just so with Andre. All the gangland incidents of his life were not life-changing Drama but *zemblanity*; steps on a dark path of Destiny. But Andre had an alternative Destiny – another life to be lived, which fed on the same talents that he deployed so zealously in his criminal career – that of a saver of souls. So the real Drama that came into his life was the young female teacher who saw the spark in his eyes and persuaded him to come on the school trip. This magnificent deviation from the seemingly inexorable track of his journey was planted like a time bomb that would eventually blow the bars out of his cage. But the bomb needed an act – several acts, actually – of ignition. Only the man himself could light the fuse. This is done by the most mysterious and powerful force in human nature – Deliberation.

In the next chapter we journey into this space – the domain of the Self. The Executive Ego that is more than an innkeeper who slavishly serves his customers, but an authority who can throw out the drunks, redecorate the premises and change his lifestyle at a stroke.[10] Any of these things requires a space and an effort for a major inversion of one's life to be possible. To achieve this, Andre did four radical things, all at once.

First, he commanded, by act of will, a reordering of his desires and life goals. The narrative was, *"I don't have to follow my practiced instincts. By choice I can devalue what has guided me up to now. I can pursue a mission based upon a new vision. I can seek the help of others to do new things."*

Second, he changed his view of himself: *"No longer the 3rd toughest guy in the system; instead I am ready to be a child on the first steps of a long climb to a new maturity."*

Third, he changed his worldview: *"No longer is my only reality this community of crime whose rules I know so well; there is a brighter world beyond its walls that I can enter."*

Fourth, he started to re-equip his repertoire of routines and actions: *"My practiced skills – many forms of refined brutality and dominance – will no longer serve me as before."*

Andre realized he had to learn and find a new set of ways of connecting with people. Counseling and role modeling led him to deeper Deliberation to discover the possibility of self-liberation from the bleak Destiny offered by his sub-culture. He found an entirely new frame for identity and action. In the UK I have seen theater arts bring about similar personal transformation in prisons, using Shakespeare as a vehicle for liberating self-determination in men who have been trapped in bad cycles of action and reaction.[11]

On British TV in 1964 they conducted a bold experiment called *Seven Up!*[12] They took 20 children aged 7, of both sexes and from all social strata, and interviewed them with a view to testing the proposition: "give me the child until he is 7 and I will show you the man." The program has been repeated every seven years since. Following this remarkable record, one can see how the DDD model plays out for each of them.

There are those whose lives seem to be foretold – such as the upper class child, passing without incident through the finishing schools of the English gentry to his allotted role of stockbroker, following in his father's footsteps. Yet, even this case shows that the life surrendered to Destiny contains an abundance of Drama in small discoveries and delights – mostly domestic – that enrich experience.[13] Others traveled similar well-worn paths and then were radically blown off course by some Drama, which triggered Deliberation that thereafter reconfigured their life journeys in new directions. And there were some whose lives were much more improvisational from start to finish. Even the Destiny of their characters seemed to be uncertain, moving between roles and identities.

Biography is the story we tell of others' lives, and the DDD model is an analytical tool to help us think about cause and effect – just as the SPQ framework unpicks the problems leaders are trying to solve, here, in the context of the leader's life, the DDD model shows the balance between three forces in all our lives: the winds of Destiny that blow us forward, the accidents of a random universe that cut across our path and the rare moments of pure choice. It helps to explain why being strategic as a leader – living and leading through pure intention – is so hard.

MO IBRAHIM'S STORY

Mo Ibrahim is a twinkly eyed, short, plump, affable, pipe-smoking Sudanese from the proud and noble Nubian people of eastern Africa.[14] You'll be hard pressed to find a more genuine, outgoing, charming leader. He is also a man of prodigious intelligence and great passion. And, one other thing – he practically invented the mobile phone, built a remarkable company and then fashioned for himself a new role as a high priest of modern ethics in Africa.

His journey through life and early education endowed him with a powerfully driven values-based compass, pointing towards social justice. "I was a Marxist," he declares proudly. But his gifts lay in engineering, not political activism. Then, in the midst of his college education, seeking an evening's light entertainment away from his books, he took a taxi to see the hit movie *Khartoum*. It was 1969 and the car was a big old Renault, which, unusually for the time, had a radio receiver which the driver could use to talk to HQ. There, in the cab, Mo engaged in a critical moment of Deliberation that changed his life. As he watched the driver talking, he pondered, "What if those radio phones, whose signals pass without wires through city concrete, could be used by you and me to talk to each other, as we walk different streets?"

The thought grew and led him to seek out one of the world's experts on the topic, a professor from Bradford in England, to supervise his further research. This step took Mo to Birmingham, where he embarked on a PhD to develop this new technology, moving afterwards to join British Telecom in London, where there was a new subsidiary to develop and implement the new mobile telephony. Becoming a master of the emerging discipline, he quit the company and set up a consulting firm in the new technology in 1989, selling it ten years later and using the proceeds to found one of Africa's first and most successful cellular operators, Celtel. Riding the crest of this growing wave – for mobile phones were fast becoming Africa's missing infrastructure – he never lost sight of his values. He declared that Celtel was, first and foremost, going to be an exemplary ethical business in a continent dogged by corruption and political graft. As he competed for country licenses, he strictly enforced over-the-table, honest dealing – "no brown envelopes!" – even at the cost of acquiring at least one major operating license.

Under his inspired democratic and enlightened leadership, Celtel developed a powerful values-based culture with liberal share ownership among its employees. When he eventually sold the company – making himself a billionaire and making millionaires of more than 100 employees – he picked up again the thread of his adolescent Marxism, now transmuted into a passion for ethical leadership in Africa. This he has done by founding the Mo Ibrahim Index of African Governance, an authoritative data-based measure of the standing of 52 countries in the continent on their application of the rule of law, human rights, economic opportunity and human development. He is passionate about the quality of leadership and also awards a $6 million annual prize, including an annuity, for African political leadership that meets its criteria of excellence, including a stipulation that the leader should have voluntarily relinquished power or quit under a fair electoral process. Google him and see for yourself how this remarkable man continues to infuse the world with his values.

THE DUKE

Andre Norman's story finds an almost equal and opposite in that of another black American, Duke Ellington, born to a quite different world. His father had been an aristocrat of servants, working for a period as a member of the White House staff. Ellington, raised in a household of doting females, adopted his father's pristine manners and style and, from the women of the family, a belief that he was favored and deserving. His musical gifts, nurtured by his adoring and adored mother, were supported through the halls of the classical academy, but Duke's willful, exploratory instincts drew him out of hours to the thriving low-down world of Harlem jazz clubs.[15]

His story resembles that of the information age pioneers: Jobs, Gates and Larry Ellison – all dropping out of college to find the Destiny dictated by their instincts. Throwing away the secure script handed to them and writing their own was the act of Deliberation that fired up the careers of all these creative individuals. The models they ended up with were very different. Gates became the richest man in the world; Jobs transformed an entire industry; Ellison ushered in a new era of software development; and Ellington became the iconic father figure for his country's indigenous musical culture.

Destiny for Ellington was the milieu of his birth and his good genes. For the former, he was the grandson of a former slave, who, when freed, moved to Washington. Following the trauma of the death of his parents' first born, Duke was seen as a "special" child and pampered by his adoring mother and aunts. He grew with an unforced natural good humor, relaxed outlook and a passion for music and art, for he was gifted in both. He was naturally unflappable, rarely ill and able to endure the sleepless nights of a band leader with the aid of a resolutely low pulse rate and iron constitution. Intelligent, large, handsome, commanding, always immaculately dressed and irresistible to women, he demanded freedom and lived life by his rules, yet he was always intensely religious.

Like Steve Jobs, his motivation and ability combined to release a continuous stream of creative products throughout his life. He wrote the classic *In my Solitude* in 20 minutes, leaning against the glass partition of a recording studio, and *Mood Indigo* in a 15-minute cab journey. Like Jobs he refused to define his niche in terms of genre or domain – he averred he was not a jazz musician, just a composer.

Drama came to him in various forms, though mostly his was an untroubled and controlled life. He maintained a wife and mistress openly but with unobtrusive skill. Music was always the main compass, and the main Drama that befell him was a radical decline in big bands. Duke was perpetually high in Deliberation, as exemplified in his decisions over how to run the band; in his unbending stand against race discrimination; in his deliberate shifting of the music to a higher quasi-orchestral plane with the legendary Sacred Concerts, performed in cathedrals in the US and Europe. He was especially deliberate about relations with the band – "on everybody's side" but careful in his handling of the big egos in the band. He maintained a modicum of distance – riding in the car with just his baritone sax buddy of 45 years, Harry Carney, while the rest rode in the bus.

Yet, this highly deliberative leader – and indeed all the greatest have this strongly in their make-up – was deeply affected by two momentous relationships. One was with his mother. Her death, when he was 36, shifted him and his music into a higher realm of contemplation and spirituality. The other was a curious, yet immensely powerful, partnership with a young man called Billy Strayhorn. This diminutive, bespectacled young African-American shyly approached the great man after a concert to show him how he would have arranged one of the Duke's own pieces. Ellington was intrigued and impressed, for Strayhorn had lovingly absorbed the essence of the great man's music. Thus began one of the most remarkable artistic partnerships in history. There was Duke, resolutely heterosexual, urbane, supremely outgoing and oozing confidence; and there was Strayhorn, small, intensely private, inarticulate and homosexual; yet, they were united in a platonic love that infused their lives for three decades. Strayhorn co-composed with Ellington some of his greatest pieces and always was on hand with the right idea to keep the creative spirit moving.

As a CLR partner he was incomparable. In his autobiography,[16] Duke wrote:

> In music, as you develop a theme or a musical idea, there are many points at which direction must be decided, and any time I was in the throes of debate with myself, harmonically or melodically, I would turn to Billy Strayhorn. We would talk, and then the whole world would come into focus. The steady hand of his good judgment pointed to the clear way that was most fitting for us. He was not, as he was often referred to by many, my alter ego. Billy Strayhorn was my right arm, my left arm, all the eyes in the back of my head, my brainwaves in his head, and his in mine. Our rapport was the closest.

Strayhorn's untimely death in 1967 affected Duke even more than his adored mother's. He reputedly banged his head against the wall in torrents of tears. If you want to hear the emotion of that loss, listen to a recording; the tape had been left running at the end of a recording session, shortly after Strayhorn's passing. You can hear the Duke in an emptying studio playing, imperfectly yet dripping with poignancy, Strayhorn's beautiful ballad *Lotus Blossom*.

STEVE JOBS

A lot has been written about Jobs since his early defeat by the big C, much of it full of hyperbole, yet it is true that he does stand, along with Ford and Edison, as one of the greatest entrepreneurs and paradigm-shifting business innovators who ever lived. He was also one of the most pathologically difficult leaders seen in modern times; the fascination he holds owes much to how his neurosis was integral to the fabric of his achievement.

But let us look again at Jobs through the lens of DDD. As we noted earlier, Jobs expressed a belief in nurture over nature, but as an adopted child this is a narrative that helped him believe his heritage was something he had control over. Jobs naturally wanted to attribute much of his success to his autonomous, aggrandizing Self, yet, from a more dispassionate perspective, one can see that both his nature and his nurture were intertwined elements of what we are calling Destiny. He was preternaturally bright – the child of a Syrian PhD student (whom he once derisively referred to as his "sperm bank") and a clever young American mother, who only surrendered him for adoption on condition that his new parents would be college-educated folks who would ensure he was educated likewise. At the last moment his adoption was switched and the promise was broken, though his new parents turned out to be a blessing of a different kind.

His father was an honest, hard-working artisan, emotionally very centered and balanced; his new mother a balanced and loving woman. From his father, a meticulous purist of a craftsman in all his hobbies and occupations, Steve derived a respect for simplicity of design and of perfection in execution. Hidden circuit boards in Apple computers had to be esthetically satisfying, just like the unseen backs and insides of the wooden cabinets his father lovingly crafted.

Deliberation and Destiny were always closely coupled for Jobs. From his childhood he fiercely contested the experiences handed to him, and generated novel ones unprompted, like dropping out of college. His adopted parents had kept the second part of the promise to give him a college education, but Steve's perverse choice was a relatively obscure, small local elite institution, at least as costly as the prestigious local Ivy League college, Stanford, he could have chosen. Once there, he naïvely bridled at the college's attendance requirements, until he impulsively quit. Yet, in typical Jobs calculating style, he persuaded the authorities to allow him to audit whatever courses he fancied. Jobs's deliberations were almost always urgent and immediate, making most of the Drama in his life self-generated.

Good Deliberation requires space, time and freedom.[17] Jobs's impulsive short-term deliberations were often under self-generated duress, but it was fortunate that, early in his career at Atari, he was handed the chance to be sent on an extended assignment to India. Here, he found space and a place where he could review the values and beliefs that had swirled through his life. And it was here he fastened on and clarified the principle that underlay his greatness as an innovator – the unity of art and technology; of spirituality in design, and in the power of intuition to cut through complexity toward truthful and powerful outcomes.

When the Drama of his pancreatic cancer overtook him, Jobs's insistent Deliberation – his belief that his obsessive and faddish dietary disciplines would remit the illness – caused a fatal delay in treatment, when early surgery could possibly have halted the disease's deadly spread to his other organs.

LIFETIMES OF TRANSITIONS[18]

It is interesting to reflect that continuous Deliberation does not always yield a great life for anyone, including leaders. Consider the chart in Figure 12.1. A life on the wide ocean – the continuous choices of sailing, in box B – is both exhausting and hazardous. Sometimes the adventure in life comes from following the river (box D) – Destiny and Drama will take you places where who knows what delights and

Figure 12.1: Patterns of transitions

	Stable	Changeful
Chosen	A. Moored in harbor	B. Sailing
Not Chosen	C. Shipwrecked	D. Following the river

opportunities may land in your lap. The danger is that if you follow the river, you end up somewhere you didn't intend and which is hard to get out of. This has been the story of many career changers I have worked with. They made a few early choices that set them on the river of a corporate or professional career. They hung on in hope, fed by the usual diet of inducements and promotions, until they awoke and found themselves in a place they didn't like. To escape takes desperate measures – like ducking out of your career and coming back to college (and into my Biography class).

Being moored in harbor (box A in Figure 12.1) is the choice not to choose. We all come to that sooner or later, and often recurrently. It is the comfort zone of accepting one's fate; though there are plenty of people who chafe angrily at the Destiny that forces them to accept a world they cannot change or escape from. This is not the lot of most leaders, though there are some, for example family business patriarchs, who accept their leadership as a duty to serve with more resignation than delight.

The last of the quadrants, shipwrecked (box C), is the intrusion of Drama – often unwelcome – such as Jobs getting fired or Mandela being imprisoned. It hurts – even good change – when you've had no chance to prepare for it. When the French CEO J-P Mustier was thrust into leadership by the sudden death of his predecessor, it was not a happy experience. He had to grow new wings. That hurts, even when you can fly to new places. Mustier did, but then another Drama befell him in the form of a rogue trader, Jerome Kerviel, who, on Mustier's watch, defrauded the bank of 4.9 billion Euros in 2007. For this, and other perturbations in the troubled months of 2009, Mustier fell on his sword and went on to reinvent his career as a champion of social enterprise.[19]

There is life after death. It is well known that many people who are "let go" by their firms find rebirth and revitalization as entrepreneurs.[20] Being shipwrecked may be the best thing that ever happens to people whom success or security has imprisoned in the choice not to choose.

Let us close this chapter with a reflection on the patterns that we see in leadership. Destiny endows them with the drives, gifts and life chances that fit the demands of their times. Drama is the wild card of who they hook up with, and the crises or opportunities that land, unprogramed, in their laps. Deliberation is found in their moments of reflection and choice. These don't have to have the obsessive frequency of Steve Jobs's impulsive cogitations; they just have to be timely. Readiness is all. There's no point in sitting around trying to force insights out of yourself, any more than a poet or artist should demand vision on tap. Let it come in its own time, but be ready.

That means cultivating an openness to experience and a Zen attitude to change.

And what of our four nautical types? Conventionally, our early years are moored in harbor; we do some sailing in young adulthood; then we follow the river, until we find a harbor we really like to rest up in for the remainder of our days.[21] That's how things used to be. Corporate careers and professional paths are nonetheless much more strewn with shipwrecks than they used to be, so the patterns are more varied. This is as true for leaders as for any of us. So find your leader and ask them their story.

When we tell our own stories it is autobiography. These stories can just be ex post catch-ups for the DDD in our lives, but mostly they are more than that. They can be self-fulfilling and self-defeating, for they are the core of what makes leadership succeed or fail. This is the story of the next two chapters.

IMPLICATIONS AND OBSERVATIONS FOR LEADERS AND ORGANIZATIONS

The SPQ framework showed what leaders have to control or effect in order to keep in adaptive equilibrium with a changing world. When we look at leaders' lives we see how narrow is the space for choice and action between the forces of Destiny and the insistent disruption of Drama. We observed the following:

- We have fewer choices and more regrets in life than we would like to admit. We have to seize our moments before we settle into acceptance.

(Continued)

- Destiny has to pass through one, but it can be directed. Many leaders come to their positions from unlikely origins by fighting and finding their way to new resolutions of the "I" of leadership.

- Destiny has both to be found and transcended. This is the power of Determination.

- Expect the unexpected. There is randomness in all processes and, at every turn, leaders can expect potentially derailing Drama.

- Choice points are easily passed over. Leaders often make big decisions unthinkingly whilst agonizing over trivial choices. It pays to be able to stop and Deliberate.

- Regrets about missed opportunities tend to be more poisonous than regrets over risks taken. Seize the day!

– 13 –

THE "I" OF LEADERSHIP – INSIDE THE MIND OF THE LEADER

Watch your thoughts; they become your words.
Watch your words; they become your actions.
Watch your actions; they become your habits.
Watch your habits; they become your character.
Watch your character for it will become your destiny.

Anon

THE STRANGE VOYAGE OF DONALD CROWHURST[1]

The Sunday Times, a British national newspaper, had found fortune in sponsoring Sir Francis Chichester, the world's first man to circumnavigate the globe non-stop and single-handed. Wishing to capitalize on this success, in 1968 the paper sponsored a race on the same lines, open to all-comers, without any prior qualification. Many experienced sailors and amateurs signed up, including Donald Crowhurst. Crowhurst, a former airman and local politician, was a keen weekend sailor and electronics inventor, who had built a business, with a friend's sponsorship, selling a new navigational device. The business was failing, and the race offered an escape from his difficulties and debts. He mortgaged his family home and business to enter the race with a new American designed trimaran – a three-hulled boat that was potentially much faster than conventional craft, but untested on such a venture and vulnerable to various technical hazards.

But Crowhurst was a slapdash, impulsive optimist. Despite various mishaps, he just about got his boat into the water on the last permissible day, though with a number of technical problems unresolved. Smiling and waving he left port and headed for the open sea. Technical difficulties with the boat immediately surfaced and intensified. He couldn't make his projected speed; when he did, the vibrations proved damaging to the boat. Problems proliferated. As he reached the mid-Atlantic, he realized the hopelessness of his situation. He was faced with certain ruin if he admitted failure, so he embarked on a bold deception. He kept two logs: one a true record of his situation and one official log, which he now used to plot an imaginary course along the race route, radioing his positions back to the race organizers whilst he drifted at anchor in the Atlantic Ocean. His plan was to wait until the race leaders came into the last leg and then to rejoin at their tail, to finish inconspicuously but not ignominiously.

The plan went wrong as sailor after sailor dropped out. With horror, Crowhurst realized that he, according to his false log, was in an unassailable lead in the race. Now he was staring at a ticking time bomb. Under the spotlight of publicity on winning his deception could not escape undetected. The bomb exploded in Crowhurst's head, for at this point he went crazy. The true log records a descent into a maelstrom of madness – 25,000 words of rambling thoughts and mystical delusions, and then silence. He went overboard on June 29th 1969. Ten days later the abandoned boat and all his copious notes were recovered.

It is possible – likely, indeed – that Crowhurst had some mental instability and the pressure pushed him over the edge. Whatever the susceptibility, this was fundamentally a disorder of the Self; one which Crowhurst ended by destroying the damaged organ.

THE CURSE OF THE SELF

As Crowhurst's case shows, the Self can be a monstrous burden. It may seem unnatural that a man can widow his wife and desert his children for such "selfish" concerns. Perhaps, though many of the world's greatest ills are conducted to relieve shame or to seek "selfish" retribution.

Psychologist Mark Leary wrote a deeply insightful book on the subject.[2] Leary points out that the Self is a modern burden. Our ancestors were blissfully free from identity problems. Life was short. The gods were mainly responsible for most of the stuff that happened – not just the weather, but things that now we attribute to our Selves, like success and failure. Choice was highly circumscribed, so there was no need to agonize about preferences. Besides, in the highly collectivized culture of the tribal group, if you screwed up it wasn't entirely your fault – blame was largely shared with the capricious gods who were driving you, or with the clan who were responsible for your adoption of the right standards of behavior. Not much room left for navel gazing really.

Now, in the modern era:

1. God is dead (or at best a disinterested bystander to the theater of human life).

2. We live forever, or act as if we do.

3. We have almost infinite choice.[3] Put a caveman in a modern supermarket and he would shake his head in disbelief and confusion.

So now, all of a sudden, we are responsible for everything that happens to us. If we are unhappy, sick or fail, it's our fault. Anxiety, neuroses, compulsive behaviors, irrational fears, shame, blame and depression dog our footsteps through the paradise of freedom we have created. Leary observes that one reason why religions have featured so highly in human cultures is that they bring relief to the Self problem. They all share a message, in one form or another, about the benefits that come from the abnegation of the Self for a higher truth.

201

The appearance of self-interest is a snare for leaders, which will only garner support by linking with the self-interest of supporters, who will fade away at the first signs of trouble or diminished payoffs. Bush and Blair both found their faiths bolstered their commitments, as did Ellington and many others discussed here. Leaders don't need to have faith in God, but they need to believe in something bigger than their Selves that they can connect their people to.

DOES THE SELF "EXIST?" A BRIEF BUT IMPORTANT DIGRESSION

This might seem a stupid question, but we had best deal with it since some very serious and intelligent people have raised it.[4] Arguments are various, but add up to something like this: there is no part of the brain that can be identified as the Self, i.e. it has no simple, organic identity. It is an illusion created by memory and consciousness. It is easily tricked and deluded, for it believes it has agency when it is being externally manipulated. Free will is a powerful illusion. Does this make humans "special?" Other intelligent creatures, such as primates and some sea mammals, have a degree of self-awareness. In humans, it is just at a much more sophisticated level.[5]

Let's deal with these one by one, since they matter.

1. The nature of consciousness is one of science's frontier topics, awaiting deeper insights from neuroscience. Functionally, it is a single, narrow channel through which all experience, memory, impression, sensation, feeling, thought and expectation have to flow.[6] Other creatures have consciousness supported by complex cortical structures. For humans, this window of experience contains a function that we can call self-awareness. We know (or think we know) we exist.[7]

2. True, we can't identify any specific modules that would be like a little person at the controls (a homunculus, as it would be termed), but we do know from neurological investigations with normal and brain-damaged people that the right

hemisphere, and specifically the right frontal lobe regions of the brain, is strongly implicated in self-awareness, and especially in self-control.[8] Further investigations for sure will tell us more about what is happening here.

3. Yes, the Self is fragile and easily disturbed or tricked,[9] especially into believing that it is free and in command of our actions, when in reality it is often playing catch-up – rushing like a politician to claim credit for good stuff that happens and to distance itself from bad stuff.[10] Yet, the Self is also an "illusion" that is very hard to shake. It is near impossible to stop a child developing a sense of personal identity or theory of mind, the precious idea that other people are motivated by their own, different thoughts and feelings. It is so real to us that we might as well treat it as real, and deal with the consequences. The same goes for "free will." Our choices may be invisibly constrained, but we do make choices, and often believe, rightly, that we could act otherwise if we wished. We can leave the philosophers to argue – to all intents and purposes we have a capacity that does everything free will is supposed to do.[11]

4. It is impossible to get the smartest ape to the same level of self-control as humans, or anything like the same level of conceptual thinking about self-identity and actions.[12] People have strenuously tried and failed. There is a huge gap between us and our closest cousins. No dark nights of ego are remotely possible for even the smartest chimps.

5. The idea of the Self as an agent makes some evolutionists quite nervous. They fear it smuggles in dualism – the separation of mind from body – which violates their assumption of biologically-based "consilience" – the unity of knowledge.[13] They are right to defend consilience but their fears are groundless. The Self is a powerful functional reality. For, clearly from an evolutionary standpoint, even though it has become a "curse" to us, it is the winner's curse, for having a sense of Self is really useful.[14] Even if easily fooled, it enables

us to do a lot of stuff that matters a lot to us. As Mark Twain put it[15] – attributing the words to his friend Macfarlane, who concluded that humans had reached a pretty special but dismal place, some years before Darwin had "startled the world" with his ideas:

> He [Macfarlane] said that man's heart was the only bad heart in the animal kingdom; that man was the only animal capable of feeling malice, envy, vindictiveness, revengefulness, hatred, selfishness, the only animal that loved drunkenness, almost the only animal that could endure personal uncleanliness and a filthy habitation, the sole animal in whom was developed the base instinct called patriotism, the sole animal that robs, persecutes, oppresses and kills members of his own immediate tribe, the sole animal that steals and enslaves the members of any tribe.

Zoologists will argue with several of these points, but you get the picture. Twain is reveling in the dark side of the Self.

The upside is what psychologists call self-regulation.[16] This is the capacity we have to control our own moods, thoughts, actions and even our goals. It is self-regulation that enables the person who succumbs to midnight bingeing to protect themselves by putting a lock on the fridge. We most profoundly self-regulate when we consider our own mortality and make life plans that go way beyond the horizon of our own needs, or even those of the people we love. We are able to regulate our moods[17] by choosing to go for a run, listen to music or switch the topic of conversation. We can imagine future states and use self-control to bring them into being. We are able to conceive of ourselves in different ways, and then act out roles (a technique perfected by the so-called "Method" actors – people like Marlon Brando, Mickey Rourke and Choi Min-sik, the Korean star) to find new states of existence and relationships.

THE SELF-REGULATED LEADER

Aung San Suu Kyi is a remarkable person.[18] She spent much of her adult life separated from her family under house arrest for her opposition to the military junta ruling Burma. Throughout, she exercised a dignified and steadfast self-control until, eventually, in 2010 she secured the victory of release and the government started its retreat from totalitarianism. During this time she rejected numerous opportunities to leave the country, even to visit her terminally ill husband, because she did not trust the authorities to allow her to re-enter Burma, so sharp a thorn in their side was she. Throughout her confinement she was debarred all media contact and other visits. She became severely ill and was hospitalized on more than one occasion. She quietly studied politics and philosophy, never allowing herself to be used as a tool by any sectarian interests, but standing as a beacon throughout the world for justice and democracy in her country.

Mandela, Stockdale, Napoleon, Gandhi and Elizabeth I are among the leaders we have considered who possessed the iron discipline to see their intentions through to completion. Unfortunately, it is not just the good guys; Empress Wu, Osama Bin Laden, Hitler, Stalin and Pol Pot also were people of immense control towards their purposes, though often more unstable emotionally. As we have noted, many leaders exhibit remarkably little discipline and indulge their whims freely, because they have the power to. But to achieve anything more than riding their luck, leaders need self-control.[19] True, many are erratic, eccentric and emotionally explosive, but when it comes to their prime purposes they do not waver.

This is perhaps one of the qualities we look for most in leaders – their ability to keep going when the going gets tough. Politicians like Bush and Blair make a virtue of it, even when their detractors call it stubborn arrogance; others like Obama and Cameron are criticized for inconsistency, which they would call flexibility and pragmatism.

These labels are, of course, narratives, and there is no point in debating them. Rather, our purpose here is to understand how they work, or don't work, in motivating the actions of leaders, in shaping the responses of followers and determining the outcomes that flow from them. We have spent some time examining leadership as strategy, but the strategy has to be thought through in the leader's mind as well as acted out in the theater of the world. Sometimes the thought precedes the action when the leader deliberates and then delivers.[20]

Sometimes it plays catch-up for events that surround the leader, and sometimes thought is a series of counterpoint adjustments to the bucking bronco the leader is riding.[21] They all matter, because they foretell the future.

A MODEL OF SELF-REGULATION

Tony Blair's report of his cogitations on hearing of the 7/7 bombings in London, which we quoted at the start of this book, was remarkable as a record of a stream of consciousness, ending with his exhortation to himself to put aside his feelings and speculations and "be a leader." From a psychological perspective, that's an interesting trick to pull off. It's a kind of "self-talk," which is something sports psychologists are very interested in – how to get athletes and players to talk themselves into a good game.[22]

Figure 13.1 is a map of how the Self operates.[23] Within this field, leaders have five critical battles to fight:

1. The battle for purpose – knowing what they really want and need.

2. The battle for control – planning, executing and adapting; minimizing errors, stress, confusion and inefficiency.

3. The battle for truth – arriving at the best-shared definition of reality that will work for them and others.

4. The battle for identity – finding and protecting the most truthful and effective narratives.

5. The battle for performance – being able to generate feasible and effective action strategies.

Sometimes it resembles a game more than a battleground, but either way the Self is in a constant state of flux and adjustment. Nothing stands still. The world buzzes around us.[24] Our bodily and emotional states drift, and sometimes jerk, through gears of feeling, memory and sensation. Our thoughts range between all of these:

Figure 13.1: The challenge of self-regulation

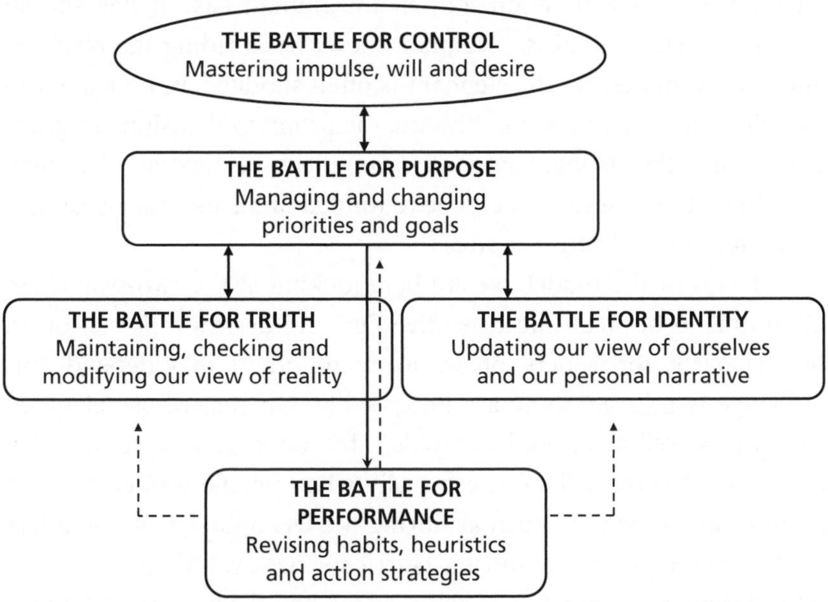

wants, perceptions, ideas of Self and possible actions; all the while setting priorities, initiating, dampening, reasoning, arguing and explaining and seeking moments of peace, fun and relaxation.

The Self-Regulation of Desire – The Battle for Purpose

Like all animals, we are governed by desires. In his brilliant book, *The Happiness Hypothesis,*[25] Jonathan Haidt uses the metaphor of a man riding an elephant to capture the difficulties we humans face with our instincts, impulses and thoughts about what we want. The elephant represents our primitive mammalian brain – it is driven by feeling and impulse to satisfy its needs. It has no language, though it can bellow its rage and murmur its contentment. It is strong and willful. If it wants to stop and feed, it will. The man who sits astride it is intelligent, conceptual, calculating, capable of planning and linguistically articulate. He has ideas about what is good for him and the elephant and tries to steer it accordingly. He represents the neocortex, especially all those parts that command the powers of reason and planned action.

The Executive Ego is the man on the elephant. All sentient creatures have an executive function, but in the human case it has special powers of self-awareness. The man knows he is riding the elephant and tries to master it. The elephant is often subdued and obedient to his will, but sometimes not. The man is prone to delusions of grandeur. When the elephant stops to graze, the man may say, "I wanted it to do that." He doesn't like to be reminded of his ultimate weakness in the face of his brutish desires.[26]

In terms of the model, we are here looking at the two-way chain of command between the Executive Ego and desires.[27] For all of us, but especially for leaders, on whom many others may depend, this exchange is critical. Some are lucky – like Obama, whose elephant seems very well behaved. His problem has often seemed to look like an excess of reasonableness, especially when people wanted to see a bit of elephantine rage, such as during the Deepwater Horizon affair, yet that served him well during Hurricane Sandy. Others, like Steve Jobs, despite yogic practice in self-control, had the burden of riding a very frisky beast. What can the Executive Ego actually control, when it comes to wants and desires? Well, it seems the man can actually train the elephant and recalibrate its needs. More than that, the man can, through a mix of pure reason and willpower, move the elephant. Look at Admiral Stockdale.

For many leaders, the story of their development was a journey of discovery, like Akio Morita of Sony finding something new that enraptured him – electronics in his case – and radically displaced other goals in his life.[28] The life journeys of many others we have considered – people like Andre Norman and Mo Ibrahim – have involved similar revelations and switches of direction. It is also common for changes in our perceptions – new awareness about the world around us (the left-hand box in Figure 13.1) – to trigger changes in goals and desires.

See how quick the explorer Ernest Shackleton was to switch all his energy and focus to the new, unwelcome goal of having to save the lives of 28 men; how Gandhi's life goals changed in an instant on a dusty African railroad; how Duke Ellington stepped up to be a leader when the band caught his predecessor skimming the takings. The ability to recalibrate, turn on a dime and take a new path is a vital leadership attribute. Many fail because they can't do this – they get stuck with the wrong goals, like John Akers of IBM. The goal-driven bias helps people overcome tremendous obstacles. Acts of heroism emerge typically when people are in dire straits.

What is much harder, and a trick that only humans can pull off, is to change your desires just by thinking about them.[29] A leader can say to herself, "I have got this wrong, I should be taking more care of my budgets and less of my staff welfare, even though doing the latter gives me more pleasure." More profoundly, one can say, "What I thought I valued has left me with an empty feeling. My purposes are not fulfilling me." Many people have simply walked out of their lives into new ones as a result of such reflections – we saw in Andre Norman one such spectacular case in the last chapter. People routinely walk out of relationships in this manner. Poor Donald Crowhurst, in effect, did this – choosing the new goal of eliminating all his desires and feelings, achieved by extinguishing his own life.

Some leaders worry a lot in their lonely, reflective spaces, and it may take a CLR partner or some other external agent to help them to examine and re-order their goals productively, by examining the deeper motives underlying them, even at the cost of personal discomfort and inconvenience. The deeper you go, the harder it gets. It's easy to switch from jam to marmalade, but much harder, say, to surrender power for peace of mind. It is tough to face up to how much one is driven by partially disguised motives, like wanting to be well thought of, or a need to act as if you are more confident in yourself than you really are.[30] In a sense – and this is where it gets rather abstract and theoretical – reflection can be one set of desires and goals talking to another, via the Executive Ego, which has to manage their bids for gratification like a judge and referee. And there is always the strong possibility that the referee is being misled. Scratch the surface of high-minded and legitimate needs and you may find more selfish and earthy desires.[31] A leader is likely to pass over the uncomfortable truth that her so-called bravery stems from a need to look attractive and be popular. As evolutionary scientists have shown, the mind deceives itself for a very good reason.[32] It is much easier to carry off a credible performance if we believe our stories.

A lot of self-talk that goes on in our heads is an attempt to find a way through the contradictory tangle of our desires. People searching for their "real" Selves are on a similar mission to map this territory – to figure out which goals serve their vital interests.

Leadership Willpower – The Battle for Control

Willpower is a distinguishing feature of many successful leaders – the ability to withstand hardship and practice self-denial whilst leading desperate people, or to bide one's time until the time is right to act – Nelson Mandela is perhaps admired for his raising this to the highest level. Lee Kuan Yew, like Mandela, was also blessed with a natural ability to maintain an iron discipline; just as George S. Patton and Steve Jobs were unable to restrain their passions.

Willpower is the task of the Executive Ego, at the top of the model. Roy Baumeister, a scholar who has devoted more study to its workings than almost any other, likens it to a mental muscle that has limited capacities.[33] It is hard mental work to persist with a difficult task; to hold temptation at bay; to make sacrifices for long-term benefits; to ward off distracting thoughts; to stick to one's beliefs by standing out against the resistance and disagreement of others.

Ego strength is clearly a prime leadership virtue, and we have already seen many instances of it. Baumeister and colleagues point out that although we differ enormously in how easy we find it to exercise willpower, we are all vulnerable to it being weakened – "depleted" as they put it. Competing demands, stress and physical tiredness can all sap our ability to plan, control, persevere, self-deny and do difficult things.[34] For this reason, leaders need to keep themselves in good shape physically and mentally. Failings in self-regulation can be fatal. The mighty Gucci empire was shredded by a series of self-indulgent conflicts amongst its family leaders.[35] But, on the other hand, you can take too much care of yourself. Jimmy Cayne, CEO of Bear Stearns

– "a dope-smoking megalomaniac" according to one associate[36] – was away playing championship bridge when the firm's hedge funds collapsed at the height of the financial crisis.

One of the most enigmatic and powerful leaders of our times has been the German Chancellor Angela Merkel, at the time of writing probably the world's most important leader in terms of her capacity to influence the global economy. Her life and her politics have been the purest expression of achievement through self-control.[37] Female, diminutive, from the former Communist East Germany, daughter of a strict Lutheran, a practicing scholar with a Doctorate in physics and chemistry, she rose steadily through the mired politics of post-unification Germany to become leader of the largely Catholic, male, Western-oriented and conservative Christian Democrat Party, and subsequently, in 2005, became her country's leader; a position she has held securely to the time of writing.

Her leadership style is quiet, intimate, cautious, dogged and thoughtful. She is intensely reflective, hard to read and seemingly extremely difficult to influence. Highly intelligent, she listens, analyzes and takes her own counsel. Twice married and childless, she has no particular political intimates, yet she is widely revered and respected – though hardly loved. She is a somewhat distant "Mutti" (mom) of the nation. For most of her term of office she has been at the eye of the most serious economic and political storm of our times – the Eurozone debt debacle. She has been beset by pleading voices – from the southern European leaders pleading for succor from German coffers, and from economists and politicians much closer to home, including the US president, urging her to moderate her austere, disciplined and unbending stance. She has resisted all. Every step she has taken through the crisis has been incremental and calculated.

Not every leader has such self-mastery. In Merkel's case many of her political opponents and some of her friends might wish to see another side. The question is: when is such control what is needed? There are other times and other leaders where a more spontaneous and creative leadership style is called for – in the Duke Ellington mode perhaps. Yet, the records of business and political history are strewn with leaders who failed the willpower test.[38]

One thing we may ask of all leaders is where do they have fun and relax? Obama has his family, basketball and, no doubt, a range of other pleasurable escapes from the burdens of office. Some leaders meditate, play chess, go to the gym, play golf or listen to music. These are all restorative and essential to stop one going crazy with wall-to-wall leadership. The Executive Ego needs respite. Indeed, we invent many activities just to achieve this. The Ego itself flips between goal-striving states and periods of reverie, when it can luxuriate in the moment.[39] These can be cultivated healthily, and the best leaders know how to maximize their mental resources by nurturing them. Many of the worst bosses in the world seem to eat, drink and cohabit with their jobs. The reason many family businesses fail is because their founders and owners have nothing else in their lives and refuse to let go, even when they have become unfit to lead. Henry Ford was just one of a long line.

When Tony Hayward of BP gaffed that "he wanted his life back" at the height of the Deepwater Horizon crisis, it was grossly insensitive to the 11 men who had tragically died in the accident. But, at another level, you see where he was psychologically, and understand the sentiment. He spoke what he should only have thought, but it did show him to be a normal guy. We want our leaders to be superhuman, of course, but we must allow them to be human, so long as it doesn't cost them or us too much.

Visions of Reality – The Battle for Truth

Vision is a leadership buzz word. It refers to the "might-be" worlds of future promise that hopeful followers want to hear. But to take followers on a journey to B, the leader needs some idea of where A is. As we have seen, this is not always a simple matter.

From a leader's point of view, there is a lot that is self-evident and uncontroversial in how people around her see the world, although, as we have said, it is the leader's role to see more deeply than others the nuances and the clues to an unfolding reality. We have noted that this requires an active strategy of attention and investigation. The leader also needs to understand that the subjective aspects of reality are all-important – the completely different value people place on features of the world, and how much we all live in a reality shaped by beliefs before facts. Yet, individuals differ greatly in how much they focus on the subjective vs. objective. There are those who live in a moral universe of good and bad acts; heroes and villains. This group would include many politicians and religious leaders, such as George Bush and Benazir Bhutto. Others – engineers, finance chiefs and many CEOs – live in a world that is all bloodless calculus and problem-solving.

In terms of the map of the Self that we have drawn, we can also see leaders differ greatly in how they absorb perceptions of the world. They extend between two poles:

Pole 1: The leader is fearlessly dedicated to facing up to realities, however harsh, and dealing with them, i.e. the leader's goals are heavily dependent on her distillation of what is going on in the world.

Pole 2: The leader is driven by a desire to reach certain outcomes and she will view reality, and encourage others to do the same, in whatever way is most compelling and motivating to support that vision.

By the way, there are also leaders who have a fundamentally impoverished view of the world – accepting what is passed down to them. Their focus is on following routines others have handed them. "I was just following orders," they protest when caught doing something wrong or stupid.[40]

Steve Jobs

Steve Jobs was a man whose mind was burning with visions, not of the world as it is, but as it might be. These were so tangible to Jobs, and he was so gifted in the arts of influence and sales talk, that he was readily able to get others to inhabit his dream world and, against all odds, bring it into being. This was not infallible and Jobs's mature life up to his untimely death in 2011 can be seen as a heroic series of battles with reality, some of which he won, and some he lost.

But a "reality distortion field" like his has its limits. For example, he firmly believed that his austere vegan – at times "fruitarian" – diet immunized him from body odor and the need for regular bathing. Braver colleagues periodically would give him a friendly nudge: "Steve. Do us a favor. Take a shower." In fact, throughout his career he had friends, especially women, who would remind him of the damaging effects of his unrestrained habits. But Jobs went through life with the attitude that the normal laws of conduct were suspended for him. He also – correctly, one might say – adhered to the view that the future is there to be invented, not predicted. His "reality distortion field" is what one sees in many charismatic leaders. Their gift is their belief in their own visions and their ability to get others to share them. Without such deluded visionaries, we would still be in the Stone Age.

Although he had a pretty monstrous ego, from an external point of view, Jobs wasn't a self-regarding egotist. He simply believed he was special, which, of course, he was. Another case of a self-fulfilling narrative perhaps. A telling incident was his agonizing over whether his or the actor Richard Dreyfuss's voice should be used in the award-winning "Crazy Ones" ad in 1997.[41] At the last moment, Jobs opted for Dreyfuss on the reasoning that this was not about him but his beloved Apple. Indeed, one can see how, for Jobs, his ego was an extended entity, residing more in his creations and ideals than in his personal being.

Jobs didn't seem to want to spend too much time reflecting on who he was, though he was intensely curious about his origins as an adopted child. Nor did he give a damn about what others thought of him, with some notable exceptions. He didn't completely lack insight, joking about himself as a "difficult" person, which undoubtedly he was, yet he was always a willing showman, ready to project himself on to the largest stage. His self dynamic was that of a man guided by his beliefs and instincts – his creative asceticism especially – more than by any fixed ideas about himself. Perhaps the most important part of his "story," though, was a sense of destiny: a belief that he was "special" (so his parents always told him), that he would change the world and that he would die young.

This is clearly a good story, for it turned out to be true – as with all compelling narratives, it had self-fulfilling elements. Jobs's beliefs were part of what sustained him through hardship, opposition, negative feedback and other setbacks. We might even conclude that this kind of goal-commitment is a necessary condition for great achievement, but it is not a sufficient condition. History is littered with glorious failures who believed they could bend reality to their will. Jobs was lucky to be able to fulfill the Leadership Formula: to be the right person, in the right place, at the right time, doing the right thing with the right people.

Felix Martensen

This name will not be known to you, but he is a real person[42] – the CEO of a large technology company operating in most countries around the world. He runs one of its largest markets in Asia. Of all the executives I have worked closely with, Felix is one of the most unusual, because he defies so many of the stereotypes of leadership, yet has figured out exactly how to fulfill the Leadership Formula.

When you enter a boardroom, it is normally instantly obvious who the leader is by people's body language and the bearing of the leader. Not so Felix, a quiet, quizzical, cool Dutchman, super smart and a real industry expert with a background not in engineering, the natural training ground for many leaders in his industry, but law and economics. I met him while he was leading another technology company, which subsequently sold out to a Middle Eastern group, before Felix moved on to his present position, in one of the world's most complex and demanding markets.

Three incidents tell the story of his style. The first was when I met him, where he opened up his board to a workshop that involved sharing their own detailed personality profiles along with other data. I have done this many times, and, although leaders' profiles are as different as fingerprints, they have common themes in most Western organizations: dominant, somewhat detached, tough, driven individuals. There were a few of these in the group, but not Felix. His profile marked him out as the least conventionally "leaderly" person in the room: cool, detached, modest, laid back and non-dominant, and decidedly democratic in his style. Felix was quite unfazed by the data and cheerfully shared his profile with his colleagues. Yes, he was a self-effacing, non-dominant, un-egotistical, democratic guy and yes, they all knew it. Indeed, it was apparent throughout the workshop that Felix was obviously not a very controlling CEO, leading from the middle. How did he achieve this?

As I got to know him, several things became clear. One, he was highly intelligent and industry savvy. Two, he held strongly to analytical reality principles – a dispassionate reader of people and situations alike. Three, he would dig his heels in once he had made a decision, because, for him, it was based upon an error-free reading of reality. His style was remarkable among CEOs for its freedom. He seemed to be untroubled by any ego concerns and neither was he wedded to his goals if his reality principle ordered them to be re-jigged.

He loved the workshop and, some months later, asked me to facilitate his top team retreat. Although I was getting to know him, again he amazed me right at the outset by saying, after a few pleasantries, "Over to you, Nigel." Of course we had discussed what might happen, but my assumption was that he would lead discussion and I would facilitate, and here he was asking me to do both. It proved to be a remarkable meeting, making three huge decisions about the future of the company, and in which he did turn out most definitely to lead, but in his unique way. He would come into each discussion, usually when it was well under way, with a considered synthesis of the material before the group, outline options and stimulate a discussion. His preferred outcomes were usually apparent, and thus inevitably carried the day based entirely on their reasonableness, not because of the power of his position.

The third example of his leadership style was his strategic approach to his new company in Asia. His departure from his previous position was very coolly taken, without rancor and entirely rationally, on the argument that his style would not work with the new, more passionate and romantic style of the new Middle Eastern owners. Being headhunted to the Asian company, where just such an emotion-led culture had held sway, was a deliberate choice to lead a transformation. This he did by a highly reasoned assessment and analysis of the market challenge and the existing talent, resulting in a plan that restructured the business and the roles and responsibilities of the executive team.

At this point he called me in to facilitate the top team retreat to consider the plan. It was bold and risky, since I did not know the people – a mix of local and Anglo-Saxon talent at various career stages – and the plan was creating major shock waves. Felix's predecessor had been a charismatic local man, and the contrast with Felix was challenging. From my pre-meeting interviews with them, there were a few astonished and angry people at the temerity of such a massive pre-empt by the new leader. Felix played it perfectly with total openness, clarity and flexibility about implementation issues. Throughout the workshop the mood changed – conflicts erupted and were dealt with coolly and correctly. People felt they understood each other better and began to figure out how to make the new structure work. Most of all they began to appreciate the straight-talking, egoless, rational style of their new Dutch leader.

The outcome was the transformation of the business and steady replacement of the non-local members of the top team with local talent. The company started to perform spectacularly well from its new platform and the new Asian leadership team found itself growing in confidence, autonomy and teamwork under the new empowered regime Felix had ushered in.

These two cases stand at the poles of a continuum of perception-based leadership from Jobs, where vision is reality, to Martensen, where reality is vision. For both of them, "seeing is being." It is worth returning to this truth, for the leader who can command people's perception has ultimate power for as long as she can do so. Yet we know that, although perceptions have the force of reality, they are still just perceptions. The world is not just a miasma of persuasive delusions.

"I" Meets "Me" – the Battle for Identity

Different though they are from each other, what these three leaders have in common is that they were not fixated on themselves – rather on the worlds they inhabited. As we move to the right side of Figure

13.1, we find a different kettle of fish. We have already encountered leaders such as George S. Patton, who inhabited their skins as costumed heroes. For many of them, the Self is huge, contested and problematic. As Mark Leary, in his *Curse of the Self*, noted, people torture themselves with doubts about their worth. And as another far-sighted psychologist, Dan McAdams, noted in his book, *The Redemptive Self*,[43] it is an almost indelible strand in the American psyche to believe that the Self is a battleground in which to triumph. It is hard to know what plagues leaders in the hour before dawn, but it is a sure bet that many of the consequences that arise for their followers and the world they inhabit come from the leader's internal battle for identity.

It was the great American psychologist William James, over a century ago, who first drew the distinction between the "I" – the Executive Ego – and the "Me" – the picture of ourselves that we construct from experience, memory and reflection.[44] Our stable idea of ourselves is a comfort for us and those who love us. It is a concoction of images and narratives that serves as a reference point, a compass and a source of gratification and heartache. It grows as we grow – as we learn about our preferences.

But again, people differ enormously in how much they attend to it. As we have seen, someone like Steve Jobs, although a powerful personality, was hardly egotistical, despite his reveling in personal showmanship. Many leaders spend little time navel gazing but live in a world of action. Yet, action does not always quiet the clamor of the Self for certainty and ease. Earlier we met George S. Patton. He was one of a breed of leaders who are driven by their sense of themselves – their beliefs about their identity and mission. A student of the classical era, and its military history in particular, he came to believe in himself as the reincarnation of some unspecified early hero. As a dyslexic but highly intelligent man, one might wonder how literal that belief was. It hardly matters. Patton saw himself as a man on a heroic mission from God, waiting for destiny to call him, yet plagued by self-doubts and depression, so intense was his sense of Self.[45] He first distinguished himself as a derring-do fearless warrior in a raid on the Mexican Pancho Villa's rebels, and again towards the end of

WWI, leading a tank division with huge purpose and aggression. He spent the inter-war years perfecting his skills as a cavalry officer and student of tank warfare, which he came, correctly, to believe to be the central element in a multi-force approach to offensive power. But peacetime found him frustratedly cooling his heels waiting for live opportunities to put them into practice. Even during WWII when he was kept with the reserve forces, he was an attack dog straining at the leash.

But in any command situation he created and maintained an iron discipline, a strict dress code and relentlessly high standards in all operational matters. When engaging with the enemy, Patton would lead from the front, striking terror into the hearts of his enemies; showing no quarter and never pausing, other than to fire before moving forward again. If he found men sheltering in fox holes, he would beat them back out on to the field of fire. The Patton attack machine became the most feared in the whole theater of war.

The Patton vision was so powerful that it sucked up everything and everybody in its path. No one under his command could escape its force. Indeed, it was this that led his more moderate junior colleague, Dwight B. Eisenhower, to overtake him in command and then have to restrain him, much as one might muzzle a half-trained Rottweiler. Patton died just after the war's end – tellingly, in a shooting accident – which was probably a blessing in disguise, since it would be hard to imagine him surviving through retirement as a genial old general, subsisting on his war stories and reminiscences.

Everything that happened to Patton passed through the powerful mesh of his beliefs about himself. Could he have altered that filter? We noted earlier that the self-concept is perhaps the only part of the "Q" factor in the SPQ framework – the leader's qualities – that can change radically and suddenly, but that turns out to be a theoretical rather than an empirical truth. Yes, it is possible that Patton could have got some kind of religion that changed his view of himself into a pacifist vegetarian poet, but not at all probable. People do have experiences of radical conversion, but the appearance of change is greater than the reality – the core "Q" factors remain unaltered.[46] You may be able to stretch your self-concept somewhat, but if you go too far from what is instinctive to you, it will become dangerously delusional. The upshot is that anyone who is strongly "traited" will have a range of possible Selves that they can change in and out of, like a wardrobe, but for most, the choice of identity will be a restricted range.

One's sense of one's Self is thus subject to inputs that amount to the reliability and consistency of thoughts, reactions and impulses.[47] If you are a flexible, relatively untraited[48] individual, then you will happily adopt whatever roles are handed to you. Many great actors are like this – rather mild and uninteresting in private, but quite compelling once they put on their theatrical costumes.[49] Actors with strong egos have a much narrower range of options, and have to work harder to suppress their characteristic impulses.

Here are some leadership examples. They are all variants on the theme of leaders who, like Patton, created the world in their own image and brooked no opposition.[50]

Henry Ford: Strong-willed, domineering father and dogmatic business strategist; perceived his own son and grandson as extensions of his ego, destroying the former and losing out to the latter in an old-stag–young-stag head to head in the boardroom.[51]

Margaret Thatcher: Early in her life she adopted from her father, a shopkeeper and local politician, the crusading defense of corner store entrepreneurship.[52] This she carried into government to destroy the protectionist culture of trade unions, the civil service and big business. Her instincts for transformation continued way beyond the tolerance of her people and even most ardent party supporters, who cheerfully and tearfully but respectfully let her glide into retirement.

Al Dunlap: Nicknamed "Chainsaw" for his ruthless conduct of business, he cultivated a tough guy image and invented a story of the hardships of his life, at odds with the facts of his comfortable middle class upbringing.[53] He promoted this image through writing, speeches and, most devastatingly, his disastrously destructive management of people and organizations.

Benazir Bhutto: The first woman Islamic political leader (she was PM of Pakistan from 1988 to 1996), assassinated in 2007 in the run-up to elections, was a charismatic, reforming and controversial figure, whose own father and two brothers had been assassinated before her.[54] She, her mother and her husband had been imprisoned intermittently. She externalized her sense of destiny. "I didn't choose this life. It chose me," she said. Her vision of her role as a destined figure – "I am a symbol of what the so-called Jihadists, Taliban and al-Qaeda most fear"[55] – for her ruled out any possibility of the life of a normal woman and mother. She bent her immense will to her idea of herself as a fighter, never betraying her emotions in public and refusing any opportunity to take any safer course. It looks close to the martyrdom of the Self.

Michael Maccoby[56] has written about narcissism as a personality trait that infects many leaders, and the costs it imposes. Yet, despite their competitive selfishness, Maccoby is right to admit that history owes much to their efforts. The key point here, though, is how easy it is for leaders to become imprisoned in their identity: their track records, their images and the words spoken about them leave them fewer escape routes than ordinary citizens, who don't have to play act and take themselves so seriously. So, the question is: when is it good, or even possible, for a leader to change their idea of themselves? As the SPQ framework tells us, this can be a critical success factor in a leader's striving to be adaptive, but it remains one of the least likely outcomes.

What It Takes to Lead – The Battle for Performance

At the foot of our Self model, we have the element that might seem to be the most critical – action. Earlier, we talked about the challenge of shot selection, which, in a way, is the easy part. The harder part is how to free ourselves from what we have in the locker. By that I mean our familiar bags of tricks – our habits, routines and heuristics.

Heuristics – "rules of thumb" – are especially important. As we noted earlier, we have mini libraries of these.[57] Evolution via culture has already stocked us up with several – such as many of the routines of greeting and interaction.[58] Life teaches us many more, and we tend to hang on to the ones that have worked for us in the past. This may not always be so smart. Enlarging and amending one's stock of practiced behaviors and tactics is something we might expect every effective leader to do. And we may be disappointed by how so many are insulated by not having to – inertia resourced by the buffer of power.

Yet, there are many leadership action junkies who are actually dominated by this realm, i.e. they care little for their self-identities or about the world.[59] Many of them are glorified technicians. In such domains as engineering, IT and finance, there are plenty of colorless leaders who rejoice in acts of execution, whilst being relatively uninterested in what is going on in the world and relatively interested in their Selves.

One such, who was not at all gray, was the boss of the UK's Royal Bank of Scotland, Fred Goodwin – "Sir" Fred Goodwin until the British Government stripped him of his title for leading the bank to massive failure and debt, which the Government bailed him out of. Born into the Scottish working class, and the first of his family to go to college, Goodwin had a meteoric career from accountant to auditor to banker.[60] With forensic intelligence, determination and single-minded focus, he transformed a small, regional bank – briefly – into the largest bank in the world after a succession of deals culminating in the acquisition of the Dutch Bank ABN-AMRO. This was the deal that destroyed him – conducted on the wrong terms at the wrong time by the wrong man, according to commentators.[61] He was the complete inversion of the Leadership Formula.

Just before the wave of the financial crash broke and brought the whole house tumbling down, I interviewed him. I quizzed him about his views on leadership and how his career had taken shape. His response was interesting. He expressed no sense of direction from his goals other than to succeed in whatever task was in the forefront of his attention. He had no particular orientation to banking and no concept of himself as a leader. He claimed he was just someone operat-

THE "I" OF LEADERSHIP – INSIDE THE MIND OF THE LEADER

ing instinctively on whatever challenge was in his viewfinder. He told me that his weekly routine with his top team was to examine all the deals available and choose those that would enhance the firm.

Here is leadership as action personified. He built the firm through moment-to-moment deal-making, just as he had built his career, and in the process created an organization in his own image. RBS was famed for its execution and it had a slogan to match – "Make it happen." It basked proudly in a proclaimed identity of being the bank whose strategy was not to have a strategy.[62] Goodwin became a vilified figure, but it is sobering to reflect that his style – obsessive, pragmatic, laser-like in its attention to detail, impatient and laden with self-belief – had infected the culture of the firm and propelled RBS into the top rank as a business of its times.

The crash of 2008 was comprehensive – and the Goodwin model was an absolute disaster in the new era of strategic intent, risk management and value-based leadership.[63] We need not dwell on this, though this sad story is a testament to the adage that history is not written by the losers. It looked like hubris, but Goodwin's overreach had two roots in the model we have been looking at. One was that his uncomplicated self-concept was entirely subordinated to his goal of success. He believed, and had learned from experience, that whatever he wanted he could make happen and succeed. He was undisturbed by a need to maintain his self-concept. People were generally scared of him and that was sufficient. He seemed not to care about their opinions of him, nor did he spend much time engaged in introspection.

Second, he was also careless of reality, believing he could shape it to his will. In conversation with him, I asked him how many emails he received a day. "None," he replied, "everything comes through my personal assistant." I was reminded of Richard Nixon, another leader who lived in a sealed-off world, shielded by the twin guard dogs Erlichman and Haldeman.[64] In Goodwin's case, the channel was not even a source of advice but a humble PA. Of course, he received tons of data that he analyzed obsessively, but that is not reality. Leaders need to do more than act; they need to reflect and find a narrative that works.

IMPLICATIONS AND OBSERVATIONS FOR LEADERS AND ORGANIZATIONS

We have come to the deepest mystery around leadership – what goes on in the leader's mind that makes them who they are, that shapes what they do. The Self has real importance, though it is hard to pin down. Key observations were:

- The Self is dangerous territory – full of traps and delusions for leaders. They need to tread carefully and confidently. Some leaders hardly engage in introspection. Most of the time that's probably not such a bad thing, but from time to time to do so is essential, to avoid putting everyone at risk.

- Some leaders need a lot of help to control themselves – it is not a sign of weakness to call upon active support.

- Leaders need to revisit their goals continually and not take for granted the "why" of what they do.

- Leadership is tough – it can drain one's purpose, constancy and control. Leaders need to take care of themselves physically and mentally and avoid distraction, temptation and depletion.

- It needs to be kept in mind that people have very different ways of handling reality – leaders should not assume others are at all in the same world.

- Being wedded to a strong sense of Self is seen as desirable in leaders, but it can be a trap and leaders need to leave ajar some doors for revision or change, at least.

- It is easy to become over-reliant on a tried and tested set of routines, heuristics and other action–belief systems. Keep the larder freshly stocked.

− 14 −

GAMES LEADERS PLAY − FINDING THE NARRATIVE

The girl who can't dance says the band can't play.

Yiddish proverb

THE INVENTED SELF: WHO AM I, REVISITED

My favorite movie of all time for sheer seat-gripping entertainment is Christopher Nolan's 2000 masterpiece *Memento*,[1] which opens with a man finding himself holding a smoking gun in one hand, standing by a recently slain corpse, and in the other a Polaroid snap of the dead man bearing the name "Teddy," in his own handwriting, and the legend: "Do not believe his lies." This is the start of a fast-moving narrative told in reverse sequence, moving backward in time so that each scene makes partial sense of the scene just viewed. The central character, Leonard, we quickly learn, has, through his trauma at the discovery of his wife's rape and murder, lost his capacity to retain short-term memories. Poor Leonard, therefore, has, every moment, to reconstruct his story from the time of the trauma and his fight

225

with her assailants. For plot convenience, his memory span is 30 seconds. It is like an undemented variety of Alzheimer's disease. He is continually reawakening to contemporary reality as if he had just landed in it. At one point, we see him standing in a room – where is he? He quickly discerns that it is a motel. It is evening. He starts to undress before a large wall mirror. Unbuttoning his shirt we – and he, of course – see for the "first" time his torso, emblazoned with tattooed messages in reverse writing reflected in the glass. He has made his body a memo pad to remind him about his mission of vengeance.

He also (re-)discovers a journal and bunch of Polaroids helpfully annotated to prompt him on what is going on in his memory-less existence. His duty of revenge is thus continually impressed upon him anew. But, as the movie proceeds, it cleverly inserts doubts into the viewer's mind about what he is really up to. What is the truth? How much is a construction? How much of his behavior is driven by his primitive needs and goals, almost unsullied by any "Me" other than the one he is continually reconstructing? The question of what really happened, one realizes, is almost immaterial to the urgency of the behavior it justifies. At one point Leonard even says, "Do I lie to make myself happy? In this case, I will."

Leonard is engaged in a constant struggle to achieve mastery over his journey. Lacking the internalized reconstructions of memory, he is forced to rely on external representations, the kit he carries with him. In one way they are more reliable than memory, only they encode beliefs as much as facts. They supply purpose and direction which otherwise would be lacking. The film is a meditation on the human condition of course, for we face the same challenge with how we balance our reconstructions of the past, our images of the present and our beliefs about the future.

Psychology tells us that not only is the past a reconstruction and the future a work of imagination, but even our grip on the present is wholly unreliable.[2] There are legions of experimental studies that show that what you detect with your senses is already filtered and distorted by all kinds of processes that flow beneath the surface of your unreliable consciousness.[3] Both the hardware and software of our identity

– our physical condition, sensory apparatus, the stuff we put into our bodies, expectations formed by previous experiences, our wants and needs – bend and warp the digitalized data that stream into our systems to make our experience of the present uniquely our own.

We might agree that external reality exists – but our ability to apprehend it remains a private show that has the special singular feeling to it of "this is mine." This idea is the most poignant aspect of our self-awareness, upon which many poets and philosophers have meditated.[4]

The personal and mutable quality of identity would seem to imply that it is never too late to reinvent yourself, and there are cases of leaders who seem to have done this. Mo Ibrahim, former boss of Celtel, and Bill Gates of Microsoft have both turned themselves into notable philanthropists. That's been a familiar story in American business history. There are more radical cases, especially in politics. We have already described Abraham Lincoln's radicalization by his first sight of slavery.[5] Simón Bolivar, the revolutionary liberator of Latin America, had a similar moment of truth in 1805.[6] Born of wealthy Spanish colonial stock, leaders of Venezuelan society, his eyes were opened by an exiled friend and tutor on a visit to Europe about the reality of Spain's plunder of Latin America. At the age of 22, Bolivar stood on a Roman hilltop and swore to his friend, with tears in his eyes, his commitment to liberate the continent's people, which he duly did, leading an army against the Spanish.

There are limits to self-reinvention. As we have seen, people with strong "compasses" feel things so strongly that no amount of counter conditioning can shake the fact of who they are. We have a big investment in our stories.[7] The longer one has lived, the greater the sunk costs. Steve Jobs claims to have reinvented himself from the epiphany of getting fired from his own company. It certainly set him on a new path and started a new chapter in the story of his life, but everyone could see it was the same old mercurial, controlling, visionary Steve. Being freed from the constraints of the increasingly corporate Apple enabled him to be even less restrained and more venturesome, leading to his success with Pixar and his brilliant second coming at Apple. Interestingly, the same DNA-encoded traits are visible. So, the rewriting is more like drawing a line in the sand than fundamental identity change. We may rewrite the old story as follows, "Well, now looking back, I see that what I was really doing was . . ." and then follows some retrofitting to suggest a degree of unrecognized destiny in earlier paths we have walked.[8]

When people talk about the "real" Self, this is what they mean – they have come to some new conclusion about the meaning of their journey. More on this in the next chapter, but for the moment what we see is people with relatively well-defined profiles continually augmenting the cover story.

THE GAMES LEADERS PLAY

The genius of *Memento* is to remind us how dependent we are on the construction of our own stories and their embeddedness in memory. Psychologists remind us that memory is not a reliable videotape but a matter of continual construction.[9] In the act of recollection, we drag up previous half-remembered material, already embellished with previous cleansing to fit the needs of the moment, and do the whole thing over again each time we recall something. This can become like the conclusion of a round of Chinese whispers, where we have a perfectly meaningful story in which only the facts are wrong! We all have had the uncomfortable experience of finding a presumed solid memory to be seriously out of whack with what actually happened. Now couple this with story-telling and what do you get? A private universe of meaning, that's what!

Story-telling is a hardwired human instinct.[10] Dreaming is a pure expression of it. These are concocted narratives. The mind, raising its awareness to a point close to consciousness, dips its ladle into the cognitive swirl of memory fragments passing through the synapses, and does what comes naturally – it concocts a story, the dream.[11] Story-telling has always been one of the most powerful tools of our species.[12] Non-literate societies depend upon stories to teach, make sense of the world, draw people together, entertain and to impel action.[13] Stories are leaders' most potent weapons. Jack Welch knew this, remarking that his leadership success owed much to the fact that he was Irish and loved to tell stories.

There are two sides to stories that we need to consider. First are the stories that leaders tell themselves to tie their self-systems together. We have already seen that these differ radically; they make a huge difference to what leaders do, and some work better than others at any point in time.[14] The second is the idea that leaders can provide a story for external consumption that is authentic[15] – i.e. integrated with their interior story – and effective – i.e. it meets their strategic purpose, fulfilling the Leadership Formula now and into the future.

Using the framework presented in the last chapter, let us look at five types of self-story that leaders exhibit – five games that can be benign or deadly, but all of which play fast and loose with the illusion we call the truth.

1. Driven by Desire

The dynamic here is the leader who wants something so much that everything is subordinated to it. Risk analysis is one of the first casualties of desire.[16] Unrealistic optimism and minimizing threats are the curse of the addicted gambler.[17] Many charismatic leaders have taken their people into very bad places through their implacable wishes.[18] The Self achieves alignment around the goal (a) by biasing the view of reality in a way that understates hazards and risks, and (b) by boosting their self-belief in their capability of managing risks and outcomes.[19] Many mergers and acquisitions get into trouble because they are driven by the overweening desires of their leaders for glory.[20] Something like this clearly was happening in the disastrous attempt at cross-cultural marriage between Chrysler and Daimler-Benz in 2007;[21] at around the same time, Fred Goodwin was masterminding the largest acquisition in the history of banking, when RBS swallowed ABN-AMRO and nearly died digesting it.[22] Leaders need to take time out for introspection and consider what their desires are doing to them. As we have seen, some lucky ones have a CLR or loving partner who will warn them. But will they listen? One of the dangers of the lonely leader is the hegemony of unchallenged desire.

2. Protecting the Executive Ego[23]

The Executive Ego, that often-overworked servant, looks after itself by taking time out, closing down, getting distracted. It is part of our self-protective biology for lapses of concentration, daydreaming, distractions and dozing off to afflict our best attempts at persistent control.[24] We called this the battle for control in the previous chapter, and leaders know that willpower is one of their sterner tests. Sensible leaders protect their time – sleep well, manage stress, relax with their families, indulge in hobbies and pastimes. Yet, there are many who apply relentless control, even to their escape routes. Heart attacks on the golf course are not unknown. It is a conundrum that self-control needs itself to be subject to self-control. The lock on the fridge is an inferior solution to restructuring one's goals. Self-care matters. The spouse or partner of many a leader has this kind of emotional support for a leader. Margaret Thatcher famously leant on her clubbable, affable and easy-going husband Denis, and made a point of maintaining domestic routines that relieved the pressures she mounted upon herself.[25] One of the reasons for the success of family firms is that their leaders have one or more "Chief Emotional Officers" standing close to the leader.[26]

3. Imprisoned by Experience

Earlier we discussed the battle for truth, and we have given special attention to the Law of the Situation, which urges leaders to interrogate reality. They also have to stand up to it, for the risky game here for leaders to play in the domain of self-regulation is that they become enthralled by experience.[27] This becomes especially dangerous when leaders find themselves chasing a moving target, such as the good opinion of analysts or even shareholder value. Trying to meet metrics you have no control over is to lose sight of what leadership means. It was part of the collective madness that created the late noughties financial crisis, when leaders should have been trying to fulfill their real purpose, which is to create real value for their people. This does not mean pleasing your followers. That is another experience trap – goals and self-concept enslaved to the delight of others.[28] British Prime

Minister Gordon Brown, for the last few years of the Labour Government in the UK after Blair's departure, was reputedly anxious, controlling and constantly trying to please one group after another, to the point where he became regarded as inconsistent, devoid of vision, untrustworthy and mercurial.[29] Many business leaders similarly spin uselessly rather than generating the kind of situation-driven strategies we have discussed.

4. Ego-mania

We have considered leaders whose personalities are too big and noisy to be ignored. They are forced to glory in who they are. Steve Jobs was like that, though not particularly self-regarding. A more dramatic example is Adolf Hitler. He became a theatrical posturer; rehearsing all the stylized routines of his demagoguery.[30] If you distill his long and impassioned speeches, they amount to a hypnotic incantation of permutated assertions: "You are Germany. Germany is great. I am Germany. We are great. We will triumph over our enemies."[31] His vision of the world was the extension and embodiment of his ego – itself a distillation of his constructed image of his nation. The circular reasoning of egotism is the hammer that sees the world as a nail. The leader cares so much about his idea of himself that he subordinates goals and perceptions of reality to that end.[32] Reality may, however, intrude at the last. One of the unforgettable newsreel sequences of the 20th century was that of the beleaguered dictator, Nicolae Ceauşescu, in 1989 standing on a balcony attempting to wave and speak to "his" people. Then you can see the dreadful dawning realization on his face that the shouts of his people are not cries of adulation but of anger, rejection and ridicule. More recently, Colonel Muammar Gaddafi seemed to believe to the last, even when cornered like a rat in a sewer, that he still had the love and respect of his people.[33]

There is a painful and paranoid inversion of this distortion. It is a depressive condition where the person obsesses about their lack of self-worth, defines the world as a punishing place to be and holds to the belief that their action system toolkit is empty of strategies, other than those that confirm their worthlessness.[34] The Self system drives towards internal consistency,[35] in extreme cases even at the cost of well-being.

5. Action Addiction

The world has changed. There was a time when a person was more defined by what they did than who they were.[36] It was enough to satisfy curiosity to say you were an office manager or an accountant. Roles were defined as sets of duties and qualifications that constituted proof of competence. Even leadership was viewed in this way.[37] Leaders were chosen as "natural" successors because of their position in the hierarchy or length of service. The leader was charged with simple challenges – grow the business – and largely unsupervised by supine boards of uninterested shareholders. Who the leader was only mattered to those directly in his (yes, his) line of fire, when they chalked up some notable success, or when they were revealed to be an abject failure. Their eccentricities remained largely hidden. Many of the worst in terms of the misery they inflicted on their workers – such as Vanderbilt, Rockefeller and Carnegie – glorified their names by major acts of philanthropy before they died.[38]

Now, we are intensely interested in who leaders are, so they cannot retreat into their roles so easily, though the old model is still alive and well in some developing economies.[39] Yet some leaders would, if they could, forget about the world and themselves and just get on with stuff. One suspects many do, but have to pretend to be more strategic. We have seen examples. Bill Gates is clearly a leader who loves the doing and the results, but has always been intensely interested in the context of the technologies that obsess him. So it was his CEO, Steve Ballmer, who was tasked with integrating this talent for action into the world of business.[40]

Of all the games, action addiction is the most benign – leaders who do a lot and think little – though it is still often harmful in its consequences. One of the continuing failures of leadership development in our age is the ability of people to get to positions of leadership by passing exams of one sort or another without ever being examined for their fitness to lead.[41]

Let us now see how these games can be moderated and consider some implications for our understanding of leadership.

THE LEADERSHIP NARRATIVE

The journey we have traveled in this book so far is one that connects the widest range of evolutionary history with the most intimate and private mental processes that go on in human minds.

So let us take stock of the argument so far. At the broadest level, leadership is an abstraction – a property of social organization and a process for getting things done through people.[42] It can take many forms, embodying the spirit of its place and time. Within any given context, individuals are selected or step forward to offer themselves up for the role and its responsibilities. Much of the time, how leaders enact their role follows the rutted path of history without seeking to change it. But every once in a while comes the leader who wants to redefine the path and how it is traveled. Indeed, leaders all face choices about how much they submit to or shape events. This is strategic leadership – the decisions people make to enact the role – a topic on which we have meditated at length.

Now, in the last chapters, we have come down to how this is represented in the life of a person and the workings of their mind. Leaders often look pretty much like each other and do similar things, so that they appear interchangeable. Yet, they may come to the same choices by very different sets of mental calculus. This is normal. We happily drive along roads in the same manner as others, but with quite different thoughts, feelings and motives.[43] When that road is leadership, this may or may not matter. It may cost one leader a lot more stress and strain, for example, to stand up and address the troops than another, though the difference may not be visible to anyone but themselves.

We have looked at this in two ways. First is the personal journey of the leader to get to their position – a mixture of Destiny, Drama and Deliberation. These three continually interplay. Much of the time our choices are either illusory or trivial – we just feel as if they matter, because we *need* to feel they matter. That's where the Self reigns – in the space where we evaluate ourselves, weigh our actions, examine our impressions of the world and consider what matters to us. We may live our lives at such a tempo that Deliberation gets squeezed out;[44] which results in the leader who chases events rather than shapes them.

And here we come to the central powerful mystery of leadership: the story, the narrative that connects past – present – future, spells out the fate of leaders, followers, nations and the course of change. Stories are concocted, disputed and revised in the great game of life. Stories become prisons that entrap leaders into ways of destruction. Stories lead people to turn dreams into reality. Think of Martin Luther King, John F. Kennedy, Lee Kuan Yew and Eva Perón. And the humble mid-level manager of an enterprise who is told to be a leader, what hope does she have? A great deal. Everyone needs their own story, otherwise you will just be part of someone else's; turning up for work to be told what your next role is to be in their narrative.

NARRATIVES VS. SCRIPTS: EMMA'S DILEMMA AND THE AGONY OF AGASSI

When researching in the oil industry, I came across a young woman engineer called Emma, who confessed to me her career perplexity. "My problem," she said, "is that everything I'm good at I don't really like; and what I really like I'm no good at." This phenomenon became stuck in my mind as Emma's dilemma. This story is noteworthy because it doesn't happen too often. Mostly, people find gratification in what they're good at, though, as we have seen, the journey to discovery can be long-winded, uncomfortable and challenging. Emma, no doubt, eventually fixed her misalignment through self-directed discovery, but there are people who have less freedom to find their own narrative.

A narrative that someone else hands you is, in the jargon of psychology, a "script."[45] Parents especially, but also teachers, are often inclined to hand their kids scripts about who they are and what they want.[46] This may be harmless observational summary, but it can also be dangerously fueled by the parent's own frustrated ambitions. As

Jung said, "The greatest tragedy of the family is the unlived lives of the parents."[47] Andre Agassi, one of the greatest all-time tennis stars, got this in spades.[48] His Armenian father – who worked on the tennis circuit stringing rackets with great expertise and knew all the players – spotted the precocious potential of his youngest child at a very early age, and thence relentlessly trained him to stardom. The only problem was that little Andre hated it, from start to finish, but was unable to resist the domineering parent.

The story is fascinating because Agassi also cannot resist the rewards of his own talent, and the momentary satisfactions of playing and winning. His life is dogged by this ambivalence, which eventually he resolves in the moving narrative he recounts in his autobiography. The journey is poignant and painful and achieved through a lot of searching self-talk.

In my Biography class, shedding the scripts that have been handed to you by family, educators and employers and writing your own story is a key process. Yet, we should surely be reassured when we are led by leaders who have been on a personal journey that means they can stand before us and give us a true and compelling account of: "This is who I am and why I am here."

THE LEADER'S STORY – CONNECTING IDENTITY WITH HISTORY

Let us look at this in three stages: making sense of the past; evaluating the present; and envisioning the future.

1. **Making sense of the past:** Using the DDD framework, any leader at any level can put together a truthful narrative about their journey to now. It will involve facing up to the moments of serendipity (happy accidents), zemblanity (willed foolishness), missed opportunities, failed choices, moments of truth, turning points and profound learning. It will show the part played by unquenchable drives in the person, irresistible forces in the world and stuff that just happens for no

particular reason. The truthful narrative is one that avoids the melodrama of moral judgment, but looks at who you are with dispassionate self-forgiveness. This can be done in a number of media, by the way, using lifelines, video narratives and mappings through art, and will be elaborated upon in the next chapter.

2. **Evaluating the present:** The stream of consciousness occurs in a singularity of attention. Stuff can pass through it at great speed. But through this channel, of course, come memories of the past and anticipation of the future; we can control, up to a point, which of these fields we camp in. One could even say that the secret of a happy, well-adjusted existence can be found by judiciously flitting between them.[49] This is something that leaders need to master in their communications – *when* and *where* to direct the focus of their followers, associates and external stakeholders. By the same token, psychologists have taken a close interest in the interdependence of thought and emotion. Self-regulation is intimately concerned with the management of mood, and modern cognitive therapies aim to restore a sense of positive self-control to this process – keeping troubling and unproductive thoughts at bay and finding positive lines of remembrance and intention that will give people a healthy sense of purpose.[50]

  Leaders need to command the muscle of the mind to range where it will help them and their people most, to effect positive action or generate a sense of value. Most important in this process is the ability (a) for the Executive Ego to replenish its strength, (b) for images of reality to be examined bravely and, if necessary, challenged, (c) for the "Me" to be regarded positively, freely and without delusion and (d) for beliefs, routines and actions to be reshaped and augmented to meet the challenge of change.

3. **Envisioning the future:** Every leader is, for every follower, a value proposition. Sometimes the value is negative or neutral, but great leaders give their people something enduring. This

will, in one way or another, connect the identity of the leader with a wider set of purposes that have shared meaning. The narrative can be one of reassurance, a call to arms or a promise – but it has to come from the heart.

The leader's story has four elements, each of which may be stronger or weaker at any time or circumstance, for we are back to the "P" of the SPQ framework. The Leadership Formula and the Law of the Situation dictate that the leader's story will be the right one for the time. These are the four connected themes:

1. Who am I and why am I here?

2. Who are we and what do we stand for?

3. Where are we going and why?

4. Why must we change?

Stories 2–4 will be no more than the exhortations of the powerful, unless Story 1 carries conviction. Let me put it another way: people get very cynical about leaders' vision and values statements if they seem inauthentic – if they are not rooted in something fundamental to the leader.

Story 1 is no potted CV, but a selective narrative that shows the leader to be real and human – to use that overworked word, authentic.[51] The leader can do this by recounting a simple experience from her past; a point of learning and meaning, something that explains what she is doing here. People want to hear, "I am not a perfect being. I know my foibles and weaknesses as well as my strengths. I have lived and learned. I have chosen to be here. I came on a journey to arrive at this point, and I want us to go forward together from here, because we have something valuable to do. I need your help to ensure that I get you to where you want to be."[52]

The ideas set out above, around the past and the present, are the springboard for the dive into the future – into the unknown – for, as has been said, the future is not there to be discovered but invented.[53] This is why the leader is not some incidental power but needs to be a trusted fellow traveler. The value proposition of leadership is that we will do something together that changes you, me and the world around us. This is what, in the literature, is called transformational leadership.[54]

Story 2 is the natural extension of Story 1. It is about the purpose, values and learning of this corner of the world that the leader shares with her people – the business entity that the leader can put her arms around. Story 3 is the mission story – where have we come from; what kind of journey are we on; what we are seeking aspirationally and realistically? Story 4 is the story that every group needs from time to time – especially when everyone is getting very comfortable with their own success.[55]

Let's be clear, as the SPQ framework implies, any of Stories 2–4 may be more or less difficult to tell at any point in time. Story 2, the business identity story, may be the hardest to tell in a time of radical transition – post-merger for example – though this is exactly when it is needed most, as a declaration of aspiration. Story 3, the mission story, is hardest to tell in times of great adversity and uncertainty, and again this may be just when it is most relevant. Working with highly stressed banking executives trying to marshal the engagement of their demoralized staff, I would tell the story shown in Figure 14.1.[56]

Figure 14.1: The valley filled with fog

Once you were easy on the hill of A, looking forward to a bright future. Now, you find you have descended into a long and deep valley, and it is filled with fog. What can you do? Three things: (1) know that there is a better place, B, somewhere ahead that you will find, but (2) only if you keep going. You cannot know how long it will take to get there, but your only hope is to keep walking with belief in a better future in your hearts; (3) you are in fog, so hold hands. Together we will come through.

Story 4 is also not what people suffering from change fatigue want to hear, but the change story is essentially one of reframing the present. It says, "where we are now feels like a place of safety, achievement and comfort (like hilltop A) but beware, the future will not be like the past. We have to shape it to our purpose rather than let it drag us to where we have no desire to be."

We have focused on what leaders can do to craft their narrative. That is a great skill, but what about their ability to read the narratives of others? This may be a greater challenge, as we shall see in the next chapter, where we pull together the implications of the "I" of leadership for effective self-control and action.

IMPLICATIONS AND OBSERVATIONS FOR LEADERS AND ORGANIZATIONS

We have been examining the many ways in which the all-important narrative of the Self is constructed. Leaders need to examine their own mental processes and take command of them. Key points from the chapter:

- Moments of truth and self-reinvention are rare but do happen. They can't be engineered, but being ready for change is a prerequisite.

- Too much desire distorts vision. Leaders need to beware of seeing the world as they would like to see it.

- Stress creeps up on you. Leaders need to ensure they have support.

- Leaders can get lost chasing a changing reality.

- Leaders can explode from ego inflation – a degree of healthy skepticism about one's self-image helps to keep you real.

(Continued)

- Being an action man or woman easily degenerates into useless spinning.

- Narratives are essential to coherent leadership – they need to be rehearsed and revised.

- Leaders need to have taken ownership and authorship of their story, and beware they are not carrying the scripts of others.

- Every leader needs four stories – in mind if not in speech – stories of identity, purpose and change.

— 15 —

THE SELF-MANAGEMENT OF LEADERSHIP – YOU, OTHERS AND ORGANIZATION

Men fear thought as they fear nothing else on earth – more than ruin, more even than death . . . Thought is subversive and revolutionary, destructive and terrible; thought is merciless to privilege, established institutions, and comfortable habit. Thought looks into the pit of hell and is not afraid. Thought is great and swift and free, the light of the world, and the chief glory of man.

Bertrand Russell[1]

DISCIPLINES – FROM INSIDE-OUT TO OUTSIDE-IN

We've been on a journey in this book from the broadest vista of history to the intricate spaces of identity. We have provided tools for thought and analysis to help leaders and the led to see what might be going wrong and why, and where to start in achieving adaptive and aligned leadership. In the spirit of realism before idealism that I hope permeates this book, we have not spent our time staring in admiration at the leadership cases here. Realism shows us how many rode their luck, were in the right place at the right time and had terrific people helping them at critical junctures. And then, inevitably, we've also viewed those who fell flat on their faces, some through no obvious fault of their own, where the tide of events turned against them, or where a moment or two of inattention and weakness cost them dearly.

My message is that leaders do not have to surrender to these fates, nor wait for the roll of circumstantial dice to see whether they're a winner or a loser, but rather to take charge.[2] What do you have to take charge of? So far, this has not been a self-help book. Now it is time to consider what disciplines might emerge from our analysis. Let us look at three levels which leaders can command. First and foremost is the Self. Second are other people. Third is the environment: the context that you share with your followers and associates. In each domain there are disciplines that may be practiced to give you your best chance of success.

Disciplines of the Self

Mirror Work[3]

It's a sad fact that the act of looking in a mirror has a negative effect on quite a few people. Why is this? Because it confronts them with the discrepancy between how they feel and how they look. No matter how old we are, we retain aspects of the identity we have carried since youth – so we seldom feel our age, especially as the years advance. To look in a mirror is to remind ourselves of imperfection and mortality. It's worse when you catch yourself on film. You are familiar with the face in the wash basin mirror – the one that fixes its make-up, shaves or adjusts its apparel. Some have an opposite problem – the trap of having movie star looks – where, living in a cage of appearances, they are plagued by the fear that superficial attraction dominates their relationships. Either way, people need to be free of image problems. This is hard when the world obsesses more with your image than you would like. This indignity is something that people with physical disfigurement suffer all too often.

What can we do to avoid image distress? Take down all the mirrors or avoid them whenever we can? Look at them and ourselves in self-critical disgust? That doesn't sound too good. A little mirror work may be therapeutic – to help us free ourselves from self-dissatisfaction and obsession with appearance.

Find yourself a nice space where there is a full-length mirror – at home or in a hotel room maybe. Stand naked or clothed in front of the mirror at maximum distance, and regard yourself dispassionately, compassionately – think of yourself as no more nor less than a self-regarding animal. Now come closer, move in stages, each time taking a new perspective on yourself. As you get to the intimate distance of friends talking, look deep into your own eyes. Smile. Frown. Try out expressions and feelings. Be a friend. Now come closer than anyone except a loved one gets, until you can see the pores of your skin. Lose your Self in the surface. That's all it is. Surface. Beneath the mask is your intangible, yet in many ways more real, identity. After all, you can't do cosmetic surgery on your mind.

The freer you are about your self-image, the easier it is to dress up. Try stuff on. Pose. Yes, the world is easily fooled by appearances, so take care of yours, but don't dress to hide from yourself. It's a game of signals.[4] Send messages that produce the effects you want. You can manipulate mood with appearance. Often, people respond positively to a leader who is looking and feeling comfortable. Franck Riboud, CEO of Danone, the French food and drinks maker, is famous for his casual attire – turning up at meetings of the great and the good in slacks and a woolly sweater. As a man who has always been sporty and active, he clearly feels comfortable in his own skin and disdainful of outward conformity as a value. People like it.

Self-Talk

Take it to the next level. In front of the mirror, get a dialog going between different aspects of your Self.[5] Ask yourself challenging questions: What do you really want out of life? How might you be fooling yourself in some of your beliefs and perceptions? Ask yourself what you might be doing that trades off short-term gain for long-term loss. Ask yourself the Compass Question – asking which aspects of your identity you are investing in and turning to for critical decisions. Consider how you are changing, and how the compass needle of your drives might be shifting. After challenging yourself, praise yourself. Close with a celebration of yourself. What good things can you say about yourself? Imagine you were a friendly ghost or spirit, or a guardian angel, like in the ultimate feel-good film, *It's a Wonderful Life*.[6] What would you say to yourself? In the movie, James Stewart plays the owner of a small town savings and loan business who decides to kill himself because of the ruin his failed business has brought to the people in the community he loves. The angel, an avuncular, chubby, middle-aged man, shows him what would have befallen the town and its people had he never lived. It is a greatly diminished world. Therapists use a similar technique – a "Praise Party."[7] You are invited to imagine all the people who have loved you coming to a party in your praise to say what they appreciate about you. Write them down and ponder what this says about your personal value proposition.

DDD Analysis

Look at your life. Draw a lifeline.[8] Draw a vertical axis line on the left. Half-way down this axis, plot a horizontal line extending to the right. On this line, number the years from 0 on the left to 80 on the right, marking the dates. Along the line, record significant events and the milestones in different areas of your life – color code them if you like, for relationships, work phases and other events. Don't be surprised if some parts – especially young adulthood – are crowded with life events, and other times are dominated by periods of calm, when you were "following the river" quite uneventfully. Now plot a wavy line that goes above and below the horizontal line to indicate your state of fulfillment throughout this journey.

Next, mark turning points. Mark those that happened by Drama and those by Deliberation. Expect more of the former than the latter! Look at the relationship between the fulfillment line, the turning points and your decisions. What does this tell you about your DDD – your personal qualities and the circumstances of your lifestyle

(Destiny), stuff that just happened to you (Drama) and times when you made a choice (Deliberation)? How much in command have you been of your life story to date? Maybe you've had a succession of happy (or unhappy) accidents? Time to take control.

Mark your life into chapters and give them interesting titles, as in a novel – "Lost in the forest," "Waking up in heaven" . . . you get the idea. Now look at the empty space from now to 80 – the unwritten chapters to come. Assuming you make it to that age, what do you want to do with this time? Perhaps you are at a life stage to ask yourself the legacy question – if I were to write my own obituary, having lived that long, what would I like it to say? What might I need to change in my life to fulfil my dreams and my potential?

Deliberation

Start your deliberation by considering how your Self is working. If you've completed the previous three exercises, a lot of the heavy lifting has been done. Let's start at the top of the Self Model in Figure 13.1. How's your Executive Ego doing? How much do you find yourself feeling stressed and overstretched? Do you suffer lapses of concentration; find it hard to stick to things; get distracted; lose energy; give in to temptations? You need to look after this hard-working innkeeper, forever at the beck and call of the world and its wants.[9]

Meditation, chilling out to music, playing sports, reading for pleasure, intimate time with your lover, country walks, pastimes with children, dancing – these are healthy pleasures.[10] They are not time wasted. Demand your calendar admits them. Simplify your work routines and get help to reduce stress and complexity. It's amazing how many bosses, with discretion and resources at their elbows, make a rod for their backs through compulsive do-it-all leadership. As we have seen, this is fundamentally self-defeating.

Now look at your goals. Write them down. What are you up to? What games might you be playing to get what you really want, whilst appearing high-minded? Are your priorities right, or is urgent stuff displacing important stuff? That probably means you are too much a slave to fulfilling the needs and expectations of others. Maybe you're not being selfish enough. On the other hand, maybe you're indulging yourself too much and not putting yourself and others through the hard disciplines that bring big, long-term rewards. Beware of disguised goals and their sneaky influence.

Now look at your idea of yourself.[11] How chained are you to ideas about who you are, or what you believe others think of you? If you've done your mirror work, you may find this kind of questioning now comes easier to you – though it could also be painful. You may realize that you are trying to sustain an image and an identity that you and others don't really believe in. Remember poor Jacques in Chapter 10, the French leader mired and suffering in his inauthentic life. Start to think of yourself as a person of possibilities. Ask the same challenging questions about your worldview – what holds it in place and how it might not be serving you.

As we have seen, these elements are bound together systemically, and it will require a disciplined dialog with yourself, or with a trusted confidant(e), to unpick its dynamics. This, of course, is what skilled coaches and counselors do. They help people see what goals, often hidden, sustain particular patterns of thought, repertoires of action, persistent feelings, ideas about oneself and views of the world. My point is that all of this can change, and may need to change for a leader to grow, adapt and succeed. Yet, it is all anchored in the reality of one's DNA, physical existence and an objective reality – stuff that can't be altered. We can't be anything we want and do anything we want.[12] Even what we believe is only partially negotiable. Yet, small changes in simple causal dynamics – reprogramming unhelpful thought patterns, for example – can have huge beneficial consequences.

Other People – The Power of Decentering

In effect, I am asking leaders to be psychologists to themselves. Not easy. Now let's do something really hard: think about other people. As we have already noted, if you are powerful, people will come to you, be nice to you and not trouble you too much.[13] Like in the song, leaders don't have to bother with people they hate. As Henry Kissinger put it, "The nice thing about being a celebrity is that when you bore them they think it's their fault." Actually, making others do the work

Figure 15.1: What's wrong with other people? Self-centered perspectives

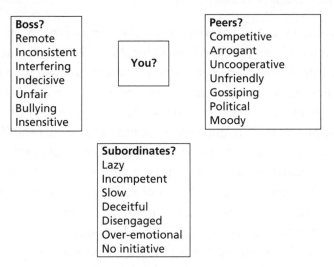

Boss?
Remote
Inconsistent
Interfering
Indecisive
Unfair
Bullying
Insensitive

You?

Peers?
Competitive
Arrogant
Uncooperative
Unfriendly
Gossiping
Political
Moody

Subordinates?
Lazy
Incompetent
Slow
Deceitful
Disengaged
Over-emotional
No initiative

is not a bad leadership strategy. One political leader I know – a woman in a top government post, in command of a ministry dominated by highly technical projects – told me she had learned that when she doesn't understand what experts are telling her, it's their problem not hers, and demands they communicate with clarity. Quite right!

But what about the problem people? The challenge depends on where you are sitting. Take a look at Figure 15.1.

I regularly ask senior executives to tell me about people they find difficult to deal with: bosses, subordinates, peers and clients. Figure 15.1 contains pretty typical lists of the adjectives they give me. This is the kind of language we regularly use to talk about other people. A couple of things are striking about these lists:[14]

1. They are distinctive and different. Although these are words that could apply to people in any of the three roles, we tend to use different kinds of criticism according to their relationship to us – up, down or peer. This is pure self-centeredness. We are critical of those aspects of others and their behavior that get in the way of our achieving our selfish goals. The boss words indicate the ways superiors interfere with or fail to help us. The subordinate words represent failings to cooperate and

perform for us. The peer words are signs of people we don't trust and feel threatened by.

2. These are not words we ever use about ourselves, except perhaps in an ironic, self-mocking, light-hearted and self-forgiving way. The people who do beat themselves up with this language are the clinically depressed, for whom it supplies a closed loop of negativity, the self-fulfilling prophecy of helplessness. This language is second or third party stuff – decidedly not first person. We use it as part of our narratives of explanation, within a moral universe where we want to be in the right and we need ways of making others predictable through our characterizations of them. They represent shorthand ways of blaming others, but doing so in ways that reflect the particular kinds of risk they pose for us – the person who has too much to do and will not deliver on time; the person who will act differently with someone else; or the person who has strong emotions which they struggle to control.

Now if this is what we are doing, it stands to reason that others are doing exactly the same – they are saying this kind of stuff about us! Outrageous! What a miasma of misunderstanding hangs over us all. How could our boss think we're lazy and deceitful; our subordinates consider us remote and insensitive; and our peers believe us to be arrogant and competitive? How little they know us! If they stood in our shoes they would see the truth of why we act the way we do.

If you can do this mental displacement for another person you are "decentering"[15] – climbing into another person's perspective to understand their narrative; their worldview; their morality play of heroes and villains, in which they, of course, are the blameless one. Decentering is a mental methodology of three steps:

1. Look at the behavior that you have just given the third party negative label to, and think about how they would describe the same behavior. What would be their explanation of themselves

and their motives? You can see how their "forthright" and "bold" turns into your "bullying" and "arrogant."

2. Step into their world and imagine the pressures they are under, the goals they are facing and the people they are trying to satisfy. Think about what rewards and punishes them. Use the frameworks we have supplied in this book – SPQ, DDD and the Self Model – to figure out how their mental universe is constructed and what they are trying to do.

3. Figure out where you stand in their universe – how they see you. You might be shocked to awaken to the possibility that you are not so much a benign presence in their world as you might like to think you are. Maybe they see you as a threat to them. In which case, maybe the way you are labeling them is really not helping. It's likely they intuit how you feel about them. This means your view of them might rest on their view of your view of them! Get it?

We can step out of this hall of mirrors by decentering. Elsewhere I have described the decentering method for dealing with difficult people, but it is a universal tool. It is actually a powerful aid to managing all kinds of relationships – with bosses, clients, subordinates, peers and, yes, spouses and other intimates too.

Why don't we do it more? One reason is that we are hardwired to put our self-interest to the fore, and it takes a deliberate effort to realize that it may be in our self-interest to understand other people's perspectives.[16] Another source of resistance is an unconscious fear of losing our sense of the rightness of our position. Yes, that is a risk. If we do this with people we dislike, we may lose the primitive basis for antipathies. Understanding is perilously close to forgiveness! If you are a boss and want to punish someone for a transgression, will it help to see why they acted as they did? Well, yes, actually. The bosses who daren't do this are fundamentally insecure.[17] We are back to the self-dialog. Maybe they need to take a hard look at themselves, as we have recommended.

Figure 15.2: Decentering: the power of perceiving from other positions

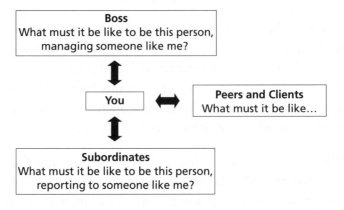

Some of the best leaders are great at decentering. It is often called empathy, but that word has too many emotional overtones. Decentering is much more analytic – a technique especially useful with people we find it hard to empathize with. The advantage of decentering for a leader is part pure Machiavelli – you become like a chess player who can anticipate your opponent's moves; or, more generously, you are better able to help others by reading their minds. Bill Clinton, Jack Kennedy, Tony Blair and Angela Merkel were all notable for their ability to read the emotions of others and engage with them. Many of these deployed their power as a kind of seductive power – making their interlocutors feel like they were truly special.

Figure 15.2 spells out the process and how it should work to create joined-up organization.

Yes, decentering can be used manipulatively, but the real purpose for leaders is to help them read their leadership situation more deeply and accurately, for the most important part of a leader's environment, as we have said, is always other people. It is also about creating the kind of cooperative relationships we discussed in Chapter 11. Decentering can be turned into a method for performance management. It becomes a management version of the couples therapy that recommends each partner thinks about the other "How can I be a better partner for you?"[18] The business version is an exchange – much more powerful than the standard appraisal niceties – where you and your subordinate have the courage to ask each other, "What could I do differently that would help you do your job better?" You don't have to do what the other says, but you sure are better off knowing.

ORGANIZING FOR AUTHENTICITY

Consider the proposition that if we get bad leaders, it's no more than we deserve. The logic of this book is that leaders select and are selected by environments. Not just leaders, but organizational cultures perpetuate themselves by drawing in people who prefer the kind of world they offer. At the same time, humans are versatile animals and we will select shots and adapt our behaviors to fit the environments we're in. It has been said that the people make the place.[19] But the place also makes the people. There have been many classic experimental and observational studies that show how people can be transformed easily by being given roles – like the classic experimental study where students role-played prisoners and guards. The study had to be terminated because the participants became too brutally identified with their roles.[20]

So, the wise leader understands that the act of shaping the world – remember Chapters 7 and 8 – is also shaping the minds and actions of the people in it. When we looked across the history of leadership, we saw how hunter-gatherer democracy produced a high degree of collaborative conformity; in contrast to the naked brutality of warrior kingdoms, where power was concentrated at the top. The experimental studies with monkeys and with humans, mentioned in Chapter 2, underline the point.[21] The adaptive Self is easily manipulated into every kind of behavior.

So the leader's job has to be to have a vision beyond performance. Or rather, to achieve performance requires a vision of how people will work together that is supported by the structure and culture of the organization. We don't have space to review all the options for the design of organizations, for there are plenty: multidivisional; hub and spoke; virtual and boundaryless; classic bureaucracy; matrix form.[22]

Each has its benefits and dysfunctions. The three rules that leaders need to bear in mind in considering structure are:

1. Does it serve our strategic intent? Does it fit our goals?

2. Does it fit its environment? Consider the law of requisite variety that says a system should only be as complex as the environment it's trying to deal with.

3. How does it chime with human nature? What aspects of human motivation does it activate or suppress?

How you organize may seem to be determined by factors beyond the leader's control – technology, for example. For most of the 20th century, car plants were hot beds of conflict, largely due to the alienating nature of assembly line technology, until the Japanese showed us a new team-oriented way of making automobiles and more besides.[23] This example proves that there are many possible ways of organizing that produce the same results, even under unavoidable constraints of technology. Most firms choose a design by copying the most "successful" model out there – until, that is, some innovator comes along and challenges the status quo.

If we can choose how to organize, then let us select ways that do the least damage to the human spirit, and which will bring out the best in leaders and followers.

The pyramidal chain of command – favored by armies, the Catholic Church and other monolithic organizations – has remarkable appeal, for its efficiency and ability to control outputs down the line with a deal of precision.[24] If the top leader has seven direct reports, and each of those has seven, and so on down a hierarchy of seven levels, you have organized an astonishing 823,543 souls in a single structure. No wonder the classic pyramid is popular.

There is another reason we like it: it appeals to our primate nature. Remember the dominance hierarchies we mentioned earlier? They have the evolutionary value of facilitating competition among aspirants to quality, to make sure the winners' genes are the best in town and get the maximum chances of being transmitted through to succeeding generations. The competition for dominance is a boys' game, taking place around a series of tournaments in which the winners get a chance to compete at the next level and the losers lick their wounds and settle for a quiet life.[25]

This is precisely what happens in many corporations. Jack Welch – in his "neutron Jack" phase – perfected a much-imitated performance management system where you keep assessing people and dropping the bottom 10%, in an attempt to keep quality in the gene pool.[26] In most big companies, performance management consists of periodic tournaments to advance people through the hierarchy.[27] But this system only works so long as true value is signaled and measured. This is more or less the case in the animal world, where the strongest and smartest win.

But there are problems with the model in business:

1. Quality is not so easy to measure, and even the most sophisticated methods we use are not reliable. The interview is especially suspect as a measure of quality.[28]

2. A lot of the tournaments are not settled on measurement at all, but someone's subjective judgment, or by a candidate getting enough votes – an election in other words.

3. It is questionable whether we can actually arrange people in a linear pecking order according to their quality. In the human world, multiple qualities count, and it is absurd to reduce individuals to a single quotient (yet, our biology makes that a very attractive illusion).

4. If you promote on performance, you are promoting on yesterday's quality not tomorrow's, sometimes called "the Peter Principle"[29] (people are promoted to their level of incompetence). In other words, qualities only have value to the degree that they fit a situation and meet a challenge (the logic of the SPQ framework).

5. If we really operated a pecking order, people would move down as often as they move up, which manifestly does not happen.

We are operating what I call "a false theory of meritocracy," pretending that superior people hold superior positions. This might not matter if everyone recognized it as a game – a game that boys are especially fond of playing.[30] Except that people do believe it is true, or should be true – an idea that messes up their minds and leads to a lot of bad behavior, including gaming the system. Oh yes, and another not inconsiderable thing: it seriously disadvantages women. Here's how:

- Leaders who believe they are superior will have an attitude of defense and feel threatened by up-and-coming leaders who might beat them down (like Henry Ford and Tom Watson).

- Leaders who believe they should be better than they suspect they actually are, to merit their standing in the hierarchy (the "imposter syndrome"[31]), will try to retain their positions by dysfunctional behaviors. Among these are dominance and fear; overwork and relentless "busy-ness" to prove their worth; and being hard to locate and pin down.

- Subordinates who believe they are too good for their lowly standing in the hierarchy and, specifically, feel they are better than their undeserving boss, are motivated to be uncooperative, will sabotage her at every opportunity and be the first to spot and point out her weaknesses when she screws up.[32]

Much of this behavior and sentiment was reported about Gordon Brown, the #2 to Tony Blair, who considered himself to be smarter than the Prime Minister (probably true), and therefore concluded (not true) that he should be in the #1 slot and spent all the later years of the Blair term of office waging a guerilla warfare campaign of backstairs gossip and malice, and occasional personal confrontation. Blair wearily gave way to Brown, though with apparent misgivings in his mind, following the SPQ logic, that his successor might not be able to satisfy the Leadership Formula. As it turned out, Brown was the right man for the financial crisis that broke during his term, but was unable to grasp or adapt to the broader demands of the leadership situation. He was duly dispatched by the electorate from office.[33]

THE SELF-MANAGEMENT OF LEADERSHIP

Human resource management systems, with their KPIs and elaborate appraisal systems, often sadly do little more than dignify the false theory of meritocracy and the bad practices it spawns. Chief amongst these is the pretense of elaborate evaluation when the final call is the subjective judgment of some senior person or group.[34] In too many organizations there are managers spending 80% of their time "performing" – meeting the KPIs and targets set for them by other anxious bosses trying to prove their own worth – and spending the remaining 20% solving the problems of the people who report to them.

But maybe it's only the very naïve who believe the system works as it pretends to, and that everyone is really just going along with it and gaming the system. Men understand and love league tables – yes, it's in their biology. As we saw in Norah Vincent's *Self-Made Man*, men are very good at cooperating and helping each other, and recognizing when someone else is good. It is not all relentless competition – rather, a readiness to engage in periodic contests when need and opportunity call. Men will often tolerate the authority of an inferior man; if they know it means little and they may get their chance before long.

But women – do they think and act this way? Might they be inclined to believe that false meritocracy could or should work, and get upset if they see someone inferior rising above them, especially another woman? Listen to the voice of Carly Fiorina,[35] who rose to become the world's most high-profile female business leader when she became CEO of Hewlett Packard in 1999. She recounts how, in her early career at AT&T, the telecoms giant, she discovered with horror how managers crudely used the merit system to trade favors – I'll advance your man if you advance mine. She sighs fervently, "I was getting my first glimpse of how prejudice can linger in an organization, and why a meritocracy is so difficult to achieve."[36] Subsequently, she makes the following telling point:

A boss isn't paid more than a subordinate because he or she is better. A boss is paid more than a subordinate because the boss has greater responsibilities.[37]

Dead right, but it is exactly this idea that is subverted by male dominance games. As elsewhere in her book, her idealism shines through. In many parts of this memoir there are accounts of tearful learning experiences. One senses what a masculine and alien world she is struggling in. Her heartfelt appeal for meritocracy is clearly not a call for the false theory, but a protest against the games men like to play. Is there a degree of naïvety in this idealism? Even to the last in her book, where she tells the story of her high-profile downfall from HP, there persists in her narrative an air of bewilderment at events around her and the boardroom putsch that displaced her. One wonders what kinds of social exchanges were going on among the influential males in and out of the boardroom that sealed her fate and why she was so flummoxed by their consequences.

It is tough to be a woman in this male universe, especially one of the few who make it to the top. A disproportionate number have foregone the pleasures of raising their own children to play this men's game.[38] It is no accident that women find their way to the top more easily in the more flat, flexible and collaborative businesses of the digital age, and in family firms where leadership is seen more as an act of service than proof of superiority.

W. L. Gore, Semco, Google and numerous smaller companies and agencies have demonstrated that we do not have to be shackled to the primitive logic of male dominance hierarchy. History has taught us the same lesson. Leaders can change a culture, which means the experience of everyone in an organization, by a comprehensive, integrated strategy. I call it head–body–legs. It's not enough to work at only one level – the body has to function as an integrated whole. Take a look at Figure 15.3.

At the top of the figure, the leader first of all needs a story, not just for herself but for all the leaders throughout the organization – a sense-making narrative that answers the four questions we set out in the last chapter. This is a story about themselves, about the identity of the business, its goals and future direction, and what is going to have to change to achieve those goals.

Second, systems have to be aligned with goals. This means avoiding the absurdities of phony hierarchies and false meritocracies, and finding ways to measure and reward what really matters in this business environment. We want systems that reward people for stepping

Figure 15.3: Leading culture: the three levels of control

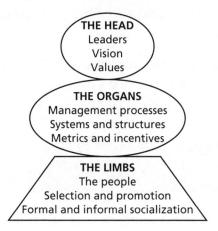

outside the bubble of "accountability" and taking charge – helping your boss when he's in trouble, or your peer when she's struggling – knowing that we should not be judging each other but helping each other to be the best we can be.

Third, leaders have to make tough calls about whom to admit and whom to dismiss from the business; whom to advance and whom to hold back, doing so with the criterion of how able and motivated they are to support the value proposition of the business. You also need ways of socializing new entrants – routines and methods for embedding them in a community of shared values.

And remember, as a leader, you are not there just to "be," but rather to "see" and "do."

I regularly work with a former theater director on leadership programs.[39] He points out that the theater director's job is not to *be* anything – certainly not to be a better actor than any of his cast – but rather to do two things:

1. To turn a bunch of disparate, emotional and egotistical actors into an ensemble, where, regardless of their different reputations and roles, they regard and treat each other as equals in a team dedicated to a single cause – the performance.

2. To coax out of them a performance of quality by continually observing, giving positive feedback and experimenting. Think of Duke Ellington.

This is a great model of leadership. Your job, as a leader, is to see what others can't see, do what others can't do and to be yourself. That's a strategy for seeing, being and doing.

IMPLICATIONS AND OBSERVATIONS FOR LEADERS AND ORGANIZATIONS

At this point, my book has turned into a self-help book, showing how the various frameworks and ideas presented here can be converted into paths for self-improvement. These are to do with identity, reading other people and developing contexts that bring out the best in the human spirit. Key points in this chapter are:

- The Self is a work in progress; it is also a hall of mirrors. Leaders can claim it as their own and take command. This is some of the hardest work a leader will ever have to do. There are truths to be faced; delusions to let go; and narratives to be claimed.

- Leaders can get very comfortable with the wonderful, reliable and supportive people they have worked hard to keep close by them. But the real test of leadership is dealing with the assholes. Decentering is not an elaborate way of letting them off the hook. If you have to administer justice, go ahead, but decentering may open your eyes to what people are really doing, and what effects you are unintentionally imposing on them.

- A lot of organizational misbehavior is context driven – people's rational responses to the demands that are made of them, and the unwitting stupidity of the thoughts that hierarchy and false theories of meritocracy implant in their minds. You can take charge of organizational arrangements that will bring people into cooperative relationships.

- The leader is a culture-carrier. That means working at three levels simultaneously: (i) at the level of you as a leader – what you say and do; (ii) at the level of systems and structures; and (iii) the implicit message you send to the people who drive the organization along. All three levels can be managed and directed.

— 16 —

CAN LEADERS SAVE THE WORLD? VISION, IDENTITY AND PASSION

More than any other time in history, mankind faces a crossroads. One path leads to despair and utter hopelessness; the other to total extinction. Let us pray we have the wisdom to choose correctly.

Woody Allen

What's the point of yet another book about leadership unless it has ambitions? So let's go for it and try to save the world! To this goal, it seems self-evident that we need leaders who can do important and difficult things for us, serving our needs without sacrificing our respect. There is, first off, the question of who the "we" is here – a matter of some importance. One can take a quite localized view of leadership and, indeed, at one level you have to, since leaders use networks of intimates before they can reach out to people they don't know. Here, let us take "we" at its most inclusive to refer to the human species and its habitat, our beautiful blue planet.

We face an unprecedented challenge at the present time. Never before have we had such awareness of the vulnerability of the

259

ecosystems of which we are a part, and the responsibility that lies upon our shoulders for their fate.

If we are to have leaders to measure up to this great challenge, what might they need? V-I-P leadership:

- **Vision** – a coherent, realistic, value-driven view of the challenge.

- **Identity** – a deep appreciation of who they are, and who we are.

- **Passion** – to care deeply about what they are doing and the ability to express that.

All three are needed together. V + I without P is uncommunicative self-absorption. V + P without I is empty sloganeering. P + I without V is egoistic declamation.

Of these three, *Identity* is the lynchpin. That has been the argument running through this book – the need for leaders to be self-aware. They might have moments of doubt, confusion and change, but they are always aware that, without a deeply felt and honest answer to the question "Who am I and why am I here?," they can carry no conviction. There is also a "we" version of this that you can take to the level of species aggregation, and which our world leaders should be able to apprehend: "What kinds of creatures are we and what are we on this planet for?"

If leaders can't live up to this challenge, we're better off without them. So here are five questions:

1. Are leaders necessary or do we need substitutes for leadership?

2. Are we in a new era that requires a new model of leadership?

3. In this context, how can we get better leaders?

4. How can we help leaders to lead better?

5. Can they change the world?

Let's take these as a logical sequence.

DO WE NEED LEADERS?

Are leaders part of the problem, part of the solution, both or neither? The last of these – "neither" – would imply they are a completely irrelevant distraction. The answer "both" is what would follow from our analysis. It also seems that we really have no choice. Leadership is in our nature. We want leaders, so we will have them, regardless of whether they are the best way to coordinate, make decisions or direct activity.

Sometimes they are; sometimes not. It depends upon the Leadership Formula. Yes, if they are the right person, doing the right thing at the right time. This, of course, bristles with conditionals. Perhaps the biggest one of all, which relates to the closing theme of this book, is: is it worth it? Leaders can be effective malignantly. Philosopher Hannah Arendt, witnessing the trial of the architects and operational chiefs of the Nazi death camps, was struck by the "banality of evil"[1] – the workmanlike efficiency and detached carelessness of those who committed these monstrous atrocities.

So there are fundamental value questions to be answered about the "why" of leadership. What is the justification for the goals they are striving for? If we let algorithms and machines make decisions and set directions on account of their impartiality, freedom from emotional contamination, absence of cognitive bias and efficiency, there are accountability problems. We have seen this in financial markets, where mathematical trading models inflate bubbles, such as the credit crunch we saw in 2007. We want leadership to have a human face, even if only to spit in when it lets us down.

There are times when, manifestly, we would be better off without leaders, as you will often hear the public lament when they see venal, greedy, lustful, punitive and selfish leaders running their institutions. We should beware of slipping into a binary view – good/bad vs. no leadership. There are other models that accord a significant role to the collective. Yet, governance by committee is usually a disaster or a pretense (look at communism). In business, there has been some mixed success for communitarian structures.[2] Leadership is not absent or evenly shared in these, for you will not have to look far to find people in leadership roles. Yet, they are subject to the higher authority of council structures.

As the SPQ logic dictates, it is necessary to specify the situational imperatives before concluding whether a model works or not. These models are not good for all seasons. Perhaps the best way of thinking about this issue is to ask what kinds of constraints and influences leaders should be subject to. Then we can enter into sensible debates about which leadership models, along with which varieties of organizational design, are most fit for purpose. What we don't want is leaders who are totally self-reliant without the relationships and influences that can offer a reality check, feedback, extended vision or any of the benefits we discussed in Chapter 11.

ARE WE IN NEED OF A NEW MODEL FOR OUR TIMES?

So what's so special about the times we live in? Quite a bit, actually.

First, through science, we have a new appreciation of how fortunate we are to exist at all. Life is such a rare miracle in the universe – at least from our standpoint on this planet – and it is a racing certainty we will never encounter other intelligent life forms outside Earth. Even to get beyond our solar system is not possible without magical technology. The thought does concentrate the mind on the importance of our stewardship of this precious planet.

Second, we also know that if there are gods overseeing human affairs, they are not much motivated to intervene to stop us destroying ourselves and the habitat upon which we depend. If we are hell-bent on nest-fouling our way to self-destruction, we shall do so, while the cockroaches look on impassively. This is creating among us a stronger mindset and culture of self-control beliefs – that not just our destiny lies in our hands, but also the fate of many other life forms (even the surviving cockroaches will endure greatly reduced income without us). The consequence is the emergence of environmentalist values, and a shift towards a reconstruction of capitalism stressing values other than competitive advantage.

Third, science has become ever-more reflexive (i.e. it applies to us), handing us new empowering tools – for energy management, agriculture, genetics, medical science and psychology. Some of these will help to ensure we avoid some aspects of a Malthusian tragedy (overbreeding and underproduction). It is the psychology that is potentially the most interesting. As we learn about how the brain and the mind function, the alluring vision arises that we may be able, at last, to seize the reins of human nature and steer away from our self-destructive ways.

Fourth, technology and information are transforming communications and manufacturing processes in ways that require quite different ways of organizing – ways that allow for customer-designed services, just-in-time production, mass customization, loosely coupled systems, hub and satellite models and "coopetition" (cooperative competition).[3]

Fifth, culture and community are changing. Let's not write off the village just yet – in fact, the yearning for community is a powerful element of the mix – when social media are making it much easier to find and connect with people of like mind and develop movements in markets and social arenas. Clearly, one of the problems facing us is how we define "us." Nation states engaged in economic competition can result in what has been called "the tragedy of the commons," where each herdsman is motivated to maximize the feeding of his cattle on common ground, leading to its destruction through overgrazing. Fisheries are an area where this confronts us today. Even the EU, an entity designed to solve such problems, struggles to avoid cultural tribalism.

The implication is that leadership is going to have to enact new processes that move us toward new solutions.[4] As our analysis implies, this requires a new kind of leadership.

IN THIS CONTEXT, HOW CAN WE GET BETTER LEADERS?

The prior question to consider is how we get leaders in the first place; then we need to ask if we could be doing better. In Chapter 3 we discussed the main paths to leadership: emergent, hereditary, conquest, elected and appointed, and how they are not all what they seem – all can slip easily into dynastic systems, such is the primitive appeal of legitimacy by bloodline. But if we follow the SPQ logic, we reach the inevitable conclusion that we need to find leaders by different means according to the demands of the time and place.

Emergent leaders are needed in all operational areas of life, and we make far too little use of them in business. We have talked about the remarkable, fluid systems of management invented by industrial family firms, such as W. L. Gore in the USA and Semco in Brazil. Both developed emergent leader models, with a commitment to small business units. Readers may recall (Chapter 6) our discussion of Dunbar's number – 150 – the size below which communitarian self-management can be readily sustained. Both of these firms spontaneously adopted a "small is beautiful" approach to business units. One firm that did this deliberately was The Flight Center,[5] an Australian originating travel agency, which, for a while, enjoyed phenomenal growth based upon its organizational model. This was devised by its maverick leader Graham "Screw" Turner, who read an article on evolutionary psychology and business, which I wrote for the *Harvard Business Review*,[6] and promptly reorganized the firm into "families" (stores), "villages" (clusters of stores) and "tribes" (aggregates of villages totaling no more than 150 people). The model maximized self-management, intra-team cooperation and sharing, and was dedicated to achieving unparalleled customer service, under the slogan "unbeatable."

Yet, we need more permanent leadership models, and the anarchistic ideal of communitarian self-government has never fulfilled people's need and desire for more visible and institutional leaders who can help shape the future through vision and strategy.

Elective democracy has become the political model for our times, and, as we have noted, operates in disguised form in many areas of "appointed" business leaders (election being by boards).[7] Election is a political process – a game of interests – and the elected leader is caught in the familiar duality at the heart of the SPQ model: shaping vs. versatility. The effective elected leader has to play a power game

– balancing her need to be an adaptive servant to the interests of her constituents, against being a person who shapes the agenda. Step too far in one direction and you fail.

There is a further complication in adversarial political systems – one that caught Barack Obama in his first term – the leader who contends for office by virtue of party support and then, on winning, may face demands for payback from the interests who helped make victory possible. Yet, the leader has been elected to represent the commonwealth, which includes minority interests who opposed their election. The stuff of politics, as we observed earlier, is the alignment of interests. Failure beckons on every side, for there are multiple ways in which elected leaders can screw up: disappoint people by not living up to inflated promises, become too detached from their supporters, become captive to a narrow vision, or run away with ego-inflated hubris about their own invulnerability. The advantage of elected leaders is the leash of accountability and possible recall.[8] Yet, once elected, they have a degree of legitimate authority that, amongst other things, can make them hard to get rid of. On this basis, as one can see in multiparty systems, an individual may be put up for election by powerful and shadowy king/queen makers, who prefer to stay in the background while their chosen leader fulfills their silent bidding.

Hereditary leaders offend modern sensibilities, unless they are mere figureheads, like most modern monarchs. Yet, as we have seen, they can be an enlightened solution and often work well in family firms[9] – rising above factional interests as the legitimate servants of the commonwealth. If we could see ourselves as one planet with a common interest, perhaps a king or queen of the world would solve the global challenges we face! Certainly, we need leaders who have the capacity to rise above divided interests, but without the concentration of power that degenerates into the Big Man parodies which have dogged history, as we saw in Chapter 3.

However, it is appointed leadership that most concerns the corporate world. Clearly, this is the only model that can fulfill the SPQ logic completely, so long as it is based upon a balanced appraisal of the needs of the situation, comprehensive and accurate meas-urement of candidate qualities and support for whatever helps the right leadership processes to be enacted. Sadly, we often see firms falling short of this ideal: superficially analyzing the situation, focus-ing on the wrong qualities and failing to be pragmatic about who does what. As we have also seen, corporate tournament promotion systems in hierarchies,[10] closely coupled with the false theory of meritocracy, can mean that all the people we really want to lead us – people with emotional intelligence, integrity and balanced intel-lects – have been killed off or sidelined long before they might become eligible.[11]

This, of course, is not an argument against rationality, but for it. What we need is a true meritocracy, which assesses people on multiple criteria, is far-sighted about the responsibilities to be shouldered and is guided by a vision that encompasses a range of future states. This is possible, and it happens. You don't need crude medieval tourna-ments. Plenty of organizations in technology companies, academia, arts and media and some specialist service organizations find leaders by a flexible and self-aware process.

Enlightened leadership is possible in all these forms – we just need to cast aside our theatrical presumptions about merit and romantic fantasies about leadership and see it as an adaptive process that needs a supportive and strategic framework of the elements we have identi-fied through the SPQ framework:

- Eye-opening sources of insights into one's leadership situation and the workings of the world;

- The courage to shape the world that comes from vision + self-knowledge;

- Knowing one's personal biases, impulses and instincts;

- Tools for self-control and disciplined responses to unexpected events;

- Partnership with diverse people so that action can be regulated creatively.

HOW CAN WE HELP LEADERS TO LEAD BETTER?

Let us come back to the "I" of leadership. As we have said, from the leader's point of view, true effectiveness comes from self-management. On the leadership journey it is necessary to have conversations. Some of the most important are with oneself. We started this book with George Bush's and Tony Blair's interrogation of the sudden flood of thought, feeling and imagery that crashes through the channel of consciousness at moments of crisis. At such times, leaders need their wits about them, literally. At any moment, a sudden revision of goals might be required: a radical recalibration of perceived reality or a new view of how one is perceived by others. There is work here for the Self to do.

Throughout this book, and at the end of each chapter, I have tried to capture practical measures that answer this question: what can be done to give leaders a frame of mind to do the right thing and secure our future. I was recently asked by a news network to give my five principles for good leadership. Any number is ridiculous, of course, so five is as good as any. To conclude, here they are:

1. Be real.

2. Decenter.

3. Build ensembles.

4. Scan and scout.

5. Frame the journey.

Be Real

The "I" of Leadership in the title is to bring the mind of the leader to the foreground, in the belief that we are the only species that can change our destiny by thinking about it. A prerequisite is that we think about ourselves, understand our own psychology and then frame our actions in ways that are strategic for us, our people and context. Our connection with others is hugely important, as is *trust*, the most important value in the leadership lexicon. The leader has to be able to answer the question: "Who am I and why am I here?" with a conviction, honesty and purpose that will create the bond of trust that the most powerful actions require.

Decenter

Everyone is the center of their lives, and therefore the leader needs to perfect the art of taking steps into the minds of others, no matter how uncongenial that may be. There are a lot of big, general tactics leaders need to master – things that have universal reliable effects such as the arts of communication, influence and action – but much of the most important action is in the micro-space of individuals and their relationships. Leaders have to read the minds and motives of individuals with dispassionate decentering, so their interventions can be more nuanced and powerful. They also need to go a step farther and read relationships – ones they are party to, and ones they are not. Within this context, leaders should be mindful of their own needs and use these skills to build the support of Critical Leader Relationships.

Build Ensembles

There is a TV game show[12] where members of the public are given a meager allowance to buy food, which is then given to top chefs who compete to improvise brilliant meals. It is relatively easy to be a great leader if you can hand pick the rarest human ingredients – the Steve Jobs way. But it is much harder to perfect the "ready, steady, cook!" art of leadership – taking the rag-bag mix of humanity handed to you and turning them into a powerful team. Sports coaches, conductors, theater directors and, yes, business leaders have to do this. It is the art of using those tactics that create a super-cooperative ethos where people will really work for each other, and then get an outstanding performance out of them. The great leaders create a world where people feel they belong; where they can do their best work and be valued.

Scan and Scout

Some leaders are naturals at the intimacy of teambuilding and managing people, with the risk that they spend all their time in the locker room with the players. But, however much the leader feels at one with the team, she should remember that she has a distinct role and different responsibilities. No matter how much the team wants her close by, she must manage distance – one of the trickiest dimensions of leadership.[13] She needs to rise above and see what they cannot see – to scan the wider world and the world to come and report back to her people how what they are doing fits in with a wider set of purposes and challenges. This is what her people need from her. She should not come back empty handed. It is imperative that she scout for the resources, talent and ideas that will enrich the enterprise.

Frame the Journey

This sense-making needs to extend in time, for the leader has to connect the past, present and future in a compelling way. She needs a narrative that encompasses her personal journey, the identity and history of the commonwealth and the future possible worlds that, together, they are bound for. To do this, she must be prepared to tear up the past that has made them great – slay the holy cows, dismantle the great edifices and build anew if need be. The past must be honored but not obeyed. It is through the "I" of leadership that history is made.

ENDNOTES

Chapter 1: It Goes with the Territory – Leadership Moments

1. Bush, G.W. (2004) *Decision Points*, Crown Publishing, p. 127.
2. Blair, T. (2007) *A Journey*, Hutchinson, p. 566.
3. See Baumeister, R.F. and Vohs, K. (eds) (2004) *Handbook of Self-regulation*, Guilford Press.
4. Van Vugt, M. and Ahuja, A. (2010) *Selected: Why some lead, why others follow, and why it matters*, Profile Books.
5. McElreath, R. and Henrich, J. (2007) Dual inheritance theory: The evolution of human cultural capacities and cultural evolution. In R.I.M Dunbar and L. Barrett (eds) *Oxford Handbook of Evolutionary Psychology* (pp. 555–570), Oxford University Press.
6. For example, Northouse, P.G. (1997) *Leadership: Theory and practice*, Sage; Heifetz, R. (1994) *Leadership without Easy Answers*, Harvard University Press; Bennis, W. (2009) *On Becoming a Leader*, Basic Books; Yukl, K. (2012) *Leadership in Organizations*, 8th edition, Prentice Hall.
7. For authoritative sources on evolutionary psychology, see Barrett, L. *et al.* (2002) *Human Evolutionary Psychology*, Palgrave; Buss, D.M. (2011) *Evolutionary Psychology: The new science of the mind*, 4th edition, Pearson. For the first book-length exposition of its relevance to business, see Nicholson, N. (2000) *Executive Instinct*, Crown Business (published in UK and RoW as *Managing the Human Animal*, Texere/Thomson).
8. The SPQ framework has been developed over years of executive development practice. The letter order is almost arbitrary – where should one start in a circle of triangular interdependency? Throughout the book as I discuss these elements, the order is not consistent because there is no need for it to be. Sometimes I shall emphasize "seeing" as the point of origin for leadership behaviors (leadership situations) and sometimes being (leadership qualities), when, ultimately, as we shall see, it is what leaders do – leadership processes – that determine outcomes.
9. The model has been introduced briefly in Spisac, B.R., Nicholson. N., and Van Vugt, M. (2012) Leadership in organizations: An evolutionary perspective.

In G. Saad (ed.) *Applications of Evolutionary Psychology in the Business Sciences* (pp. 165–190), Springer.

10. McAdams, D.P. (1993) *The Stories We Live By: Personal myths and the making of the self*, Guilford Press.

11. This actually paraphrases an important insight from what is called perceptual control theory – the idea that behavior in humans and other animals is directed by actions that reduce discrepancies between percepts and goals; see Powers, W.T. (1973) *Behavior: The control of perception*, Aldine.

12. Useem, M. (1998) *The Leadership Moment*, Three Rivers Press.

13. Axelrod, A. (2006) *Patton: A biography*, Palgrave Macmillan.

14. Hogan, R. and Chamorro-Premuzic, T. (2011) Personality and the laws of history. In T. Chamorro-Premuzic, *et al.* (eds) *The Wiley-Blackwell Handbook of Individual Differences*, 1st edition (pp. 501–521), Wiley.

15. Lowenstein, R. (1995) *Buffett: The biography*, Random House.

16. Wilson, T. (2002) *Strangers to Ourselves: Discovering the adaptive unconscious*, The Belknap Press of Harvard University Press.

17. Self-talk is an activity much used by sports people; see Cunningham, S.B. (1992) Intrapersonal communication: A review and critique. *Communication Yearbook # 15* (pp. 597–620), Sage.

18. Biographical approaches to leadership include Gardner, H. (1996) *Leading Minds: An anatomy of leadership*, Basic Books; Mumford, M.D. (2006) *Pathways to Outstanding Leadership: A comparative analysis of charismatic, ideological and pragmatic leaders*, Erlbaum.

19. Sparrowe, R.T. (2005) Authentic leadership and the narrative self, *The Leadership Quarterly*, **16**: 419–439; also, Ligon, G.S. *et al.* (2008) Development of out-standing leadership: A life narrative approach. *The Leadership Quarterly*, **19**: 312–344.

Chapter 2: Leadership in the Wild – The Evolution of Power

1. Isaacson, W. (2011) *Steve Jobs: The exclusive biography*, Little, Brown.

2. Southwick, K. (2003) *Everyone Else Must Fail: The unvarnished truth about Oracle and Larry Ellison*, Crown Business.

3. Bower, T. (1996) *Maxwell: The final verdict*, Harper Collins; also Greenslade, R. (1992) *Maxwell: The rise and fall of Robert Maxwell and his empire*, Carol Publishing.

4. Miller, G. (1997) Protean primates: The evolution of adaptive unpredictability in competition and courtship. In A. Whiten and R.W. Byrne (eds) *Machiavellian Intelligence II* (pp. 312–338), Cambridge University Press.

5. Miller op. cit.

6. See Sebag Montefiore, S. (2003) *In the Court of the Red Tsar*, Weidenfeld & Nicolson.

7. Source material on his early life from Simon Sebag Montefiore, *Young Stalin* (Weidenfeld & Nicolson, 2007); and Sebag Montefiore ibid.

8. London, J. (1903) *The Call of the Wild*, Macmillan.

9. London, J. (1906) *White Fang*, Macmillan.

10. Goldsworthy, A. (2010) *Effective Leadership: Learn from the animals*, Dog Ear Publishing.

11. Mazur, A. (2005) *Biosociology of Dominance and Deference*, Rowan & Littlefield.

12. Self-sacrifice for one's kin is a key insight in modern Darwinism, called "kin selection"; see Hamilton, G.D. (1964) The genetical evolution of social behaviour. *Journal of Theoretical Biology*, 7: 1–52.

13. Zahavi, A. and Zahavi, A. (1997) *The Handicap Principle: A missing piece in Darwin's puzzle*, Oxford University Press.

14. For a complete exposition of these varieties, see Miller, G. (2000) *The Mating Mind*, Heinemann.

15. This "shifting game" is the basis for co-evolutionary processes. See Henrich, J. (2004) Cultural group selection, coevolutionary processes and large-scale cooperation. *Journal of Economic Behavior & Organization*, 53: 3–35; Richerson, P.J. and Boyd, P. (2005) *Not by Genes Alone: How culture transformed human evolution*, University of Chicago Press; Sober, E. and Wilson, D.S. (1998) *Unto Others: The evolution and psychology of unselfish behavior*, Harvard University Press.

16. See Miller (2000) op. cit.

17. Mazur op. cit.

18. De Waal, F.B.N. (1982) *Chimpanzee Politics: Power and sex among apes*, Harper & Row.

19. Ibid; also Goodall, J. (1986) *Chimpanzees of the Gombe: Patterns of behavior*, Belknapp Press of the Harvard University Press; Harcourt, A.H. and Stewart, K.J. (2007) *Gorilla Society: Conflict, compromise, and cooperation*, University of Chicago Press.

20. Tomasello, M. (1999) *The Cultural Origins of Human Cognition*, Harvard University Press.

21. Pierce, B.D. and White, R. (1999) The evolution of social structure: Why biology matters. *Academy of Management Review*, 24: 843–853.

22. Pierce, B.D. and White, R. (2006) Resource context contestability and emergent social structure: An empirical investigation of an evolutionary theory. *Journal of Organizational Behavior*, 27: 221–240.

23. Thomas-Hunt, M.C. and Phillips, K.W. (2004) When what you know is not enough: Expertise and gender dynamics in task groups. *Personality & Social Psychology Bulletin*, 30: 1585–1598.

24. Erdal, D. and Whiten, A. (1996) Egalitarianism and Machiavellian intelligence in human evolution. In P. Mellars and K. Gibson (eds) *Modelling the Early Human Mind*, McDonald Institute for Archaeological Research; Boehm, C. (1999) *Hierarchy in the Forest: The evolution of egalitarian behavior*, Harvard University Press.

25. Hackman, J.R. (2002) *Leading Teams: Setting the stage for great performances*, Harvard Business School Press.

26. Semler, R. (1993) *Maverick: The success story behind the world's most unusual workplace*, Warner Books.

27. The subject of business school cases, and discussed by Gary Hamel and Bill Breen in *The Future of Management*, Harvard Business School Press, 2007; see also W.L. Gore and Associates Ltd., CEIBS Case study, CC-303-008.

28. Meindl, J., Ehrlich, S.B. and Dukerich, J.M. (1985) The romance of leadership. *Administrative Science Quarterly*, **30**: 78–102.

29. Collins, J.C. and Poras, J.I. (1994) *Built to Last*, Random House.

30. Welch, J. and Byrne, J.A. (2003) *Jack: Straight from the gut*, Business Plus.

31. Howell, J.P. and Dorfman, P.W. (1981) Substitutes for leadership: Test of a construct. *Academy of Management Journal*, **24**: 714–728.

32. Van Vugt and Ahuja op. cit.

33. Perrow, C. (1984) *Normal Accidents: Living with high risk technologies*, Basic Books.

34. Ross, L. (1977) The intuitive psychologist and his shortcomings: Distortions in the attribution process. In L. Berkowitz (ed.) *Advances in Experimental Social Psychology*, Volume 10 (pp. 1311–1321), Academic Press.

35. See Nicholson, N. (2005) Meeting the Maasai: Messages for management. *Journal of Management Inquiry*, **14**: 255–267.

36. Lowenstein op. cit.

37. Dunbar, R. (1996) *Gossip, Grooming and Evolution of Language*, Faber & Faber.

38. McDonald, L.G. and Robinson, P. (2009) *A Colossal Failure of Common Sense: The inside story of the collapse of Lehman Brothers*, Crown Business.

39. De Waal, F.B.N. and Lanting, F. (1997) *Bonobo: The forgotten ape*, University of Chicago Press.

40. McClean, B. and Elkind, P. (2003) *The Smartest Guys in the Room: The amazing rise and scandalous fall of Enron*, Portfolio.

41. Goleman, D. *et al.* (2004) *Primal Leadership: Learning to lead with emotional intelligence*, Harvard Business School Press.

42. O'Brien, M. (2011) *John F. Kennedy's Women: A story of sexual obsession*, Now and Then Reader.

43. Gray, J.H. and Densten, I.L. (2006) How leaders woo followers in the romance of leadership. *Applied Psychology: An International Review*, **56**: 558–581.

44. Machiavelli is strong on this point – see Bull, G. (1961) (trans.) *Machiavelli: The Prince*, Penguin.

Chapter 3: A Very Short History of Leadership

1. Kiester, E. (2009) *Before They Changed the World*, Fair Winds Press; Jacobs, W.J. (1973) *Hannibal: An African Hero*, McGraw Hill; and Galsworthy, A. (2000) *The Punic War*, Cassell; also BBC Radio 4, *In Our Time*, October 11, 2012.
2. Kiester op. cit.; Levine, C. *et al.* (2003) *Elizabeth: Always her own free woman*, Ashgate Publishing.
3. Eldredge, N. (1995) *Reinventing Darwin: The great debate at the high table of evolutionary theory*, Wiley.
4. Cziko, G. (1995) *Without Miracles: Universal selection theory and the second Darwinian revolution*, MIT Press.
5. Henrich, J. and Gil-White, F.J. (2001) The evolution of prestige: Freely conferred deference as a mechanism for enhancing the benefits of cultural transmission. *Evolution and Human Behavior*, **22**: 165–196.
6. Schyns, B. and Meindl, J.R. (eds) (2005) *Implicit Leadership Theories: Essays and explanations*, Information Age Publishing.
7. Ryan, A. (2012) *On Politics: A history of political thought from Herodotus to the present*, Norton.
8. Skinner, Q. (1981) *Machiavelli: A very short introduction*, Oxford University Press.
9. Kirkpatrick, S.A. and Locke, E.A. (1991) Leadership: Do traits matter? *Academy of Management Executive*, **5**: 48–60.
10. For a review, see Northouse op. cit.
11. See Hollander, E.P. (1992) Leadership, followership, self, and others. *The Leadership Quarterly*, **3**: 43–54.
12. Bass, B.M. (1998) *Transformational Leadership: Industrial, military, and educational impact*, Erlbaum.
13. Greanleaf, R.K. (1991) *Servant Leadership: A journey into the nature of legitimate power and greatness*, Paulist Press.
14. Khurana, R. (2007) *From Higher Aims to Hired Hands: The social transformation of American business schools and the unfulfilled promise of management as a profession*, Princeton University Press.
15. Scandura, T.A. and Williams, E.A. (2000) Research methodology in management: Current practices, trends, and implications for future research. *Academy of Management Journal*, **43**: 1248–1264.
16. The co-evolution of human culture has become a major theme in evolutionary theory and research. Key sources are: Richerson, P.J. and Boyd, R. (2005) *Not by Genes Alone: How culture transformed human evolution*, University of

Chicago Press; Sober, E. and Wilson, D.S. (1998) *Unto Others: The evolution and psychology of unselfish behavior*, Harvard University Press.

17. Sperber, D. (1996) *Explaining Culture: A naturalistic approach*, Blackwell.

18. Sebag Montefiore (2007) op. cit.

19. Sebag Montefiore (2003) op. cit.

20. Ferguson, N. (2011) *Civilization: The six killer apps of western power*, Allen Lane.

21. McGrue, W.C. (2002) *Chimpanzee Material Culture: Implications for human evolution*, Cambridge University Press.

22. This actually shapes the course of gene evolution, through the alteration of the balance of selective forces. An emerging influential body of knowledge is accumulating under the rubric of Dual Inheritance Theory to examine this process; see McElreath, R. and Henrich, J. (2007) Dual inheritance theory: The evolution of human cultural capacities and cultural evolution. In R.I.M. Dunbar and L. Barrett (eds) *Oxford Handbook of Evolutionary Psychology* (pp. 555–570), Oxford University Press; and Richerson and Boyd op. cit.

23. Sampson, A. (2000) *Mandela: The authorized biography*, Vintage.

24. Landes, D. (1988) *The Wealth and Poverty of Nations*, New York: Norton.

25. Henrich, J. op. cit.; Richerson and Boyd op. cit.; Sober and Wilson op. cit.

26. Tattersall, I. (1998) *Becoming Human: Evolution and human uniqueness*, Oxford University Press.

27. Coon, C.S. (1997) *The Hunting Peoples*, Penguin; Chagnon, N.A. (1997) *Yanomano*, Wadsworth.

28. Boehm op. cit.

29. Diamond, J. (1997) *Guns, Germs and Steel*, Norton; Diamond, J. (1991) *The Rise and Fall of the Third Chimpanzee*, Random House.

30. One was Anthony Willoughby, a lifelong explorer and innovative practitioner in "territory mapping" as a technique he devised for interrogating company (and tribal) strategy. The other was Jo Owen, bestselling author of management books including *How to Lead* (Pearson, 2005). This experience is also described in Nicholson (2005) op. cit.

31. Anderson, D.M. (1995) *Maasai: People of cattle*, Chronicle Books; Saitoti, T.O. (1986) *The Worlds of a Maasai Warrior: An autobiography*, Random House.

32. Hofstede, G. (1998) *Culture's Consequences*, Sage.

33. Boehm op. cit.

34. Meder, A. (2007) Great ape social systems. In W. Henke, I. Tattersall and T. Hardt (eds) *Handbook of Paleoanthropology*, Volume 2 (pp. 1235–1271), Springer-Verlag.

35. Tudge, C. (1998) *Neanderthals, Bandits and Farmers*, Weidenfeld & Nicolson; Diamond, J. (1997) op. cit.

36. Ibid.

37. Harris, M. (1979) *Cannibals and Kings*, William Collins.

38. Utas, M. (ed.) (2012) *African Conflicts and Informal Power: Big men and networks*, Nordic Africa Institute, Uppsala, Sweden and Zed Books.
39. The man was Neil Kinnock MP and the date was July 17th 1988.
40. Stevens, A. and Price, J. (1996) *Evolutionary Psychiatry*, Routledge.
41. Bruner, E.J. (1997) Stress and the biology of inequality. *British Medical Journal*, **314**: 1472–1476.
42. Wilkinson, R. (1996) *Unhealthy Societies: The afflictions of inequality*, Routledge; and Wilkinson, R. and Picket, K. (2009) *The Spirit Level: Why equality is better for everybody*, Allen Lane.
43. Herman, R.T. and Smith, R.L. (2010) *Immigrant Inc.: Why immigrant entrepreneurs are driving the new economy*, Wiley.
44. Landes op. cit.
45. Neyer, F.J. and Lang, F.R. (2003) Blood is thicker than water: Kinship orientation across adulthood. *Journal of Personality and Social Psychology*, **84**: 310–321.
46. Kieser, A. (1987) From asceticism to administration of wealth: Medieval monasteries and the pitfalls of rationalization. *Organisation Studies*, **8**: 103–123.
47. All of this is admirably recounted in Landes op. cit.
48. Stewart, G.L. *et al.* (1999) *Team Work and Group Dynamics*, Wiley.
49. Bellow, A. (2003) *In Praise of Nepotism: A natural history*, Doubleday.
50. Westphal, J.O. and Zajac, E.J. (1995) Who shall govern: CEO/board power, demographic similarity, and new director selection. *Administrative Science Quarterly*, **40**: 60–83.
51. Thornton, G.C. and Byham, W.C. (1982) *Assessment Centers and Managerial Performance*, Academic Press.
52. Kiester op. cit.
53. Kiester op. cit.; and Burchard, P. (1999) *Lincoln and Slavery*, Atheneum.
54. See Sonneborn, S. (2010) *The End of Apartheid in South Africa*, Chelsea House Publishers.
55. Kaiser, R., Hogan, R. and Craig, S.B. (2008) Leadership and the fate of organizations, *American Psychologist*, **63**: 96–110.
56. Kiester op. cit.

Chapter 4: Leadership as Strategy – Situations, Processes and Qualities (SPQ)

1. Tedlow, R.S. (2003) *The Watson Dynasty*, Harper Business.
2. Carroll, P. (1994) *Big Blues: The unmaking of IBM*, Three Rivers Press.
3. Slater, R. (1999) *Saving Big Blue: Leadership lessons & turnaround tactics of IBM's Lou Gerstner*, McGraw Hill.
4. *LA Times*, 28th January 1993.

5. Strategic "agility" has become a fashionable concept in the management literature, see Doz, Y. and Kosonen, M. (2008) *Fast Strategy: How strategic agility will help you stay ahead of the game*, Pearson Prentice Hall.
6. Eldredge op. cit.
7. Laland, K.N. (2007) Niche construction, human behavioural ecology and evolutionary psychology. In R.I.M. Dunbar and O. Barrett (eds) *The Oxford Handbook of Evolutionary Psychology* (pp. 35–48), Oxford University Press.
8. Amburgey, T.L. and Rao, H. (1996) Organizational ecology: Past, present and future directions. *Academy of Management Journal*, **39**: 1265–1286.
9. Morita, A. (1987) *Made in Japan*, Collins.
10. For a trenchant criticism of business school education, see Mintzberg, H. (2005) *Managers Not MBA: A hard look at the soft practice of management and management development*, Berrett-Koehler.
11. Michael West and I published many papers together around these themes, most of which are represented in Nicholson, N. and West, M.A. (1988) *Managerial Job Change: Men and women in transition*, Cambridge University Press.
12. Nicholson, N. (1984) A theory of work role transitions. *Administrative Science Quarterly*, **29**: 172–191.
13. Blumenthal, K. (2012) *Steve Jobs: The man who thought different*, Bloomsbury.
14. Addison, P. (2007) *Winston Churchill*, Oxford University Press.
15. Murnighan, J.K. (2012) *Do Nothing! How to stop overmanaging and become a great leader*, Portfolio Penguin.
16. Barr, M. (2000) *Lee Kuan Yew: The beliefs behind the man*, Georgetown University Press.
17. See, for example, Judge, T. *et al.* (2002) Personality and leadership: A qualitative and quantitative review. *Journal of Applied Psychology*, **87**: 765–780; also Hogan, R. *et al.* (1994) What we know about leadership: Effectiveness and personality. *American Psychologist*, **49**: 493–504.
18. Nicholson, N. (2002) To the manner born. *Financial Times*, November 8; and Nicholson, N. (2001) Gene politics and the natural selection of leadership. *Leader to Leader*, No. **20**, Spring, pp. 46–52.

Chapter 5: Who am I? Leadership Qualities and the Compass Question

1. Clinton, W.J. (2004) *My Life*, Vintage; Obama, B. (2004) *Dreams from My Father: A story of race and inheritance*, Random House.
2. Clinton op. cit.
3. Rees, A. and Nicholson, N. (2004) The Twenty Statements Test. In C. Cassell and G. Symon (eds) *Essential Guide to Qualitative Methods in Organizational Research*, Sage.

4. McCann, S.J.H. (2001) Height, societal threat, and the victory margin in Presidential Elections (1824–1992). *Psychological Reports*, **88**: 741–742.

5. Kirkpatrick and Locke op. cit.

6. Morrell, M. and Capparell, S. (2003) *Shackleton's Way*, Nicholas Brealey.

7. Eagley, A.H. and Johnson, B.T. (1990) Gender and leadership style: A meta-analysis. *Psychological Bulletin*, **108**: 233–256.

8. Buss, D.M. (1991) Evolutionary personality psychology, *Annual Review of Psychology*, **42**: 459–492; MacDonald, K. (1994) Evolution, the five-factor model, and levels of personality, *Journal of Personality*, **63**: 525–567.

9. Arvey, R.D. *et al.* (2006) The determinants of leadership role occupancy: Genetic and personality factors. *The Leadership Quarterly*, **17**: 1–20.

10. Fiorina, C. (2007) *Tough Choices: A memoir*, Portfolio; Burrows, P. (2004) *Backfire: Carly Fiorina's high-stakes battle for the soul of Hewlett-Packard*, Wiley.

11. See Mayer, J.D. (2003) Structural divisions of personality and the classification of traits. *Review of General Psychology*, **7**: 381–401. Traitedness can be considered a "metatrait" – the trait of having or not having a given trait; see Baumeister, R.F. and Tice, D. (1988) Metatraits, *Journal of Personality*, **56**: 571–598.

12. A related concept is "self-monitoring". People high on this attribute are found to be more adaptable in their social behavior; see Mark Snyder (1974) Self-monitoring of expressive behavior, *Journal of Personality and Social Psychology*, **30**: 526–537.

13. See Lawrence, A.H. (2001) *Duke Ellington and His World*, Routledge; Jewell, D. (1997) *Duke: A portrait of Duke Ellington*, Elm Tree Books.

14. Hogan, J. *et al.* (2011) Managerial derailment. In S. Zedeck (ed.) *APA Handbook of Industrial & Organizational Psychology* (pp. 555–575), American Psychological Association.

15. Judge, T.A. *et al.* (2009) The bright and the dark sides of leader traits: A review and theoretical extension of the leader trait paradigm. *The Leadership Quarterly*, **20**: 855–875; Padilla, A. *et al.* (2007) The toxic triangle: Destructive leaders, vulnerable followers, and conducive environments. *The Leadership Quarterly*, **18**: 176–194.

16. Manes, S. and Andrews, P. (1994) *Gates: How Microsoft's mogul reinvented an industry – and made himself the richest man in America*, Touchstone.

17. Judge, T.A. *et al.* (2004) Intelligence and leadership: A quantitative review and test of theoretical propositions. *Journal of Applied Psychology*, **89**: 542–552; Riggio, R.E. *et al.* (eds) (2008) *Multiple Intelligences and Leadership*, Lawrence Erlbaum.

18. Eichenwald, K. (2005) *Conspiracy of Fools*, Broadway Books.

19. Research supports the idea of "moral identity" as a differentiator. See Aquino, K. and Reed, A. (2002) The self-importance of moral identity. *Journal of Personality and Social Psychology*, **83**: 1423–1440; Reed and Aquino, 2004; Aquino, K. *et al.* (2007) A grotesque and dark beauty: How moral identity and mechanisms

of moral disengagement influence cognitive and emotional reactions to war. *Journal of Experimental Social Psychology*, **43**: 385–392.

20. De Pree, M. (1999) *Leading without Power*, San Francisco: Jossey-Bass.

21. Carlson Nelson, M. (2008) *How We Lead Matters: Reflections on a life of leadership*, McGraw Hill.

22. Brandt, R.L. (2011) *The Google Guys: Inside the brilliant minds of Google founders Larry Page and Sergey Brin*, Portfolio.

23. "The bounty of Africa," Lunch with the FT, Mo Ibrahim. *Financial Times Magazine*, February 16–17 2008; "The man giving Africa a brighter future," *Observer Magazine*, February 1, 2009; "Roots radical," *Business Strategy Review*, Summer, 2006, pp. 62–65.

24. Carlson Nelson op. cit.

25. Bennis, W. and Thomas, R.J. (2002) *Geeks and Geezers: How era, values and defining moments shape leaders*, Harvard Business School Press.

26. Holland, J.L. (1997) *Making Vocational Choices*, 3rd edition, Psychological Assessment Resources Inc.

27. Woodbury, L. and De Ora, W. (2011) *The Invisible Branson*, Quantum Publications.

28. Strauss, B. (2012) *Masters of Command: Alexander, Hannibal, Caesar, and the genius of leadership*, Simon & Schuster.

29. Westphal and Zajac op. cit.

30. See Toyoda, E. (1985) *Toyota: Fifty years in motion*, Kodansha International; Sanders, S. (1975) *Honda: The man and his machines*, Little, Brown; Akio Morita op. cit.

31. Crossing boundaries and knowledge and development.

32. Koestler, A. (1959) *The Sleepwalkers: A History of Man's changing vision of the Universe*, Hutchinson.

33. Slater op. cit.; Carroll op. cit.

34. Vincent, N. (2007) *Self-Made Man: My year disguised as a man*, Viking.

35. Geary, D.C. (2010) *Male/Female: The evolution of human sex differences*, Academic Press.

36. Conway, M.A. and Pleydell-Pearce, C.W. (2000) The construction of autobiographical memories in the self memory system. *Psychological Review*, **107**: 261–288.

37. Gordon, G. and Nicholson, N. (2008) *Family Wars*, Kogan Page.

38. Hogan, J. *et al.*, op. cit.

39. Kiester op. cit.

40. Jackson, A. (2012) *Churchill*, Quercus.

41. Addressed to the English army at Tilbury Fort, 1588.

42. Van Velsor, E. and Leslie, J.B. (1995) Why executives derail: Perspectives across time and cultures. *Academy of Management Executive*, **9**: 62–72.

Chapter 6: The "Eye" of Leadership – The Law of the Situation

1. Hill, L.A. (1992) *On Becoming a Manager*, Harvard Business School Press.
2. Kiester op. cit; Brown, J.M. and Parel, A.J. (eds) (2011) *The Cambridge Companion to Gandhi*, Cambridge University Press.
3. Attributed to American philosopher Peirce; also known as Thomas Theorem, after a variant from sociologists W.I. and D.S. Thomas.
4. Nicholson and West op. cit.
5. Nicholson, N. and Arnold, J. (1989) Graduate entry and adjustment to corporate life. *Personnel Review*, **18**(3): 23–35; and Graduate early experience in a multinational corporation. *Personnel Review*, **18**(4): 3–14.
6. Isaacson op. cit.
7. Parker Follett, M. (1924) *The Creative Experience*, Peter Smith.
8. Martin, R. (1977) *The Sociology of Power*, Routledge & Kegan Paul.
9. Many writers have discussed the "bases for power" and how leaders use them, starting with French, J.R.P. and Raven, B.H. (1959) The bases of social power. In D. Cartwright (ed.) *Studies in Social Power* (pp. 118–149), University of Michigan Press.
10. McClean and Elkind op. cit.
11. J.F. Kennedy helped to make this aphorism famous, yet it is an inaccurate reading of the Chinese characters, see Mair, V.H. (2010) *Danger + opportunity ≠ crisis: How a misunderstanding about Chinese characters has led many astray*; blog Pinyin.info.
12. National Commission on the BP Deepwater Horizon Oil Spill and Offshore Drilling (2011) *Deepwater: The Gulf oil disaster and the future of offshore drilling*. Report to the President.
13. NowPublic (2010) *Tony Hayward quotes: BP CEO gaffes or remarks that went wrong?* June 2nd, NowPublic website.
14. Called "perspective taking" in the social psychology literature, see McHugh, L. and Stewart, I. (2012) *The Self and Perspective Taking*, New Harbinger Publications.
15. Gabarro, J.J. (1985) When a new manager takes charge. *Harvard Business Review*, **May/June**: 110–123.
16. Slater op. cit.
17. Lala, R.M. (2004) *The Creation of Wealth: The Tatas from the 19th to the 21st century*, Viking.
18. Hall, D.J. and Salas, M.A. (1980) Strategy follows structure! *Strategic Management Journal*, **1**: 149–163.
19. Barley, S.R. (1990) The alignment of technology and structure through roles and networks. *Administrative Science Quarterly*, **35**: 61–103.

20. Pfeffer, J. (1992) *Managing with Power: Politics and influence in organizations*, Harvard Business School Press.
21. Daft, R.L. (2012) *Organization Design and Theory*, 11th edition, Southwestern Publishing.
22. Daft op. cit.
23. Dunbar, R.I.M. (1992) Neocortex size as a constraint on group size in primates. *Journal of Human Evolution*, **20**: 469–493.
24. Called by one early sociologist, *gemeinschaft*; see Tonnies, F. (1957) *Community and Society: Gemeinschaft und Gesellschaft*. Translated and edited by C.P. Loomis, pp. 223–231, Michigan State University Press.
25. Dorfman, P.W. *et al.* (2004) Leadership and cultural variation: The identification of culturally endorsed leadership profiles. In R.J. House *et al.* (eds) *Culture, Leadership, and Organizations: The GLOBE study of 62 societies* (pp. 669–722), Sage.
26. Mooney, J. and Ellison, G. (1992) *James Mooney's History, Myths, Sacred Formulas of the Cherokees*, Bright Mountain Books.
27. See Addison op. cit.; and Jackson op. cit.
28. Morrell and Capparell op. cit.
29. Jewell op. cit.; Lawrence op. cit.
30. Goia, T. (1999) *The History of Jazz*, Oxford University Press.
31. Goleman *et al.* op. cit.
32. Schneider, B.W. (1987) The people make the place. *Personnel Psychology*, **40**: 437–453.
33. For this metaphor I am indebted to Weinberg, G.M. (1985) *The Secrets of Consulting*, Dorset House Publishing.
34. Hambrick, D.C. and Mason, P.A. (1984) Upper echelons: The organization as a reflection of its top managers. *Academy of Management Review*, **9**: 193–206.
35. "The sword and the word," *The Economist*, May 12th, 2012.
36. Hogan, R. (2010) Putting leadership in an (evolutionary) context. Presentation to SIOP annual conference, Atlanta, GA; Winsborough, D. *et al.* (2009) An evolutionary view: What followers want from their leaders. *LIA*, **29**(3): 8–11.
37. Hersey, P. (1997) *The Situational Leader*, Center for Leadership Studies.
38. Heller, R. and Hayward, A. (2001) *Jack Welch*, DK Adult.
39. For a classic discourse on the topic, see Moore, G.E. (1905–1906) The nature and reality of objects of perception. *Proceedings of the Aristotelian Society*, **6**: 68–127.
40. Ball, S.W. (1988) Evolution, explanation, and the fact/value distinction. *Biology and Philosophy*, **3**: 317–348.
41. Pinker, S. (1997) *How the Mind Works*, Norton.
42. See Nicholson (2000) op. cit.

43. Tumasjan, A. *et al.* (2011) Ethical leadership evaluations after moral transgression: Social distance makes the difference. *Journal of Business Ethics*, **99**: 609–622.

44. Goldgar, A. (2008) *Tulipmania: Money, honor and knowledge in the Dutch Golden Age*, University of Chicago Press.

45. Coleman, M. *et al.* (2008) Subprime lending and the housing bubble: Tail wags dog? *Journal of Housing Economics*, **17**: 272–290.

46. Nicholson, N. (2009) Leading in tough times. *Business Strategy Review*, **Summer**, 38–42.

Chapter 7: The Adaptive Leader – Leadership Processes

1. See Obama, B. (2006) *The Audacity of Hope*, Crown Publishing.

2. Maraniss, D. (2012) *Barack Obama: The story*, Simon & Schuster.

3. Ibid.

4. McAdams, D.P. (2006) *The Redemptive Self*, Oxford University Press.

5. Klein, E. (2012) *The Amateur: Barack Obama in the White House*, Regency Publishing.

6. Woodward, B. (2012) *The Price of Politics*, Simon & Schuster.

7. Andrew Kirell on mediate.com, October 3rd 2012.

8. See, for example, Rand Paul: Obama BP criticism "un-American" – politics – Decision 2010, MSNBC. 21 May 2010; and Drake, B. (2010) "Public Pans Obama's Response to Oil Spill, But Gives Worse Marks to BP." Politics Daily, 27 May.

9. Donald, A. (2007) *A Lion in the White House: A life of Theodore Roosevelt*, Basic Books.

10. In note 8, Chapter 1, I acknowledged the arbitrariness of the letter order – here it makes sense to start by considering Qualities.

11. Hershberger, S.L. *et al.* (1995) Traits and metatraits: their reliability, stability and shared genetic influence. *Journal of Personality and Social Psychology*, **69**: 673–685; Bouchard, T.J. (1997) Genetic influence on mental abilities, personality, vocational interests and work attitudes. In C.L. Cooper and I.T. Robertson (eds) *International Review of Industrial and Organizational Psychology*, Volume 12, Chichester: Wiley.

12. See, for example, Swann, W.B. and Hill, C.R. (1982) When our identities are mistaken: Reaffirming self-conceptions through social interaction. *Journal of Personality & Social Psychology*, **42**: 59–66.

13. Conger, J.A. and Kanungo, R.N. (1998) *Charismatic Leadership in Organizations*, Jossey-Bass.

14. Odiorne, G.S. (1974) *Management and the Activity Trap*, Harper & Row; see also Murnighan op. cit.

15. Eldredge op. cit.
16. Rothbaum, F. *et al.* (1982) Changing the world and changing the self: A two-process model of perceived control. *Journal of Personality and Social Psychology*, **42**: 5–37.
17. Gandhi, M.K. (1982) *The Story of My Experiments with Truth: An autobiography*, Penguin Books.
18. Jewell op. cit.
19. Mandela, N. (1995) *Long Walk to Freedom: The autobiography of Nelson Mandela*, Back Bay Books.
20. Gordon and Nicholson op. cit.; also Collier, P. and Horowitz, D. (2002) *The Fords: An American epic*, Encounter Books.
21. Kaplan and Kaiser op. cit.
22. Heifetz, R.A. *et al.* (2009) *The Practice of Adaptive Leadership: Tools and tactics for changing your organization and the world*, Harvard Business School Press.
23. Trompenaars, F. and Hampden-Turner, C. (2001) *21 Leaders for the 21st Century: How innovative leaders manage in the digital age*, Capstone Publishing.
24. Vise, D.A. and Malseed, M. (2005) *The Google Story*, Delacorte Press.
25. Backman, C.W. *et al.* (1963) Resistance to change in the self-concept as a function of consensus among significant others. *Sociometry*, **26**: 102–111.
26. Isaacson op cit.
27. Lawrence op. cit.
28. Lansing, A. (1999) *Endurance: Shackleton's incredible voyage*, 2nd edition, Basic Books; also Morrell and Capparell op. cit.
29. Gigerenzer, G. *et al.* (1999) *Simple Heuristics that Make us Smart*, Oxford University Press.
30. Bull op. cit.
31. Mintzberg, H. (1973) *The Nature of Managerial Work*, Harper Collins; see also Hales, C. (1993) *Managing Through Organisation*, Routledge.
32. Lawrence op. cit.
33. Jewell op. cit., p. 35.
34. Ibid., p. 83.
35. Lawrence op. cit., pp. 341–343.

Chapter 8: Dynamic Leadership – Shaping and Discovery

1. Here I concentrate on shaping, but equally leaders select situations that are right for them, see Ickes, W., Snyder, M. and Garcia, S. (1997) Personality influences on the choice of situations. In R. Hogan *et al.* (eds) *Handbook of Personality Psychology* (pp. 165–195), Academic Press.
2. Hambrick and Mason op. cit.; see also Hambrick, D.C. and Cannella, A.A. (2004) CEOs who have COOs: Contingency analysis of an unexplored structural form. *Strategic Management Journal*, **2**: 959–979.

3. Byrne, J.A. (2009) *Chainsaw: The notorious career of Al Dunlap in the era of profit-at-any-price*, Harper Business.

4. Collins, D.R. (1992) *Lee Iacocca: Chrysler's good fortune*, Garrett Educational.

5. Slater op. cit.

6. Follett op. cit.

7. Stewart, W. (1997) *Aung San Suu Kyi: Fearless voice of Burma*, Lerner Publications.

8. Hall, D.J. and Salas, M.A. (1980) Structure follows strategy! *Strategic Management Journal*, **1**: 149–163.

9. Lala op. cit.

10. Slater op. cit.

11. Dongyoup, L. (2006) *Samsung Electronics: The global Inc.*, YSM.

12. Munk, N. (2005) *Fools Rush In: Steve Case, Jerry Levin, and the unmaking of AOL Time Warner*, Harper Business.

13. See Gordon and Nicholson op. cit.

14. See Nicholson (2000) op. cit.

15. Burrows op. cit.

16. See Collins op. cit.

17. Settoon, R.P. *et al.* (1996) Social exchange in organizations: Perceived organizational support, leader–member exchange, and employee reciprocity. *Journal of Applied Psychology*, **81**: 219–227.

18. See, for example, Owen, J. (2012) *The Leadership Skills Handbook: 50 skills you need to be a leader*, Kogan Page.

19. See Collins, J.C. and Poras, J.I. (1996) Building your company's vision. *Harvard Business Review*, September–October, 65–77.

20. This inside capture of a majority by a cohesive minority faction is well known in the social psychology literature. See Nemeth, C.J. (1986) Differential contributions of majority and minority influence. *Psychological Review*, **93**: 1–10.

21. Conger, J.A. (1990) The dark side of leadership. *Organizational Dynamics*, **Autumn**, 250–276.

22. Perceptual control theory develops this idea and its implications. See Powers op. cit.

23. Published in 2000 by Texere/Thomson and in the US by Crown Business as *Executive Instinct*.

24. Pfeffer op. cit.

25. Nicholson, N. and Imaizumi, A. (1993) The adjustment of Japanese expatriates to living and working in Britain. *British Journal of Management*, **4**: 119–134.

26. Nicholson, N. (1987) The transition cycle: A conceptual framework for the analysis of change and human resource management. In J. Ferris and K.M. Rowland (eds) *Personal and Human Resources Management*, Volume 5, JAI Press.

27. Ibarra, H. (1999) Provisional selves: Experimenting with image and identity in professional adaptation. *Administrative Science Quarterly*, **44**: 764–791.
28. Gardner op. cit.
29. Campbell, J. (2009) *Margaret Thatcher: Grocer's daughter to iron lady*, Vintage.
30. Plomin, R. (1994) *Genetics and Experience: The interplay between nature and nurture*, Sage.
31. Lowenstein op. cit.
32. See Nicholson (2000) op. cit.
33. The psychology of the credit crisis was prefigured in our work on the psychology and management of traders. See Fenton-O'Creevy, M., Nicholson, N., Soane, E. and Willman, P. (2004) *Traders: Risks, decisions and management in financial markets*, Oxford: Oxford University Press.
34. Buckley, A. (2011) *The Financial Crisis: Causes, context and consequences*, Pearson.

Chapter 9: Reading the World – A Leadership Conundrum

1. Rees, L. (2012) *The Dark Charisma of Adolf Hitler: Leading millions into the abyss*, Ebury Press.
2. Kaplan, R.E. and Kaiser, R. (2006) *The Versatile Leader: Make the most of your strengths – without overdoing it*, Pfeiffer.
3. Tomalin, C. (2002) *Samuel Pepys: The unequalled self*, Viking.
4. Sternberg, R.J. (2006) *Cognitive Psychology*, Wadsworth.
5. This is the idea that genius is 90% perspiration, 10% inspiration, or the idea that 10,000 hours will make anyone a master. See Gladwell, M. (2011) *Outliers: The story of success*, Back Bay Books; also Howe, M.J.A. (2001) *Genius Explained*, Cambridge University Press.
6. Heifitz, R. *et al.* (2009) *The Adaptive Leader: Tools and tactics for changing your organization and the world*, Harvard Business School Press.
7. Hirsch, A. (2005) *Season of Hope: Economic reform under Mandela and Mbeki*, University of Natal Press.
8. Goffee, R. and Jones, G. (2000) Why should anyone be led by you? *Harvard Business Review*, **September–October**, 63–70.
9. Robinson, H. (1994) *Perception*, Routledge.
10. Brock, S. and Mares, E. (2007) *Realism and Anti-realism*, McGill-Queen's University Press.
11. Ninio, J. and Philip, F. (2001) *The Science of Illusions*, Cornell University Press.
12. See Strauss op. cit.; Galsworthy op. cit.
13. Gergen, K.J. (1999) *An Invitation to Social Construction*, Sage.
14. Henrich (2004) op. cit.

15. Gordon and Nicholson op. cit.

16. Brooks, D. (2011) *The Social Animal*, Random House.

17. It seems that one does not even need confederate subjects, see Mori, K. and Aria, M. (2010) No need to fake it: Reproduction of the Asch experiment without confederates. *Journal of International Psychology*, **45**: 390–397.

18. Gates, W.H. (1999) *Business @ the Speed of Thought: Succeeding in the digital economy*, Warner Books.

19. Ackerman, R. *et al.* (2010) *A Sprat to Catch a Mackerel: Key principles to build your business*, Jonathan Ball.

Chapter 10: Born to Lead? Leaders Lost and Found

1. Glendinning, V. (2012) *Raffles and the Golden Opportunity*, Profile Books.

2. Plate, T. (2010) *Conversations with Lee Kuan Yew*, Marshall Cavendish; and Barr op. cit.

3. Northouse op. cit.

4. Meindl *et al.* op. cit.

5. First performed at the Duke of York's Theatre, London, 1902.

6. See Nicholson (2000) op. cit.

7. See Hamel op. cit.

8. See Wilson, T. op. cit.; and Iyengar, S. (2010) *The Art of Choosing*, Twelve.

9. See Bennis, W. (1989) *Why Leaders Can't Lead: The unconscious conspiracy continues*, Jossey-Bass; see also Murnighan op. cit.

10. Stockdale, J.B. (1984) *Vietnam Experience: Ten years of reflection*, Hoover Press.

11. Collins, J. (2001) *Good to Great*, Harper Collins.

12. Stockdale, J.B. (1993) *The World of Epictetus*, The Trinity Forum, Reading.

Chapter 11: Who's Your Buddy? Critical Leader Relationships

1. Eisner writes about this in Eisner, M.D. and Cohen, A.R. (2010) *Working Together: Why great partnerships succeed*, Harper Collins.

2. Akio Morita op. cit.

3. Slater, R. (2004) *Microsoft Rebooted: How Bill Gates and Steve Ballmer reinvented their company*, Penguin.

4. Khurana, R. (2002) *Searching for a Corporate Saviour: The irrational quest for charismatic CEOs*, Princeton University Press.

5. See Kantor, J. (2012) *The Obamas*, Back Bay Books.

6. Sally, D. (2002) Co-leadership: Lessons from Republican Rome. *California Management Review*, **42**: 84–99.

7. Endlich, L. (1990) *Goldman Sachs: The culture of success*, Little Brown.
8. Around 15% of family firms have co-leadership, according to MassMutual Financial Group/Raymond Institute (2002) American Family Business Survey.
9. See Nicholson, N. (2008) Evolutionary psychology and family business: A new synthesis for theory, research and practice. *Family Business Review*, **21**: 103–118.
10. O'Hara, W.T. (2004) *Centuries of success: Lessons from the world's most enduring family businesses*, Adams Media.
11. Alvarez, J. and Svejenova, S. (2005) *Sharing Executive Power*, Cambridge University Press.
12. Katzenbach, J.R. (1997) *Teams at the Top: Unleashing the potential of both teams and individual leaders*, Harvard Business School Press.
13. See Maister, D. *et al.* (2000) *The Trusted Advisor*, Simon & Schuster.
14. O'Toole, J. *et al.* (2002) When two (or more) heads are better than one: The promise and pitfalls of shared leadership. *California Management Review*, **44**: 65–83.
15. Bevelin, P. (2003) *Seeking Wisdom from Darwin to Munger*, PCA Publications.
16. Eisner and Cohen op. cit.
17. Stone, F. (2004) *The Mentoring Advantage: Creating the next generation of leaders*, Dearborn Publishing.
18. Campbell op. cit.
19. Maccoby, M. (2003) *The Productive Narcissist: The promise and peril of visionary leadership*, Broadway.
20. Prager, A.J. and Roberts, L.J. (2004) Deep intimate connections: Self and identity in couple relationships. In D.J. Mashek and A. Aron (eds) *Handbook of Closeness and Intimacy*, Lawrence Erlbaum.
21. Langer, E. (1989) *Mindfulness*, Addison-Wesley.
22. Conger, J.A. and Riggio, R.E. (2006) *The Practice of Leadership: Developing the next generation of leaders*. Jossey-Bass.
23. Villalonga, B. and Amit, R. (2006) How do family ownership, control and management affect firm value? *Journal of Financial Economics*, **80**: 385–417.
24. Wolff, M. *et al.* (2012) The Master Mogul of Fleet Street: 24 tales from the pages of Vanity Fair, *Vanity Fair*.
25. Heenan, D. and Bennis, W. (1999) *Co-leaders: The power of great partnerships*, Wiley.
26. Caro, R.A. (1990) *The Path to Power: The years of Lyndon Johnson*, Volume 1, Vintage.
27. Powell op. cit.
28. Ederer, F. and Patacconi, A. (2010) Interpersonal comparison, status and ambition in organizations. *Journal of Economic Behavior & Organization*, **75**: 348–363.

29. Evidence on what makes a "happy" or "good" marriage is equivocal. Generally, for an easy and comfortable life, partnering with someone perceived to be similar to oneself seems the best policy. See Burleson, B.R. and Denton, W.H. (1992) Anew look at similarity and attraction in marriage: Similarities in social-cognitive and communication skills as predictors of attraction and similarity, *Communication Monographs*, **59**: 268–287.

30. Harvey, M. *et al.* (2009) Mentoring global female managers in the global marketplace: Traditional, reverse, and reciprocal mentoring. *International Journal of Human Resource Management*, **20**: 1344–1361.

31. Hicks, M.D. (1996) *The Leader as Coach: Strategies for coaching and developing others*, Personnel Decisions International.

32. Center for Creative Leadership (2007) *Active Listening: Improve your ability to listen and lead*, Pfeiffer.

33. Whitmore, J. (2002) *Coaching for Performance*, 3rd edition, Nicholas Brealey.

34. From the "Eschatological Laundry List" in Sheldon Kopp's (1976) *If You Meet the Buddha on the Road, Kill Him*, Bantam Books.

Chapter 12: Destiny, Drama and Deliberation – The Lives of Leaders

1. This material is based upon interviews with Andre. See Andre's website for other materials about him and his life: http://andrenorman.com

2. My colleague was Jules Goddard, co-author with Tony Eccles of the splendid *Common Nonsense, Uncommon Sense*, London: Profile Books, 2012.

3. *Decision Points* op. cit.

4. For a wonderful secular tale of awakening to reality, see the classic novella by Dr Samuel Johnson (1899) *Raselas: Prince of Abyssinia*, Cassell & Co.

5. On the Sloan Fellowship Program at London Business School.

6. These are themes explored in the field of life-span developmental psychology. See Baltes, P.B. *et al.* (1980) Life-span developmental psychology. *Annual Review of Psychology*, **31**: 65–110.

7. Tedlow, R. (2006) *Andy Grove*, Penguin.

8. Wrosch, C. and Freund, A.M. (2001) Self-regulation of normative and non-normative developmental challenges. *Human Development*, **44**: 264–283.

9. Defined as "the faculty of making unhappy, unlucky and expected discoveries by design" (Hamish Hamilton 1998; pp. 234–235).

10. Rob Kurzban portrays the Self as a West Wing duality where the President colludes in his own ignorance, for deniability purposes, by the willed concealment of his Press Secretary, in *Why Everyone (Else) is a Hypocrite*, Princeton University Press, 2010.

11. *The London Shakespeare Workout*, founded by Dr Bruce Wall in 1997, see www.lsw;productions.co.uk

12. Produced by Granada Ventures; directed by Michael Apted, published by Network DVD.

13. In life-span development psychology, what I am calling Drama is termed "non-normative life events," see Wrosch and Freund op. cit.

14. Based upon interviews plus sources.

15. This material is based upon Jewell op. cit. and Lawrence op. cit.

16. Characteristically and appropriately entitled *Music is My Mistress*, Doubleday, 1973.

17. Bandura, A. (2006) Toward a psychology of human agency. *Perspectives on Psychological Science*, 1: 164–180.

18. I have previously noted that life stories can be seen as nested and contiguous cycles of transition, in Nicholson (1987) op. cit.

19. Based upon interviews with Mustier and press reports; Mustier was vindicated by the court rejecting Kerviel's defense in his trial, completed in October 2012.

20. Cooper, A.C. and Dunkelberg, W.C. (1986) Entrepreneurship and paths to business ownership. *Strategic Management Journal*, 7: 53–68.

21. This is the classic normative career path, described by Levinson, Sheehy and others, yet increasingly people depart from this norm, and it never has applied particularly well to women. See Sugarman, L. (1986) *Life-span Development: Concepts, theories and interventions*, Methuen; also Nicholson and West op. cit.

Chapter 13: The "I" of Leadership – Inside the Mind of the Leader

1. Tomalin, N. and Hall, R. (2003) *The Strange Last Voyage of Donald Crowhurst*, Hodder & Stoughton.

2. Leary, M. (2004) *The Curse of the Self*, Oxford University Press.

3. For a wide-ranging analysis of the dysfunctional consequences of excessive choice in modern life, see Iyengar op. cit.

4. See Kurzban op. cit.; Metzinger, T. (2009) *The Ego Tunnel: The science of the mind and the myth of the self*, Basic Books; Hood, B. (2011) *The Self Illusion: Why there is no "you" inside your head*, Penguin.

5. For a comprehensive review of the evidence, see Tomasello op. cit.; also Heyes, C.M. (1998) Theory of mind in non-human primates. *Behavioral and Brain Sciences*, 21: 101–148.

6. Donald, M. (2001) *A Mind So Rare: The evolution of human consciousness*, Norton.

7. Bandura, A. (2008) The reconstrual of "free will" from the agentic perspective of social cognitive theory. In J. Baer, J.E. Kaufman and R.F. Baumeister (eds)

(2008) *Are We Free? Psychology and the free will*, Oxford University Press, pp. 86–127; also Leary, M. and Buttermore, N.R. (2003) The evolution of the human self: Tracing the natural history of self-awareness. *Journal for the Theory of Social Behavior*, **33**: 365–404.

8. See Heatherton, T.F. (2011) Neuroscience of self and self-regulation. *Annual Review of Psychology*, **62**: in press; Stone, V.E. *et al.* (1998) Frontal lobe contributions to theory of mind. *Journal of Cognitive Neuroscience*, **10**: 640–656.

9. John Bargh's work has demonstrated the gullibility of our sense of self. See, for example, Bargh *et al.* (2010) Motivation. In S.T. Fiske *et al.* (eds) *Handbook of Social Psychology*, Volume 2, 5th edition (pp. 268–316), Wiley.

10. Kurzban op. cit.

11. Bandura op. cit.

12. See Tomasello op. cit.

13. Wilson, E.O. (1998) *Consilience: The unity of knowledge*, Vintage Books.

14. Psychologist Nick Humphrey first made the argument that a sense of self is a corollary of our very functional ability to read other minds in Nature's psychologists. In B.D. Josephson and V.S. Ramachandran (eds) (1980) *Consciousness and the Physical World* (pp. 55–75), Pergamon.

15. Reader, V. (ed.) (1959) *The Autobiography of Mark Twain* (p. 127), Harper & Row.

16. Karoly, P. (1993) Mechanisms of self-regulation: A systems view. *Annual Review of Psychology*, **44**: 23–52; Baumeister and Vohs op. cit.

17. Gross, J. and Oliver, J. (2003) Individual differences in two emotion regulation processes: Implications for affect, relationships, and well-being. *Journal of Personality & Social Psychology*, **85**: 348–362.

18. Stewart op. cit.

19. Van Knippenberg, B., De Cremer, D., Hogg, M.A. and Van Knippenberg, D. (2005) Leadership, self, and identity: A review and research agenda. *The Leadership Quarterly*, **15**: 825–856.

20. Epstein, S. *et al.* (1996) Individual differences in intuitive-experiential and analytical-rational thinking styles. *Journal of Personality & Social Psychology*, **71**: 390–405.

21. Brehm, J.W. (1956) Postdecision changes in the desirability of alternatives. *Journal of Abnormal & Social Psychology*, **52**: 384–397.

22. Cunningham op. cit.

23. This, of course, is a schematic convenience, but does represent distinct strands in the literature on (a) Executive functions, (b) Perceptual control, (c) Self-concept and (d) Heuristics and action; for a complete exposition, see Nicholson, N. (2011)The evolved self, co-evolutionary processes and the self-regulation of leadership. *Biological Theory*, **6**(4): 12–44.

24. Famously called "blooming, buzzing confusion" by William James in *Principles of Psychology* (1890), p. 462.

25. Haidt, J. (2006) *The Happiness Hypothesis*, Random House.
26. Trivers, R.L. (2000) The elements of a scientific theory of self-deception. *Annals of New York Academy of Sciences*, **907**: 114–192.
27. Goals are nested and regulated by ego processes; see Carver, C.S. and Scheier, M.F. (1998) *On the self-regulation of behavior*, Cambridge University Press.
28. Akio Morita op. cit.
29. Baumeister, R.F. (1998) The self. In D.T. Gilbert *et al.* (eds) *Handbook of Social Psychology*, 4th edition (pp. 680–740), McGraw-Hill; Gross, J.J. (1998) The emerging field of emotional regulation: An integrative review. *Journal of General Psychology*, **2**: 271–299.
30. Changing goals by achieving insight into subconscious goals is the classic method of much therapy; for one of the earliest expositions, see Rogers, C.R. (1940) The processes of therapy. *Journal of Consulting Psychology*, **4**: 161–164.
31. Manderlink, G. and Harackiewic, J.M. (1984) Proximal versus distal goal setting and intrinsic motivation. *Journal of Personality & Social Psychology*, **47**: 918–928.
32. Trivers op. cit.
33. Baumeister, R. and Tierney, J. (2011) *Willpower: Rediscovering our greatest strength*, Penguin. The muscle metaphor is helpful, up to a point, but has been criticized for being overextended; it may actually be more a matter of competition with other goal-seeking processes; see Kurzban, R. (2012) Can we stick a fork in the "glucose-as-willpower-fuel" model? *The Evolutionary Psychology Blog*, www.epjournal.net/blog/2012/10.
34. Fischer, P. *et al.* (2007) Ego depletion and positive illusions: Does the construction of positivity require regulatory resources? *Personality and Social Psychology Bulletin*, **33**: 1306–1321.
35. Gordon and Nicholson op. cit.
36. Said by Alan Greenberg, according to a press report in *The Guardian* newspaper by Charles Ferguson, "Heist of the century: Wall Street's role in the financial crisis," May 20th 2012.
37. Angela Merkel biography.
38. Judge, T.A. *et al.* (2009) The bright and dark sides of leadership: A review and theoretical extension of the leader trait paradigm. *The Leadership Quarterly*, **20**: 855–875.
39. This is the subject of a little-known but original body of work on "reversal theory," see Apter, M. (1989) *Reversal Theory: Motivation, emotion and personality*, Routledge. Julius Kuhl (1992) similarly distinguishes between self-regulatory types in a theory of self-regulation: Action versus state orientation, self-discrimination, and some application. *Applied Psychology: An International Review*, **41**: 97–129.

40. Ray, J.J. (1978) Do authoritarians hold authoritarian attitudes? *Human Relations*, **29**: 307–325.

41. Isaacson op. cit., pp. 331–332.

42. Name and circumstantial details changed to protect confidentiality.

43. McAdams (2006) op. cit.

44. James, W. (1890) *The Principles of Psychology*, Volume 1 (1950 edition, Dover).

45. Axelrod op. cit.

46. Caspi, A. (2000) The child is father to the man: Personality continuities from childhood to adulthood. *Journal of Personality & Social Psychology*, **78**: 158–172.

47. Baumeister (1998) op. cit.

48. Mayer op. cit.

49. Sarbin, T. (1950) Contributions to role-taking theory: 1. Hypnotic behavior. *Psychological Review*, **57**: 255–270.

50. Greenwald, A.G. (1980) The totalitarian ego: Fabrication and revision of personal history. *American Psychologist*, **35**: 603–618.

51. Collier and Horowitz op. cit.

52. Campbell op. cit.

53. Byrne op. cit.

54. Bhutto, B. (2007) *Daughter of the East: An autobiography*, Simon & Schuster.

55. Ibid., p. xii.

56. Maccoby op. cit.

57. See also the body of German scholarship on action theory, which sees action schemata as being nested in the cognitive level, see Frese, M. and Zapf, D. (1994) Action as the core of work psychology: A German approach. In M.D. Dunnette *et al.* (eds) *Handbook of Industrial & Organizational Psychology*, Consulting Psychologists Press.

58. Interaction rituals, discussed by Erving Goffman (1982) *Interaction Ritual: Essays on face-to-face behavior*, Pantheon; and explained by evolutionists – see, for example, Cappella, J.N. (2006) The biological origins of automated patterns of human interaction. *Communication Theory*, **1**: 4–35.

59. Kets de Vries, M.F.R. and Miller, D. (2006) Neurotic styles and organizational pathology. *Strategic Management Journal*, **5**: 35–55.

60. Material from personal interview plus source materials.

61. See Wikipedia on Goodwin for numerous press reports; also Craig, D. and Elliott, M. (2009) *Fleeced! How we've all been betrayed by the politicians, bureaucrats and bankers and how much they've cost us*, Constable & Robinson.

62. Comment made by many executives attending a top management development course at London Business School.

63. The new thinking can be found in such works as Kay, J. (2010) *Obliquity: Why our goals are best achieved indirectly*, Profile Books; and Smith, D. (2010)

The Age of Instability: The global financial crisis and what comes next, Profile Books.

64. Reeves, R. (2002) *President Nixon: Alone in the White House*, Touchstone.

Chapter 14: Games Leaders Play – Finding the Narrative

1. Directed by Christopher Nolan, Newmarket Films, 2000.
2. Metzinger op. cit.; Wilson, T. op. cit.
3. Ibid.
4. See, for example, Metzner, R. (2010) *The Unfolding Self: Varieties of transformative experience*, Pioneer Imprints.
5. Kiester op. cit.
6. Lynch, J. (2006) *Simón Bolivar*, Yale University Press.
7. Ibarra, H. and Lineback, K. (2005) What's your story? *Harvard Business Review*, **83** (January): 64–71; McAdams (1993) op. cit.
8. Ibarra, H. (2003) *Working Identity: Unconventional strategies for reinventing your career*, Harvard Business School Press.
9. McDonald, H.E. and Hurt, E.R. (1997) When expectancy meets desire: Motivational effects in reconstructive memory. *Journal of Personality & Social Psychology*, **72**: 5–23.
10. Gottschall, J. (2012) *The Storytelling Animal: How stories make us human*, Houghton Mifflin.
11. States, B.O. (1993) *Dreaming and Storytelling*, Cornell University Press.
12. Gottschall, J. and Wilson, D.S. (eds) (2005) *The Literary Animal: Evolution and the nature of narrative*, Northwestern University Press.
13. Gottschall, op. cit.
14. Sparrowe op. cit.; Ligon *et al.* op. cit.
15. Ibid.
16. Slovic, P. (2000) *The Perception of Risk*, Earthscan Publications.
17. See Sharot, T. (2012) *The Optimism Bias*, Constable & Robinson; Ladouceur *et al.* (2002) *Understanding and Treating the Pathological Gambler*, Wiley.
18. Charismatic leaders distorted perceptions and bad consequences for others; moral disengagement is part of this process. See Moore, C. (2008) Moral disengagement in processes of organizational corruption. *Journal of Business Ethics*, **80**: 129–139.
19. Langer, E. (1975) The illusion of control. *Journal of Personality & Social Psychology*, 321–328; also Zuckerman, M. and Kuhlman, D.M. (2000) Personality and risk-taking: Common bio-social factors. *Journal of Personality*, **68**: 999–1029.
20. Vermeulen, F. (2008) Songs of the sirens. *Business Strategy Review*, **19**: 22–27.
21. Vlasic, B. and Stertz, B.A. (2001) *Taken for a Ride: How Daimler-Benz drove off with Chrysler*, Harper Collins.

22. Martin, G. and Gollan, P.J. (2012) Corporate governance and strategic human resources management in the UK financial services sector: The case of RBS. *The International Journal of Human Resource Management*, **23**: 3295–3314.

23. Tory Higgins has led a substantial research stream into how the Self regulates between "promotion" and "prevention" functions; see How self-regulation creates distinctive values: The case of promotion and prevention decision-making. *Journal of Consumer Psychology* (2002) **12**: 177–191.

24. Rueda, M.R. *et al.* (2004) Attentional control and self-regulation. In R.F. Baumeister and K.D. Vohs (eds) *Handbook of Self-regulation* (pp. 447–465), Guilford.

25. Campbell op. cit.

26. Westhead, P. and Cowling, M. (1998) Family firm research: The need for a methodological rethink. *Entrepreneurship Theory & Practice*, **23**: 31–56.

27. See Odiorne op. cit.; Murnighan, op. cit.

28. Baumeister, R.F. (1982) A self-presentational view of social phenomena. *Psychological Bulletin*, **93**: 3–26.

29. This unflattering portrait figures in Blair's memoir (op. cit.) as well as those of his political ally, for a while, Peter Mandelson (2011) *The Third Man: Life at the heart of New Labour*, Harper Press; also see Jonathan Powell (op. cit.); see also Richards, S. (2010) *Whatever It Takes: The real story of Gordon Brown and New Labour*, Fourth Estate.

30. See Rees op. cit.

31. This can be seen in Leni Riefenstahl's brilliant and terrifying film of the Nuremberg Rally, *The Triumph of the Will* (1934).

32. See Maccoby op. cit.

33. See Hilsum, L. (2012) *Sandstorm: Libya in the time of revolution*, Penguin.

34. Giesler, R.B. *et al.* (1996) Self-verification in clinical depression: The desire for negative evaluation. *Journal of Abnormal Psychology*, **105**: 358–368.

35. Baumeister (1998) op. cit.

36. This argument was developed empirically by Louis Zurcher in *The Mutable Self* (Sage, 1977) using the Twenty Statements Test, a symbolic interactionist methodology asking respondents to give twenty answers to the question, "Who am I?" See also Rees and Nicholson op. cit.

37. Guillén, M.F. (1994) *Models of Management: Work, authority, and organization in a comparative perspective*, University of Chicago Press.

38. Dowie, M. (2002) *American Foundations: An investigative history*, MIT Press.

39. Jackson, T. (2004) *Management and Change in Africa: A cross-cultural perspective*, Routledge; McCord, W. and McCord, A. (1980) *Paths to Progress*, Norton.

40. Manes and Andrews op. cit.

41. Board, D. (2012) *Choosing Leaders and Choosing to Lead: Science, politics and intuition in executive selection*, Gower.

42. See Van Vugt *et al.* (2008) Leadership, followership, and evolution: Some lessons from the past. *American Psychologist*, **63**: 182–196.
43. Kanfer, R. and Heggestad, E.D. (1999) Individual differences in motivation: Traits and self regulatory skills. In P.L. Ackerman *et al.* (eds) *Learning and Individual Differences: Process, trait and content determinants*, American Psychological Association.
44. Odiorne op. cit.
45. This concept is central to the psychodynamic theorizing under the name of Transactional Analysis; see Steiner, C. (1974) *Scripts People Live*, Grove Press.
46. Brooks, R. and Goldstein, S. (2001) *Raising Resilient Children: Fostering strength, hope and optimism in your child*, Contemporary Books.
47. Carl Gustav Jung, post-Freudian psychoanalyst.
48. Agassi, A. (2009) *Open: An autobiography*, Knopf.
49. Rueda op. cit.
50. See Baumeister and Tierney op. cit.; Rachlin, H. (2000) *The Science of Self Control*, Harvard University Press.
51. Gardner, W.I. *et al.* (2005) Can you see the real me? A self-based model of authentic leader and follower development. *The Leadership Quarterly*, **16**: 343–372.
52. Goffee and Jones (op. cit.) develop an argument about the benefits of leaders showing themselves to be open and strong enough to admit to flaws.
53. "The best way to predict the future is to invent it," Alan Kay, 1971.
54. Bass op. cit.
55. See the failure of success literature, e.g. Audia, P. *et al.* (2000) The paradox of success: An archival and laboratory study of strategic persistence following radical environmental change. *Academy of Management Journal*, **48**: 837–853.
56. See article by Nicholson (2009) op. cit.

Chapter 15: The Self-Management of Leadership – You, Others and Organization

1. Russell, B. (1917) *Why Men Fight* (p. 179), The Century Company.
2. Taking charge is a good definition of leadership, see Gabarro op. cit.
3. This term can be found through Web search but it does not really connote the method I have developed and set out here.
4. See Rafaeli, A. and Pratt, M.J. (1993) Tailored meanings: On the meaning and impact of organizational dress. *Academy of Management Review*, **18**: 32–55.
5. Cunningham op. cit.
6. Directed by Frank Capra, Paramount Pictures, 1946.
7. I am indebted to psychologist Alison Hardingham for this idea; see Hardingham, A. *et al.* (2004) *The Coach's Coach: Personal development for personal developers*, CIPD.

8. Birren, J.E. and Cochran, K.N. (2001) *Telling the Stories of Life Through Guided Autobiography Groups*, Johns Hopkins University Press.

9. There are LOTS of self-help books around this stuff. To mention one would be invidious to the others.

10. Both Mark Leary and Jonathan Haidt in their books (op. cit.) analyze the benefits of the self-liberation such activities confer on one.

11. The Twenty Statements Test is a good vehicle for this; see Nicholson and Rees op. cit.

12. As behavior genetics show us; see Plomin op. cit.

13. See Fiske, S. and Markus, H.R. (eds) (2012) *Facing Social Class: How societal rank influences interaction*, Russell Sage Foundation.

14. I have a structured method for doing this with executives, which leads them to grasp the concept of decentering properly; see also, by the author, How to motivate your problem people. *Harvard Business Review*, **81** (January): 56–67.

15. Concept borrowed from Piaget, as described ibid.

16. McHugh and Stewart op. cit.

17. See Maccoby op. cit.; also Lipman-Blumen, J. (2005) *The Allure of Toxic Leaders*, Oxford University Press.

18. Gottman, J. (1999) *The Marriage Clinic*, Norton.

19. Smith, D.B. (ed.) *The People Make the Place: Dynamic linkages between individuals and organization*, Erlbaum.

20. Zimbardo, P. (2007) *The Lucifer Effect: Understanding how good people turn evil*, Random House.

21. Pierce and White (1999; 2006) op. cit.

22. Daft op. cit.

23. Womack, J.P. *et al.* (2007) *The Machine that Changed the World*, Free Press.

24. Donaldson, L. (2001) *The Contingency Theory of Organizations*, Sage.

25. Brown, D. (1991) *Human Universals*, Basic Books.

26. Called, brutally, "rank or yank."

27. Rosenbaum, J.E. (1979) Tournament mobility: Career patterns in a corporation. *Administrative Science Quarterly*, **24**: 220–241.

28. Marchese, M.C. and Muchinsky, P.M. (1993) The validity of the employment interview: A meta-analysis. *International Journal of Selection & Assessment*, **1**: 18–26.

29. See Peter, L.J. and Hull, R. (1969) *The Peter Principle: Why things always go wrong*, Morrow.

30. See Miller op. cit.

31. Clance, P. (1985) *The Imposter Phenomenon: Overcoming the fear that haunts your success*, Peachtree Publications.

32. Manzoni, J-F. and Barsoux, J-L. (2009) Are your subordinates setting you up to fail? *Sloan Management Review*, **50**: 43–51.

33. Rawnsley, A. (2010) *The End of the Party: The rise and fall of New Labour*, Penguin.

34. Khurana, R. (2001) Finding the right CEO: Why boards often make poor choices. *Sloan Management Review*, **43**: 91–96.

35. Fiorina, C. (2007) *Tough Choices: A memoir*, Penguin.

36. Ibid p. 45.

37. Ibid p. 54.

38. Alban-Metcalfe, B. and Nicholson, N. (1984) *The Career Development of British Managers*, British Institute of Management, London.

39. See Piers Ibbotson's insightful book on what the theater can teach us about leadership, *The Leadership Illusion*, Palgrave Macmillan, 2008.

Chapter 16: Can Leaders Save the World? Vision, Identity and Passion

1. Arendt, H. (1963) *Eichmann in Jerusalem: A report on the banality of evil*, The Viking Press.

2. Kanter, R.M. (1972) *Commitment and Community: Communes and utopias in sociological perspective*, Harvard University Press.

3. Brandenburger, A. and Nalebuff, B. (1996) *Co-Opetition: A revolution mindset that combines competition and cooperation*, Currency Doubleday; Kates, A. and Galbraith, J.R. (2007) *Designing Your Organization: Using the STAR model to solve 5 critical design challenges*, Jossey-Bass.

4. For a positive answer to these questions, see Matt Ridley's *The Rational Optimist: How prosperity evolves*, Fourth Estate, 2010.

5. Described in Johnson, M. (2005) *Family, Village, Tribe: The story of the Flight Centre Ltd.*, Random House.

6. Nicholson, N. (1998) How hardwired is human behavior? *Harvard Business Review*, **76** (4): 134–147.

7. Finkelstein, S. *et al.* (2009) *Strategic Leadership: Theory and research on executives, top management team, and boards*, Oxford University Press.

8. Nye, J.S. (2008) *The Powers to Lead*, Oxford University Press.

9. Sorenson, R.L. (2000) The contribution of leadership style and practices to family and business success. *Family Business Review*, **13**: 183–200; Nicholson, N. (2008) Evolutionary psychology, corporate culture and family business. *Academy of Management Perspectives*, **22**: 73–84.

10. Rosenbaum op. cit.

11. An argument developed by the author in *Executive Instinct* (*Managing the Human Animal*) op. cit.

12. *Ready, Steady, Cook*, BBC Television, 1994–2000; with variations in other countries.

13. Antonakis, J. and Atwater, L. (2002) Leader distance: A review and a proposed theory. *The Leadership Quarterly*, **13**: 673–704.

INDEX

Index compiled by Terry Halliday